D1037507

Poet's Love

BY THE SAME AUTHOR

The Schubert Song Cycles
with thoughts on performance, 1975
Farewell Recital, 1978
Am I Too Loud? 1962
Singer and Accompanist, 1953
Careers in Music, 1950
The Unashamed Accompanist, 1943 (revised edn, 1957)

Poet's Love

The Songs and Cycles of
SCHUMANN

★

GERALD MOORE

HAMISH HAMILTON
LONDON

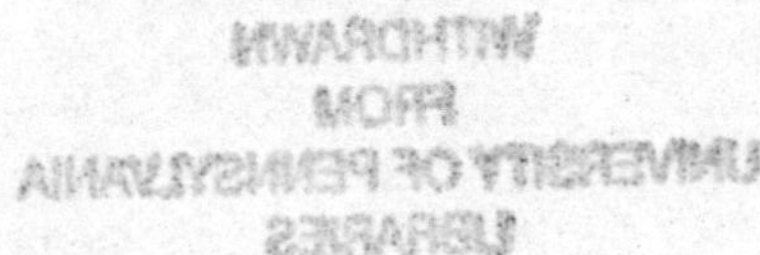

First published in Great Britain 1981
by Hamish Hamilton Ltd
Garden House 57–59 Long Acre London WC2E 9JZ

British Library Cataloguing in Publication Data

Moore, Gerald, *b. 1899*
Poet's Love.
1. Schumann, Robert. Songs
I. Title
784'.3'00924 ML410.S4

ISBN 0-241-10512-9
ISB 0-241-10518-8 Pbk

Typesetting and origination by Polly Productions, London
Printed and bound in Great Britain by
Richard Clay (The Chaucer Press) Ltd, Bungay, Suffolk

To ENID

CONTENTS

Groups I, II, III, IV and V are from Edition Peters Vol. 1, Groups VI and VII from Vol. 2, and VIII from Vol. 3.

PREFACE

There are two reasons for my giving this book the title 'Poet's Love'. In the first place to have called it 'The Songs of Robert Schumann' would have confused it with a book of that title which I regard as the definitive analysis on the subject; I refer, of course, to the penetrating study by Eric Sams[1]. In a Foreword to this I wrote, 'It will be read and read again as long as Robert Schumann's songs are loved'.

However, the Sams work differs from mine in that I have approached the subject from the angle of the singer and pianist and have concerned myself mostly with questions of ensemble, *tempi*, rhythmic flexibility, mood, colour and feeling.

Here I should emphasize that the interpreter is the servant of the composer. He sees the work 'from the inside'; to some extent he must be ingenuous; a singer for instance must believe in what he is singing and he only examines it clinically in so far as experience makes him aware of some weakness in construction, balance, stress or impulsion, that he hopes he may be able to disguise.

My essays in the following pages are written on this basis.

Many of the songs herein are inspired and are true reflections of the Schumann genius. Not all are of that superlative level though they can still be regarded as fine songs for singing.

Dichterliebe is, to me, Robert Schumann's crowning achievement as a song writer in its poetry and depth of emotion. Had he written nothing else, these sixteen songs proclaim him as a worthy successor to Franz Schubert, hence my taking 'Poet's Love' for title and beginning my book with it.

Schumann never sought to move us by rhetorical argument, his unique art was to portray innermost heart-rending emotions in such a recondite manner that the listener feels poet and composer are speaking to him alone. For this reason, many of the songs which move us most, are grasped with more understanding when we hear them in a salon or very small hall, rather than a spacious auditorium: an observation not intended as pejorative since it equally applies to many of the choicest songs of Franz Schubert and Hugo Wolf.

The magic of *Mondnacht, Die Lotosblume, Du bist wie eine Blume, Mein schöner Stern, Nachtlied, Stirb, Lieb' und Freud'*, the transcendental *Dichterliebe*, the dumb grief that brings *Frauenliebe und Leben* to an end, all demand intimacy of communication between singer and listener.

---

[1] Methuen & Co. Ltd.

This close contact, this gentle intercourse is the hall-mark of Schumann's genius and perhaps gives rise to the criticism that he makes light of the deleterious aspects of some of the poetry. He is frequently accused of his failure to recognize Heine's cynicism, though this surely cannot apply to *Ich grolle nicht*, *Das ist ein Flöten und Geigen*, *Ich hab' im Traum geweinet*, or to *Ein Jüngling liebt en Mädchen* if the latter is sung and played with understanding.

But there is some foundation for this criticism. Poetry was regarded by him, literary though he was, as an inferior art form; he held that 'it must wear the music like a wreath'. No wonder then, that sometimes he is loth to depart from the symmetry of a frame he has fashioned in order to respond to the sinister demands of his poet. The most flagrant example is Heine's *Mein Wagen rollet langsam* Opus 142 no. 4 (My carriage moves slowly). It has a languid and graceful movement, soothing to the somnolent passenger, who becomes absorbed in tender thoughts of his inamorata: without warning three ghosts appear at the carriage window, float in, mocking, gibbering and grimacing. Do they frighten the day-dreamer or disturb his train of thought? Not in the slightest degree. Richard Strauss sets the same verses under the title *Waldesfahrt* Op 69 No. 4 (Woodland Journey) and the spectres he elicits, hopping, floating, skipping for three pages of pianistic pyrotechnics, do most decidedly startle their victim and incidentally scare the living day-lights out of the pianist.

It can be said that scant justice is accorded to the Lorelei in *Waldesgespräch*, the third song in Eichendorff's *Liederkreis* for she is, when all is said and done, the be-all and end-all of the song. It is a splendid song but the terror is missing. Much is left to our imagination.

That our composer recoiled altogether from the melodramatic would be a false assumption. Heine's interpretation of the fate of *Belsatzar* is terrifyingly realized by Schumann and *Die feindlichen Brüder* is almost as blood-curdling. But for masterpieces in this genre we turn to *Der Spielmann* and *Der Schatzgräber* and find it hard to understand why they are so rarely heard.

It must be conceded that Schumann generally is much more at ease when the exigence is subtle and he can respond on the same level: this proviso is evident in some of the Eichendorff lyrics.

This poet indeed set problems; he enjoyed, when one imagines everything is going swimmingly, introducing a shudder into the last verse. In *Im Walde* we are warned of an impending sombre change of mood by the lowering clouds; well reflected by a continually drooping vocal line. But in *Auf eine Burg* the poet withholds the parting sting until the very last word and Schumann encounters it appropriately by ending the composition on an unresolved dominant discord.

Eichendorff's gambit, as Somerset Maugham said of Ibsen, is the sudden arrival in the last act, of a stranger 'who comes into a room and opens all the windows, whereupon the people who were sitting there catch their death of cold'. (And live unhappily ever after).

Schumann's vocal line often burgeons into a bloom of rich colour from a tiny seed; the loveliest of his melodies are iniated, maybe, by a simple note oft repeated: – *Der Nussbaum, Aus meinen Tränen spriesen, Wenn ich in deine Augen seh.*. (Hugo Wolf gratefully inherited this essence, it is seen particularly in his Italian Song Book). His melodies undulate with refreshing spontaneity and should be affectionately handled by the singer. They beg to be allowed to breathe, and if strangulated by the strict beat of the metronome are rendered lifeless. For this reason I have stressed in the following pages, not the desirability but the absolute necessity for *tempo rubato*. There must be dispensation from the restriction of the bar line. The melody soars wonderfully and freely. Freely yes, but not freedom unlimited, it is subject to the discipline of form and good taste. None of the great artists for whom I played were ever guilty of distortion; they sang with a natural *rubato*, a *rubato* so subtle that it was scarcely discernable.

A special brand of humour is to be remarked, at once elegant and witty. On its toes in *Die Soldatenbraut*; *Aufträge*; *Die Kartenlegerin*; Philine's song *Singet nicht in Trauertönen* (from *Wilhelm Meister*); *Viel Glück zur Reise Schwalben*; more masculine in *Sitz ich allein*; *Setze mir nicht*; *Schlusslied des Narren*; *Der Hidalgo* whose love-making is not to be taken seriously, though the lady he seduces might disagree.

One cannot doubt that Schubert was Schumann's model, for it is a fact that he took continued delight in Schubert's work. When the master died in 1828 Schumann's sobbing was heard throughout the night (Joan Chissell: *Schumann*, J.M. Dent). Of all writers he comes nearest to the Viennese composer in his genius for weaving a spell of magic out of – well – nothing: the postlude to the final song of *Frauenliebe und Leben* for instance. It is true that the heart-breaking recitative of the singer has reduced us to tears, but how does the song end after the voice's last note? The answer is by a postlude of twenty-one bars of music which is seemingly undistinguished. And yet it must be proclaimed that they are twenty-one bars of pure magic. Why are they magical? Only a Schubert or a Schumann could tell us.

It is fascinating how these two sublime composers with so much in common, differed in one aspect in their writing. Schubert's introductions are of great moment and place signal responsibility on the player. We see again and again how they prepare the way for the singer and listener by painting a picture or evoking a mood, sometimes one might say, giving a *précis* of the story. With Schumann, apart from a few exceptions, it is quite different. Some of his masterpieces, in fact most songs from *Dichterliebe*, have little or no introduction at all. He preferred the pianoforte to continue when the singing was ended, as if to carry on the thoughts of the silent singer.

No composer, before or since, knew the pianoforte more intimately than he and he made his postludes of much more consequence than his introductions. They are of shining eloquence.

It may be complained that I treat the music too clinically but one is always accused of this when refusing to leave things to chance. 'It will be all right on the night' is a slip-shod attitude that never appealed to me. If I needed vindication I can recall Alfred Brendel saying 'Thinking about the music does not exclude the emotions, it stimulates them'.

Note

All the songs herein are to be found in Vols I, II, and III of Peters Edition. The cycles are in Vol I except the Heine *Liederkreis* Op. 24 the first eight songs of which are in Peters Vol. II: the last song of this cycle *Mit Myrten und Rosen* is in Peters I, page 141.

DICHTERLIEBE (Poet's Love)

(Heine)

Op. 48. Edition Peters Volume I.

1/IM WUNDERSCHÖNEN MONAT MAI

In the darling month of May when
buds were bursting into bloom
and birds were trilling, I told
her of my love and longing.

The very first song is intimate in feeling, pregnant with a longing that is expressed by the mounting line at the end of each verse; it is an outstretching made more acute by the *crescendo* up to the high points.

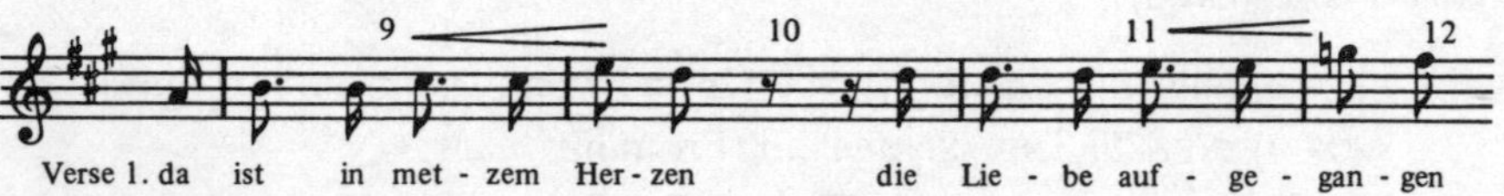

It would be an exaggeration in so short a song, simply because it is strophic, to attempt to vary the expression between the two verses; only bars 22 and 23 (Sehnen und Verlangen) beg for more time and a more persistent *crescendo* than their correlation (11 and 12).

The composer contents himself with a *piano* by way of instruction and the swellings in tone, shown above, never exceed a *mezzo forte*. However subdued dynamically, the singer tenderly relishes the buds of spring, therefore 'sprangen' has verbal energy while still remaining *piano*; 'Vogel sangen' also.

Always *legato* there should be no rigidity of pace so that the semiquavers in 5 and 7

make the second half of the bar longer than the first half (without the listener noticing it).

Many songs mentioned within the covers of this book, will find the pianoforte's treble clinging relentlessly to the voice, doubling the vocal line; it is a habit of Robert Schumann which the sensitive accompanist does his best to disguise. I am ever ready to urge the pianist to sing, and he has his chance to do so in the prelude, interlude and postlude to this song, but at the voice's entry his tune must be *sotto voce* and generally kept to a lower tonal level than the voice. At no time should we be made aware that he is playing on a percussive instrument; the fingers touch the keys, the tone floats.

The conventional 'ushering in' of the singer by a *ritardando* at the end of the introduction is to be deprecated as a rule, though here it is not displeasing. To slow up slightly on the last three notes of bar 4 lends an air of tenderness, provided this slackening of the tempo is not overdone.

As if echoing the singer's 'Sehnen und Verlangen' the postlude brings the song to an end on a note of interrogation with a discord marked by Schumann with a *fermata*. This chord is held at some length, not only with the sustaining pedal but by the fingers, and is not released until the tone has died away, upon which we embark on the next song where the long held discord is resolved.

2/AUS MEINEN TRÄNEN SPRIESSEN

From my tears flowers will blossom,
Only love me, child of my heart, and
the flowers are yours: my sighs shall
become a choir of nightingales
singing at your window.

The discord is resolved, but not the doubts.

With but seventeen bars of music the singer would be unjustified in loading the song emotionally. Though short it can be regarded as in two sections. The first half is treated in a uniform *piano*, *legato* of course, with a light and airy quality coloured by consideration of the flowers and nightingales, rather than the tears and sighs. It is factual, not intense.

'Und wenn du mich lieb hast, Kindchen' needs a deeper, warmer feeling; this is unfolded by imparting more vibrancy to the voice, not by loudening. The singer will be helped here by an awareness of the pianoforte's descending passages in bars 9 and 10 and by its pensive chromatic drop on 'klingen' (14).

This descending passage is a feature of the accompaniment and one should be more conscious of it than the parenthetical treble which clings to the melodic line of the voice.

Three of the singer's phrases end on the dominant seventh and are answered on the pianoforte.

They are all marked *pp.* and the resolution should not be sounded until the singer's tone has ceased.

Is the accompanist's semiquaver in bar 13 ('Fenster soll') to synchronize with the singer's 'soll'? The writer invariably plays it *after* the voice.

3/DIE ROSE, DIE LILIE, DIE TAUBE

The rose, the lily, the dove, the sun,
these were pure joy to me,
but she who is so gentle and so sweet,
it is she now who has captured my heart,
for she is all these –
rose, lily, dove, sun, in herself.

With hardly a break after the last song the singer suddenly bursts forth in a cascade of fervent fluttering words.

We recall 'Queen lily and rose in one' in Tennyson's 'Maud' and ask ourselves if it is not extravagant? Well, it once swept us off our feet: Schumann similarly, in the Heine lyric, felt its impact. Despite its ardour it is too slight to be sung with hearty vigour; spirit is engendered by energy of enunciation, rather than by loudening of tone, (it is marked *mezzo forte* and carries one small *crescendo*) for the song is a bird, it flies past, has gone almost before we glimpse the colour of its wings, and lasts little more than half a minute. For this very reason it would be ill-advised to speed through in record time, indeed it will be more convincing if the singer allows himself latitude and thereby makes it more intelligible. He controls the rhythm, the rhythm does not run away with him; the composer's instruction is *Munter* (lively) not *Presto*. (Chopin's A flat Valse op 64 no. 1 is known as the 'Minute Valse' but it has infinitely more grace and gives more pleasure if it takes more time to perform than its nickname prescribes.)

So the singer slackens tempo at 'Liebeswonne' (bar 4), at 'Die Eine' (8), and at 'Sonne' (12) thus he may take three breaths if he wishes. If he boasts he can contain this shortest of all songs with one breath in the middle, so much the worse for him and Schumann.

4/WENN ICH IN DEINE AUGEN SEH

When I look into your eyes pain and sorrow vanish; when I kiss your lips I am restored. When I lay my head on your breast heavenly joy fills my being; but when you say 'I love you' I cannot but weep bitterly.

There is a long silence after the third song before the introductory chord of the fourth is played, a silence to prepare us for a transition from animation to a tranquillity we have not yet experienced. So tender is the opening phrase that the *crescendo*, unless initiated with quiet care by the pianist at 'doch wenn ich küsse deinen Mund', can develop into a too strident *forte* at bar 7. The high notes (preferable to the lower alternatives) on 'ganz und gar' should not tempt the singer to excess: this is not a crowning point, infinitely bigger and more dramatic climaxes come later in the cycle.

We saw that the second song was conceived by the singer as a gently descending curve dynamically, gaining emotional depth by reticence; the same graph is again in evidence, but much steeper. 'Wenn ich mich lehn' an deine Brust' should be a complete antithesis to the preceding *forte* and is so melting that the *crescendo* (marked on bar 8) should be ignored: it is the most intimate moment of all and is murmured in natural speech rhythm.

The heart-swelling moment 'doch wenn du sprichst' is whispered softly and falls like balm on the ear

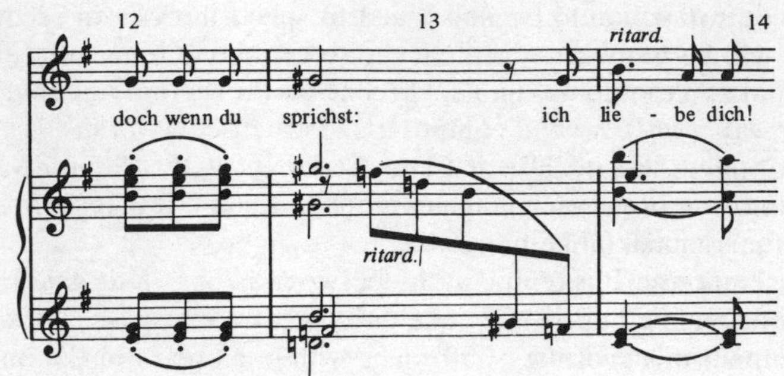

Time seems to stand still, so lovingly is the moment prolonged. The falling quavers in the pianoforte move reluctantly to 'ich liebe dich' which is breathed upon the air.

Heine's piteous 'so muss ich weinen bitterlich' is not underlined by Schumann, in fact it is almost thrown away unless the singer makes some concession to the bitterness by command of articulation: he breaks his tone – without breathing – between 'weinen' and 'bitterlich' and gives the latter an energetic 'b', still keeping to his *mezza voce.* In effect, the message is 'I weep because you are not to be trusted'.

A rhythmic pattern ♪. 𝅘𝅥𝅯 ♪ ♪ ♪ ♪ exchanged between voice and pianoforte, often on a repeated note, is a distinctive feature.

5/ICH WILL MEINE SEELE TAUCHEN

I will plunge my soul into the bell of the lily
and it will resound to a whispered song of love,
a song as tremulous as her lips when she kissed me
in that rapturous hour.

This is indeed Schumann at an inspired moment. The combination of the *legato* line and the rippling undercurrent of the accompaniment is enchanting. Heine's hinted eroticism is ignored, a plaintiveness of mood, even a languishing is inherent in this conception. It is marked *Leise* (softly or delicately) and the singer will wisely leave the music to speak for itself. We are grateful if he gives us a light lyrical tone without inflexion and a smooth line.

Debussy's instruction to pianists that their instrument should 'be without hammers' applies to much of the *Dichterliebe* (songs 1, 2 and 4 are instances) and it is borne in mind here. The melody in the accompaniment can be allowed to sing sweetly when running counter to the voice, but, as we have earlier suggested, less obviously when doubling.

The pianoforte bass moving in contrary motion to the voice in bars 7 and 15 should be noticed. Only in the postlude does the passion of the poet find expressive response. It is recognized by the swelling bass moving down step by step and arriving at its lowest note precisely as the treble tune takes an upward leap of an octave. These bars are stirring and made unmistakably so, but are never out of proportion.

6/IM RHEIN, IM HEILIGEN STROME

That sacred stream the Rhein, mirrors the holy city of Cologne. In its great cathedral hangs a picture painted on golden leather which brought sunshine to my life. Flowers and angels hover round Our Lady: her eyes, lips and cheeks are just like my darling's.

So far the songs have been miniatures, exquisite and restrained, but numbers 6, 7 and 9 need a larger frame.

The music's rolling movement not only characterizes the mighty river, more conspicuously it suggests the diapason of the cathedral organ in the pianoforte bass — majestic and sonorous. Sonorous too is the *forte* of the singer to match the pedal notes of the organ.

Nearly always rhythm is tight and the composer's notation observed: the figure most in evidence is ♪♩. ♪♩. and is never ♪ ³♫ ♪ ³♫ as if it were a triplet. Both singer and partner are vigilant in this regard.

'Das grosse heilige Cöln' must not weaken in tone though the passage lies low in the voice.

Colour most certainly changes at allusion to the picture, a tender colour without resorting to the ethereal quality of the previous song.

'Flowers and angel's floating' is depicted in an even more reverential manner and the semiquavers are treated with unhurried consideration. It would be altogether lacking in conviction if we heard 'um unsre liebe Frau' sung in strict time with vigorous sixteenths.

In fact 34 is the longest bar in the song except for the final 'Liebsten genau'. Anticipating this loving passage is a pianoforte interlude: it is marked *piano* at bar 27 but a *mezzo forte* is more desirable making possible a demulcent *diminuendo* down to a *piano* at the singer's entry (31).

Once more the organ is evident in the postlude and maintains its sonority without weakening.

7/ICH GROLLE NICHT

I'll not complain though my heart is breaking.
Love lost forever! Though you glitter with diamonds
I have long known there is no answering ray of light
in the blackness of your heart; long known that a
serpent feeds on this heart of yours. I saw, my love,
how wretched you are.

This is the only poem in the cycle where the betrayed reviles the faithless one and is the least recondite. Schumann has responded with strength and equally plain speaking. Perhaps for that reason, it is the most popular song of them all; it is exciting and easy to understand.

It is not easy to perform.

The prosaic accompaniment in block harmony gives a deceptive impression of squareness and uniformity when, in fact, it is at once pliant and febrile. Advice tendered in a previous song that the music should be allowed to speak for itself would be misleading in this instance, for now the singer has to mould every utterance.

Tempo rubato is essential. The words 'grolle nicht' are of supreme importance, for they are the root of the matter and must be allowed ample time to grip the hearer. The three quavers (bar 2) push forward to 'Herz', but the 'auch' though only a subordinate bridge between the 'Herz' (long held) and 'bricht' needs to be truly unhurried, otherwise enunciation of the consonants in 'bricht' will be indistinct. So the pianist, aware of the 'ch' in 'auch' waits for the vowel on 'bricht' before sounding his first chord in 4. The singer takes all the time he needs to give cutting meaning to these distressing words.

Even the repeated introductory chords are not played exactly as written, *tempo subito* would be far too abrupt a way to bring the singer in.

I have gone into some detail over the treatment of these four bars because the elasticity desirable throughout the song is epitomized here. After thought and practice the partners will find it natural.

'Das weiss ich längst' connects the verses by a vituperative *crescendo* on the sustained 'längst', it culminates in a heavy chord after which a steep decrease in tone is made on the pianoforte so that the singer's 'Ich grolle nicht' can this time be delivered with less intensity. Not only has he uttered the words three times previously with vehemence, but he foresees a prolonged build-up to a huge climax in the offing. A *mezzo forte* at the most is all to the good.

Schumann is conservative in his instructions. Here and there he has a *forte*, sometimes a *mezzo forte* but on the climax a *fortissimo* though wanted is not indicated. Just as surely as the singer will be unwilling to hold back – and rightly – on the towering 'am Herzen frisst' so must he occasionally redress the balance by restraint, hence my recommended reduction in volume at the start of the second verse.

There is one *piano*, authentic and vital, 'ich sah dich ja im Traume', initiating the great build-up, but the tone is far from dulcet, it is as if sung with clenched teeth; one should be made aware of the spleen as the phrases mount to the desperation of 'am Herzen frisst'. The top notes in the score are printed as alternatives but they must be sung; an effort too should be made to maintain this *fortissimo* to the very end. This suggestion is unreasonable, but at least we do not want to feel that an intentional *diminuendo* is being made. True, the final 'nicht' is low in pitch but the accompanist helps by lightening his tone. An imperceptible reduction of strength from the pianist not only allows the 'nicht' to stand out boldly, it gives him a heaven-sent opportunity for a massive growth of sound leading up to his last three detached defiant chords.

8/UND WÜSSTEN'S DIE BLUMEN, DIE KLEINEN

If the flowers knew of my grief they would weep with me, the nightingales too would sing and the stars come down to comfort me, but my pain is known to none of them, it is known only to her who has broken my heart.

As opposed to the previous song's bold front where the lover struck an heroic attitude, here he weeps; consequently in three of the four verses the singing is consistently delicate. So slight are these quatrains that three vocal phrases suffice for each; phrases similarly shaped, starting high in the stave and dejectedly, gently dropping.

Like a trembling heart the accompaniment flutters under the smooth melancholy melodic line with playing light as a butterfly. *Una corda* is necessary but with the sustaining pedal used very sparingly.

Bitter truth is truly revealed in the last verse and in affirmation has less impetuosity. 'Sie alle können's nicht wissen' is slower and has more substance, reinforced by a more generous use of the sustaining pedal in the accompaniment. As if to bear out the words 'Torn, Torn is my heart in two' the singer's dramatic declaration coupled with the rending chords in the pianoforte seem to bring the music to a stop.

Nevertheless it is in the postlude that suppressed passion erupts. Playing of uninhibited spirit is demanded.

I suggest a comma between 32 and 33. It imposes a break in time (not in continuity of sound) so that the hand can be raised to give extra emphasis on the first note of the bar. It gives the sweeping passage a dash of desperation.

Schumann gives no indication of the tempo he wanted. I like an approximate speed of ♩ = 120, this is not too hurried to disturb the singer's lyrical line, and also it enables the pianist to articulate each semiquaver with clarity.

9/DAS IST EIN FLÖTEN UND GEIGEN

Hark to the fluting, the fiddling, and the blaring of trumpets within there at my beloved's wedding feast. Amid the din and the drumming you can hear the angels weep.

Assuredly the music of the dance on such a festive occasion would be of a more joyous nature and set in a bright major key; but we are hearing it with the jaundiced ears of the rejected lover. The drum beat on the first of each bar thuds sickeningly in his head: the tight rhythm of the repeated chords with their mocking gaiety, the scraping of the fiddles in the treble, all contrive to drive him from the scene distraught with jealousy. As he retreats, the hateful noise of the merry-makers dies away.

The dance band and the eavesdropper are separate entities; the players play and blow away oblivious of the rejected lover's existence. All through, the drum in the bass thuds on the first beat marking time, not with the uncivilized frenzy of a percussion player in a modern 'punk' or 'pop' group, but with remorseless persistence.

At the beginning the accompaniment is marked *piano* under the voice's *mezzo forte* and this is as it should be, for the vocal arch sails up to 'Geigen' and is clearly heard. Trumpets are, naturally enough, marked *forte* for both partners but when 'Trompeten schmettern darein' is repeated at a lower and more disadvantageous pitch, the voice will be covered if the pianist is unmindful; the long pianoforte descent into the depths (and most resonant range of the instrument) can well be reduced in volume.

'Herzallerliebste mein' (the love of my heart) is made the more tortured by the piercing high notes of the fiddles but this poignant moment is marked *piano* in the vocal line against a *forte* in the accompaniment, a problem compounded by the level of the pianoforte tessitura which is pitched far higher than the level of the voice. Balance between voice and piano must be carefully considered. The solution (to bars 25, 26 and the corresponding 59, 60) is to make the reverberating bass consistent with a *forte* but the treble tempered and rendered less shrill than the instruction implies. These high notes will be evident in any case.

Vivid meaning is attached to the postlude. One can picture the wretched man retreating, pursued by the clangour. Finally the sound of the drum dies down as the music wails to a silence. No *rallentando* is made, for the band has not ceased playing.

10/HÖR' ICH DAS LIEDCHEN KLINGEN

When I hear the song my loved one sang,
sorrow rends my heart; in my dire longing
I go out into the woods to relieve my
overwhelming woe with tears.

The 'song she sang' rings faintly in the introduction; it is a haunting air and when the poor man takes it up, the syncopated accompaniment echoes the tune a semiquaver later than the voice.

Heine's utterance is so gracefully poised that no depth of vocal tone is needed to project it: 'das Liedchen klingen' – 'die Liebste sang' – 'die Brust zerspringen' bring the tone forward to the lips with their consonants and encourage delicacy of delivery.

He is a sensitive artist who allows the music to speak for itself since Schumann has said all there is to say. Only on 'Tränen' (bar 18) and purely for emotive articulation, should he give himself latitude, though it calls for no more force than the drooping 'mein übergrosses Weh'.

The accompaniment is always on a lower plane than the voice, a floating background, though its syncopated motif (bars 9–12) should be heard.

As if the singer's feelings were too deep for words, it is left for the postlude to attempt to reflect them and it is here the pianoforte takes up the burden and sings. The haunting air is heard again and sinks down disconsolately until with a *crescendo* (the first and only) it surges up with an effort, as if trying to shake off the shackles of despair: the apex is reached on bar 26

A singer would instinctively treat this tortured moment *a piacere* as if it were a *recitative* and so should it be played. The top D is lingered on, but it is the A with the accompanying discord that is the crucial point, and it is given more time than its neighbour. Bar 26 is the beginning of a long descent into the bass, lasting for five bars, a passage of resignation bringing the song to an end.

11/EIN JÜNGLING LIEBT EIN MÄDCHEN

A boy loves a girl but she fancies another who, in his turn, loves someone else and marries her, Out of spite the girl weds the first man who comes her way. The lad is forlorn. It's an oft told tale but when it happens, a heart is broken.

The jauntiness of the rhythm does not screen the bitter irony of the words. Cheerfulness is artificial, only skin deep, for it is the forsaken one who gives voice to it, in the belief that the poison in his soul will be disguised. To some extent, therefore, the colour needed is not dissimilar to that brought to bear in describing the wedding dance (Song 9). Certainly there is no thought of a *legato* line or mellifluence of tone. Indeed a hard quality is wanted and the singer may be inspired, or goaded, by the spiky nature of the accompaniment with its jarring false accents. Yet it should be borne in mind, that under the guise of objectivity, an old tale ('eine alte Geschichte') is being told. The song for the first twenty bars, to use a stage expression, should be 'thrown away' until 'Der Jüngling ist übel d'ran' where the rigid tempo is relaxed as marked, and where we may hear a hint of compassion. A *legato* line now becomes more and more evident; emotion increases as the singer says, in effect, 'this is my story, it is my heart that is breaking'.

Thereafter the stiff rhythm and relentless irony are resumed in the postlude, whose message clearly asserts 'Who cares?'.

12/AM LEUCHTENDEN SOMMERMORGEN

On a shining morning in summer I walk in the garden. The flowers look at me, pitying my silence and whisper, 'Be not angry with our sister, you sad pale man'.

Enchanting music more than compensates for the exaggerated sentimentality of the words. The syncopation which played so eloquent a part in number 10 (and which will be used with unforgettable inspiration in the postlude to the last song of the cycle) is to be heard in every bar of this miniature masterpiece. The wond'rous month of May (number 1) has been followed by summer and the full blooms, too heavy for their slender stems, droop their heads with the falling semiquavers of the pianoforte.

Sommermorgen is an invaluable foil, a bridge between the serrated *'Ein Jüngling liebt ein Mädchen'* and the tortured visions of number 13. *Mezza voce* obtains throughout, but the jewelled phrase, shown below, gains brightness by eager articulation.

An enharmonic modulation occurs in the above and I illustrate the vocal line to warn the singer to beware of his intonation at bar 10 where there is a tendency to flatten on 'ich'.

Schumann asks for a *pp* at 'Be not angry with your sister' and this must be reckoned with before the very first note of the song; it is the softest singing since the phrase 'Ich liebe dich' was breathed in the fourth song.

For the pianist it is a test since his postlude must be on the same whispered level. Only at bar 23 does he emerge from his *pianissimo* when the motif of the historic postlude to the final song is announced.

So telling is this moment that the composer asks for a *piano*. Slight prolongation of the semiquaver rest in bar 23, impresses us that something significant is about to happen. We hold our breath.

13/ICH HAB' IM TRAUM GEWEINET

I wept in my dreams, I dreamt you were lying in your grave; when I woke my cheeks were still wet with tears.
Again I dreamt. This time I dreamt you had abandoned me and on waking my bitter tears flowed for so long.
Again I wept in my dream, I dreamt you loved me still. I woke, but my weeping still goes on.

The first two verses consist of a dialogue between voice and pianoforte, but each speaks in a different vein; the unaccompanied voice has a mournful smoothness and a line that affectingly obeys the pitiful nuance on 'geweinet'; the pianoforte answers tersely with a *staccato* shudder. Only the mention of tears seems to elicit a more sympathetic response from the accompaniment, here the chords are no longer *staccato* and although short are warmed by the sustaining pedal and thus support the singers' expressive unhappy *crescendo*. (Bars 22, 23)

Strict time is discarded at 'floss noch von der Wange herab', a *rallentando* is marked and the phrase begs to be delivered expressively.

The second quatrain is like the first musically, except for 'Ich wachte auf' which is more precipitate.

Each phrase of the singer is made vivid by strict observance of Schumann's notation, this is mandatory.

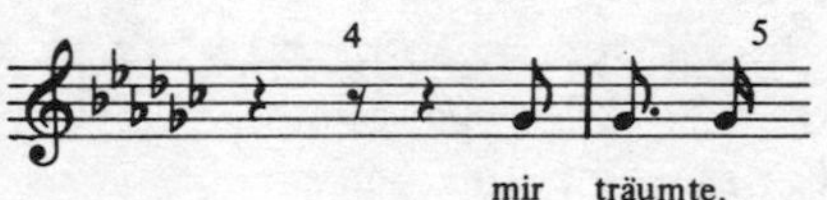

I give the above illustration purely to draw attention to bar 4 where nothing is happening, that is to say nothing except a silence, a pregnant silence which, if shortened, dissipates the suffering it is intended to convey. To spinelessly make his entry one jot before the sixth beat on 'mir' and break the suspense, would be shameful on the part of the singer, especially as this situation arises several times.

Deepest feeling is generated in the final verse. The pianoforte, for the first time, mournfully sounds the haunting opening strain, the singer takes it up with ever increasing passion, supported now by crushing chromatic chords, before climbing to 'strömt meine Tränen flut' one of the most desperate climaxes of the cycle.

It is now the pianist's responsibility to sustain the suspense in his postlude. He has two long silences to cope with – one of eight beats, one of ten beats – and must steel himself for the ordeal. (I confess when playing these last bars I count the beats like a child.)

14/ALLNÄCHTLICH IM TRAUME

Each night in my dreams you greet me warmly and I cast myself sobbing at your feet. Pearly teardrops are in your eyes. Secretly you whisper a word and give me a spray of cypress: I wake; gone is the cypress and I cannot recall that one word.

Dreams of agonizing affliction are succeeded here by dreams which despite Heine's tears are recollected (by Schumann) in repose, not so much despairingly as regretfully.

Abundant rests in the vocal line – silences to be recognized – should not persuade the singer that they are there for his convenience, or intended as favourable opportunities for him to breathe.

No doubt quick breaths could be taken in bars 1 and 2 without our being aware of them but the phrase would lose its stillness. Taken in one breath, singing mentally through the rests, tranquillity of mood is conveyed though the listener may be unaware how it has been accomplished. Naturally the same principle is followed in the second verse, though it differs slightly in punctuation.

There are no accents, nor is prominence given to the high note of each group of three (the up-beats). Absolute smoothness obtains if these suggestions are followed.

The forgotten word ('und's Wort hab' ich vergessen') at the close, should not be overdone; the helplessness of it should be more apparent than the underlying sadness.

Again the accompaniment moves with the voice though its line is sustained through the vocal rests. In bar 2 the chord before 'seh'ich dich' comes several times and the pianist should take a delight in playing it as undisturbingly as possible. His soprano voice in the two interludes sings plaintively.

Suggested tempo ♩ = 52

15/AUS ALTEN MÄRCHEN

A white hand beckons me to an enchanted land
where gay flowers bloom, green trees sing, and
the air resounds with the chirrup of birds:
misty shapes rise from the earth to dance in
fantastic throng; springs gush loudly from
rocks of marble. O land of rapture, I
long to come to you for I see you clearly.
Alas it is all a dream. It dissolves like
foam with the morning sun.

In Schubert's *Winter's Journey*, that vast outpouring of misery unparalleled in the field of song, the few moments of hope and peace of mind through illusory, stand out in contrast to the bleak distress of the rest of that cycle.

Such is the value of this song here, succeeding numbers 13 and 14 in a chain of dreams. It is animated and gay like number 11, but where mock cheerfulness was the burden of *Ein Jüngling liebt ein Mädchen*, we are now exhilarated, unaware that the dazzling promise is 'such stuff as dreams are made on'. Never before in the cycle has there been an occasion for singing with such sparkling eagerness. 'Vivacious' is the instruction and at once we are swept along by the infectious swing of the introduction, with its glittering high tessitura.

Typically Schumannesque and significant are the off-beat quavers in bars 2 and 3, they seem to spur the movement forward and are prominent again and again.

It can easily be understood that the jaunty pattern hardly conduces a steady *legato* line: all important are clarity of articulation and rhythmic precision. Both artists can ensure the latter by giving *full* value to their crotchets (quarter notes) and by lightening the quavers.

One phrase will be seized instinctively by the singer, it is an opportunity to give us a *legato* line.

With that zestful *crescendo* on 'singt' and 'klingt' do we detect a slight *portamento*? So much the better, for by contrast the next two passages are dainty and *staccato*, with those little off-beat prods again in evidence.

The sudden modulation to G major can be given more sustained tone from singer and player. This is deceptively slower in appearance because of the pedal point D naturals and F sharps in the bass (bars 29 to 31 and 33 to 35 respectively) but the pace should never lose impetus. Above all, the temptation to slacken speed at bar 65 and make a *rallentando* leading into the section labelled 'with deep feeling' must be resisted.

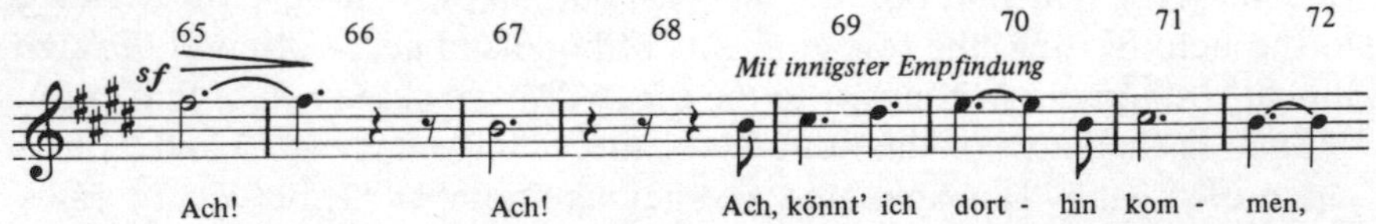

The singer can do nothing on those held notes (65–67) to keep the tempo moving; responsibility rests on the pianist. Schumann himself has cooled the high pressure without moderating the tempo. Even so, that off-beat quaver in the accompaniment makes its presence felt from time to time: particularly in the last four bars of the postlude it palpitates with a suggestion of helpless regret.

I readjust the tonic chord, so that it is sustained without using the pedal, the quaver can thus be detached in character.

The fingers keep a firm hold on the final chord in obedience to the *fermata*. A *rallentando* is unwanted.

16/DIE ALTEN BÖSEN LIEDER

Fetch me a coffin that we may bury the bad old songs and evil dreams. It must be a coffin bigger than the great tun at Heidelberg, for I have much to lay to rest in it. Fetch me a bier of thick firm timber with planks longer than the bridge at Mainz. Fetch me too, twelve giants stronger than Saint Christopher in the cathedral of Cologne, they are to bear the coffin away and sink it in the deepest sea.
Why should this coffin be so huge, so heavy? It holds all my love and all my grief.

An occasional musical relationship between one or two of the songs in the cycle can be noticed, but the first two pages here recall none of the others.

The octave introduction, resolute and powerful, proclaims that weakness of spirit and feminine tears are now cast aside, and for the first time in all the sixteen songs Schumann wants a *fortissimo*. The figuration of alternate *legato* and *staccato* quavers moving in pairs in the accompaniment (3, 4, 5) is an assertion of determination, establishing a consistent rhythmic pattern to last practically unaltered for thirty five bars; toilsome bars describing with some magniloquence the suffering which the poet endured.

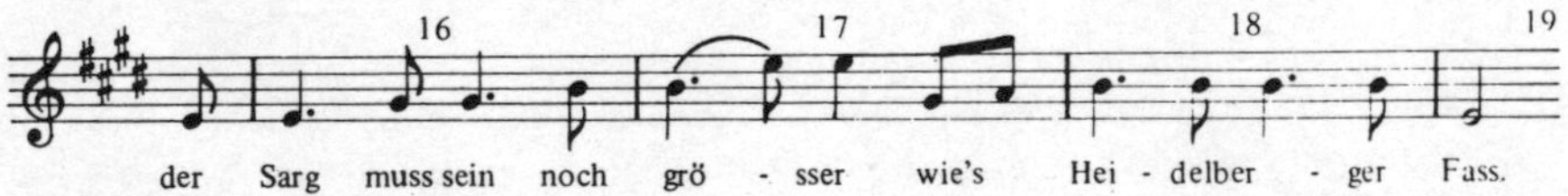

The vocal line laboriously climbs an octave and drops back in three splendid phrases; first 'bigger than the tun' (E major), again one tone higher 'longer than the bridge' (F sharp minor), a further tone higher 'strong as St. Christopher' (G sharp). In these instances the singer husbands his resources, he needs a big *crescendo* on each ascent, but makes sure that the final phrase is the biggest of all.

Only at 36, with these Herculean labours now effected do we return to the home key, when the movement suddenly becomes majestic.

In bar 39 a mighty splash on the diminished seventh chord speaks – or rather thunders – for itself, and the pianist waits for his partner's G natural (second syllable of 'herab') to be well established before his ensuing chord, because it is certain the voice will be engulfed by that tremendous *sforzando*.

'Why so heavy and huge, this coffin?' is a whispered question, very low in the stave. In a long slow *portamento* comes the reply:

A word is necessary in regard to the disposition of the grace note in 47, since singers are sometimes uncertain about it. This *portamento* (Adagio) from the low C sharp up a full octave, heralds an awaited explanation of the preceding poetic frenzy. There is no necessity for this grace note to be apologetic, and the singer, master of the situation, allows it a full quaver beat. It is traditional. A calm breath is taken before 'ich' (again a full beat) before proceeding, all sung without deference to bar lines; the bar is protracted so that poetic justice may be done.

The answer is so momentous that one doubts if it should be sung *piano* as marked? Surely 'und meinen Schmerz hinein' rendered in a soft sad undertone is the negation of the new found mettle, and I suggest that the tone should continue to swell to a *mezzoforte*, reaching a sonorous meaningful 'Schmerz hinein'. It needs dramatic emphasis.

No composer created more eloquent postludes than Schumann. Often they are songs without words, summarizing the emotional content of a cycle or *Lied* with a felicity which is peculiarly his own; the pianoforte epilogue to *Frauenliebe und Leben* is an instance.

But the inspired peroration to *Dichterliebe* is not imbued with tear-choked retrospection; it breaths a different air; we float from darkness into light. No longer a reflection of self-pity, it is a new structure; in truth there are moments of nostalgia but they are gentle and without smart, with a fragile beauty.

The pianist waits and waits, long after the singer's tone has died away before he melts into that syncopated motif heard at the close of number 12; but now it is in a higher key, enabling the solo melody to sing gently and limpidly above the soft waves in the accompaniment.

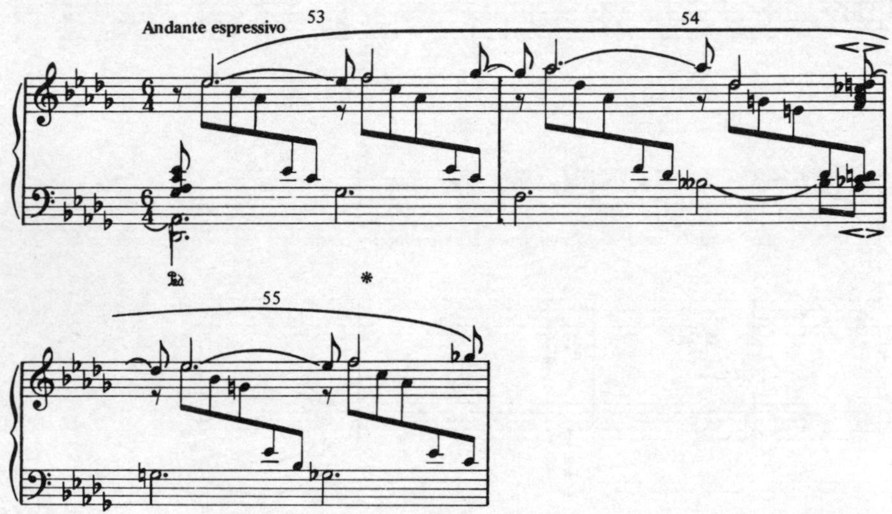

Bars 53 to 58 are tranquil and meditative. We effect the sigh on 54 (it is marked as a stress) by making a very slight pause on it. To infer that the sign calls for a tonal accent would be a misconception, for the calm serenity must be unruffled.

Gradually the melodic line melts into two bars of recitative to be played as if improvised.

The notation seen above does not correspond with that used in the Peters Edition. I have presumed to give some idea how these two marvellously eloquent bars are best unfolded, by allowing sixteen quavers to a measure that is only allotted twelve (if we are to be confined to the 6/4 time signature). Every note sings persuasively but I regard the grace notes (as they are defined in the printed score) as crucial, to be played with infinite tenderness. Actually they are a little – but only a little – faster than the prescribed quaver.

Now the heart is uplifted as three eager waves aspire (61, 62, 63) gaining momentum until their crowning point of reassurance is reached on 64.

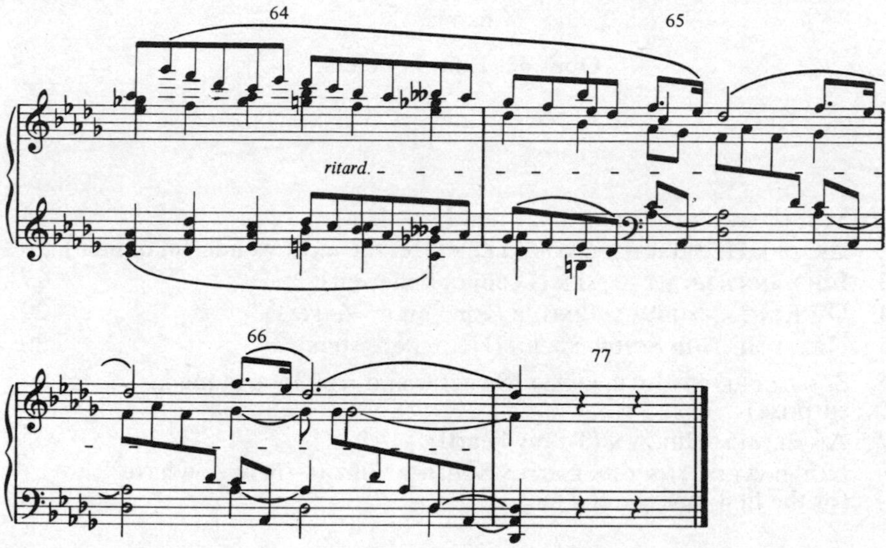

I feel the fourth beat of 64 is the glowing apex; the sixth beat is its complementary and soothing answer, to be played with affectionate care.

What is that lulling strain thrice heard in the soprano that brings us to a peaceful close? Does it recall, however faintly, ‘Hör’ ich das Liedchen klingen’, the air the beloved sang?

FRAUENLIEBE UND LEBEN
(Woman's love and life)

(Chamisso)

Opus 42. Edition Peters.

1/SEIT ICH IHN GESEHEN

Since first I saw him I feel blind to all else. I see him and only him in a waking dream by day and in the blackest darkness of night. To me all else is without meaning, colourless. Rather than play with my sisters, I would sit in my little room alone, and weep. I am blind to everything and everyone since first I saw him.

The self-styled lowly girl who seeks solitude that she may indulge in tears for love of him who in her eyes is set so far above her, must indeed be a modest maiden. Schumann draws a demure and unpretentious character in the first song, for the structure is so simple, the pattern so pure, that taken at face value, we might easily assume there is no significance to be found in it. Not until the final song of the cycle, when the postlude repeats this theme, do we discover what latent depths are concealed beneath its subdued surface.

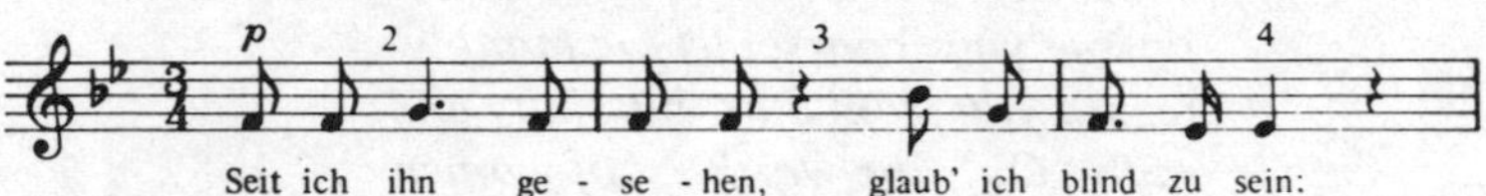

I like taking the above *legato* (it is my recommendation, not Schumann's) for the three bars should be felt as one phrase. My *penchant* for 'thinking through' a rest, without taking a breath (so easy for the accompanist!) could be considered, but a breath at this slow tempo (♩ = 40) is more fitting provided it is taken quietly and unobtrusively. An abrupt silence – snapping off tone suddenly after 'gesehen' would be unfeeling, there is ample time to make the comma gently. In the little prelude

Schumann clearly indicates that the sustaining pedal carries the tone almost to the third beat. It is a clue for the singer.

All through each verse the vocal line moves unpretentiously a step higher with each utterance until the wide liberated interval of the seventh, to the words 'taucht aus tiefstem Dunkel' (in blackest darkness), from whence it curves down again.

That expressive moment 'seh' ich ihn allein' (I see only him) has a *retard*. It is a Schumann idiosyncracy never to compensate this instruction with an *a tempo* mark in his songs. Here obviously tempo is resumed on the third beat of bar 7.

2/ER, DER HERRLICHSTE VON ALLEN

He is the finest of all men, tender and kind, handsome to behold, noble in mind and heart. He shines in my heaven like a star, glorious and remote. Pursue your course, let me humbly regard you from afar, blissfully and sadly. Only the worthiest of women should be your choice and I will bless her even though my heart should break.

The restraint of the first song is cast off in this protestation of love. The shy, chaste maid voices her innermost thoughts, bares her heart in a sudden uninhibited disclosure of passion.

It is a fine song for singing. After an introduction of a few light repeated chords, the melodic line has a splendid sweep, to be attacked with gusto.

(a)

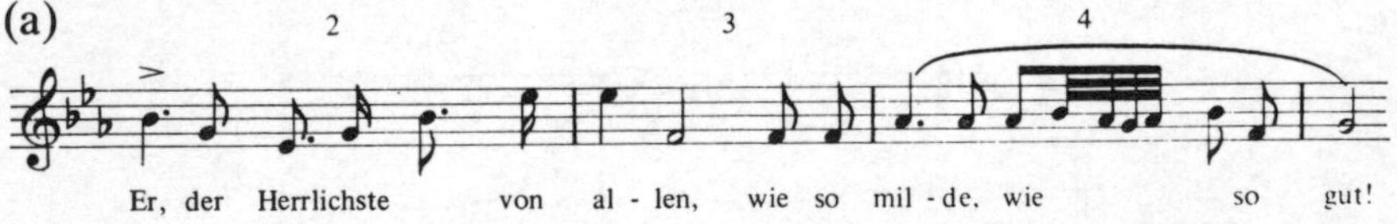

(b)

In my example (a) I turn the crotchet or quarter note in bar 4 into a quaver to make ample room for the 32nd notes of the 'turn'. Furthermore I recommend slowing the pace that these small notes may be well and truly heard, for they are an expression of great ardour. In example (b) this 'turn' is shown as it appears in the Peters Edition, it is called the Chambonnières ornament. Since the singer encounters this *gruppeto* eight times in the song it will be as well if she does not make it a meaningless scramble. There are hints, in any case, that the composer wished for some freedom of impulse by several *ritardandi.* A yielding, though not marked, is desirable at 37 'hoher Stern der Herrlichkeit' (my glorious star) in preparation for the self-effacing 'Only the worthiest of women' which is a quiet section of some fifteen bars, before the renewed enthusiasm of the recapitulation.

In the accompaniment the repeated quaver chords are heard in every bar and they should be played unpercussively to allow the voice to sail freely above. The interludes, however, hear the pianoforte treble singing clearly above the left hand. Octaves in the bass are naturally important, needing specific prominence when responding heroically to the girl's transports.

Only in the postlude do the impetuous repeated chords of the treble melt, without loss of exaltation, into four bars of repose.

3/ICH KANN'S NICHT FASSEN, NICHT GLAUBEN

I cannot grasp it or believe it; it
must be a dream, how, from all others he
has chosen and blessed me. It must have
been in a dream that I heard him say 'I am
yours forever!' O let me die in this dream
cradled in his arms, weeping with endless joy.

Schumann is more concerned with the incredulity of the bewildered girl than with the 'unendlicher Lust' of the poet's last line, and if we accept his interpretation, it is an exciting composition.

The breathlessness of the over-wrought maid is portrayed with utter simplicity

Despite the instruction 'With violent emotion' the composer asks only for a *forte*. No attempt is made to give us a *legato* line except at the sixth bar, the singer always treats her line with imaginative flexibility; it would be unthinkable for her to deliver 'A dream deceives me' at the hectic speed of ♩. = 112; she must ease up here, as we can see by the complementary bar 14, where a *ritardando* is demanded.

In the animated sections ('Ich kann's nicht fassen nicht glauben' etc. is heard thrice) the pianist plays a vivid part. His hands do not drop on to the keys, they spring *up*, as if the keys were red hot.

Considering the brevity of the song, Schumann is unusually liberal with his instructions, surely an indication that he had flexibility of tempo in mind. Very tender, therefore, is the passage recalling the loved one's promise, 'I am yours forever', with the singer lingering lovingly on the words. Again it would be unfeeling in the extreme and an uncomfortable contradiction to rap out 'gewieget an seiner Brust' (cradled against his breast) with aggressive exactitude.

A dynamic climax – 46 and 47 –

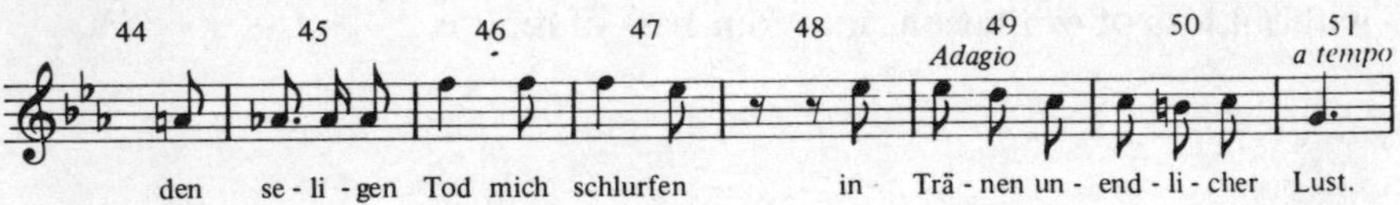

should also be generously expanded, anticipating the *Adagio*. 'Tränen' (savouring the expressive consonants T–R) is more conspicuous than 'Lust' on which the fast tempo is immediately resumed.

Uncertainty is suggested in the pianoforte interlude with its sensitive hesitations (71 and 75) and I feel this is confirmed by the girl's final phrase even though it ends (reluctantly?) in the major.

The tears are more evident than the joy.

4/DU RING AN MEINEM FINGER

Dear little golden ring on my finger
I press you devoutly to my lips and heart.
When I had done with childhood's blissful
dreams and found myself alone in the
world, it was you who opened my eyes
to life's meaning.
I shall serve him, live for him, belong
only to him: I shall become transfigured
by the light he sheds.

It was suggested on a previous page that 'Ich grolle nicht' though a fine song and understandably the most celebrated in *Dichterliebe*, by no means reached the level of several other songs in sublimity of conception. It can be presumed that in the cycle we are dealing with, 'Du Ring an meinem Finger' holds a similar high place in popular esteem. Some of its critics regard it as sickly sentimental; this charge surely cannot be levelled at Schumann's door but rather at Chamisso's. To counterbalance the palpitation of number 3, a mood truly placid is to be welcomed.

The main tune is heard three times, though it is given a slight variation at the close.

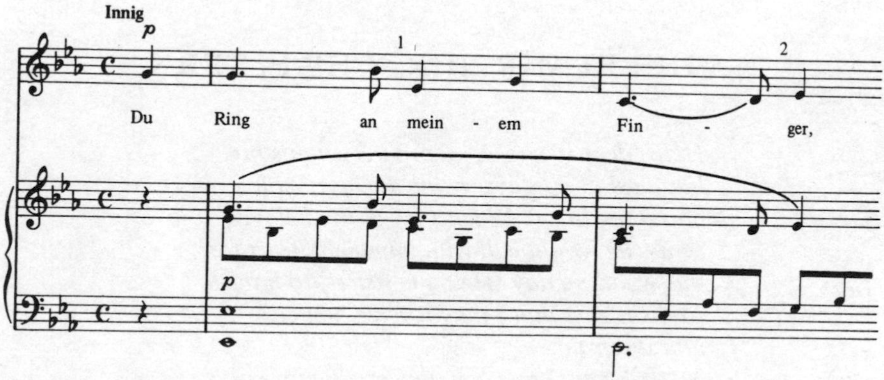

It tends to become monotonous if the two partners do not exercise some care. As can be seen, the vocal line is rather serrated in bar 1 and thoughtless singing will tend to give false stresses, so that we hear 'Du Ring AN meinEM Finger', and in bar 5 'ich drükke DICH fromm an DIE Lippen'. There is no intention on my part to imply that the first and third beats should be accented, on the contrary, these quiet phrases need honeyed smoothness; have curves that should not deteriorate into sharp angles.

The soprano voice in the accompaniment moving in unison with the vocal line, is to be veiled rather than emphasized; it is the alto voice (*molto legato*) that is of more import.

Surprisingly enough, this serenest of songs bears distinct relationship with number 3, the most ebullient in the entire cycle. This affinity is evident when Schumann forsakes the habitual quietude and with quickening pulse wants more impetuosity for eight bars (25–32). He uses a structure of repeated chords and a modulation

which we heard in 'Er, der Herrlichste von allen' in the same tonality but there with more fire. The song ends with a quiet return to the familiar refrain.

5/HELFT MIR, IHR SCHWESTERN

Help, dear sisters, to adorn me on this my happiest of all days, twine the myrtle blossom about my brow. When I lay in my beloved's arms, he would call with impatient heart for this wedding day. Help me sisters, to banish foolish fears that I may receive him clear-eyed and unafraid.
My beloved, have you appeared before me?
Sun, will you lend me radiance that I may do honour to my lord?
And you, dear sisters, strew flowers before him and tender him rosebuds.
Though I bid you a sad farewell, I leave you joyously.

What a fussy accompaniment!

But how harmonious for the occasion! One can sense through its busyness the nervous excitement of the bride, can picture her loving helpers bustling round her, making last minute adjustments to the wedding gown.

Arching arpeggios seem to signify the graceful curves of the bride's train. The dotted quaver is dwelt on as long as the player dares without disturbing the over-all rhythm of the bar; a fluttering hesitation consistent with the maiden's innocent trepidation. This suggested hesitation undoubtedly necessitates a shortening of the following semiquaver (the 16th) but that is preferable to a lazy semiquaver or loss of energy, which would impart an uncharacteristic easy-going assurance.

Yet, above all this pother, the melodic line sings with joy. A dream, far beyond all hope, is unbelievably realized.

The four bar phrase is repeated musically note for note until modulating at bar 10 to the dominant. Hitherto the rise and fall have been confined to a sixth in range, but now come two mounting arches, the first of them with a stretch only a little wider, but the second soaring like a bird.

The singer should glory in it and most certainly allow herself some latitude for 'ungeduldig den heutigen Tag' (impatience for this day) and the top G should ring out thrillingly.

At 27 the repeated quaver chords come into play and are structurally akin to those of the second song and to the middle section of 'Du Ring an meinem Finger'. Bar 30 here, deliberately recalls bars 12 and 16 of 'Er, der Herrlichste.'

However, there is a difference, for now the singer cannot permit herself to broaden the 'turn' as she did in the earlier song; it would savour of calculation where impatient zest must be the prevailing spirit. In any case bar 30 is not a goal in itself but is embraced in the stride of sweeping passages and ever-widening intervals from 24 to 34, culminating in the climax:–

A *diminuendo* is seen in the accompaniment on 34 but this mark is *not* for the voice, which sails on triumphantly.

The postlude, played with quiet solemnity, is founded on the main theme in the style of a wedding march.

Strangely enough it is in the same key as the Bridal Chorus in the third act of *Lohengrin* and I invariably call this to mind when I play it. Could Wagner have heard *Frauenliebe und Leben* or is it one of those coincidences?

Schumann writes *Ziemlich schnell* at the beginning and a suggested tempo is 𝅗𝅥 = 72. The postlude should be 𝅗𝅥 = 52 considerably slower, but is prepared for by the singer's *ritardando*.

6/SÜSSER FREUND

Sweet friend, you look at me wonderingly
and cannot understand why there are tears
in my eyes: they are pearls of joy.
How anxious my heart is, but how blissful!
Hide your face on my breast that I may whisper
in your ear what gives me joy.
Do you see now, my beloved, why I weep? Let
me hold you closer to me that you may feel
my beating heart.
Here beside my bed there is room for a cradle
and from it, when my dream comes true, your
eyes will smile up at me. Your eyes!

A more unaffected touch than Schumann's in this most intimate of songs could not be imagined. The augmented interval prompts the idea at once of debility and an appeal for compassion, and is used frequently, coming six times, for example, in the first 21 bars.

Should the singer be inclined to treat this featured interval (bars 2 and 5) with a *portamento* it is to be hoped she will think again, for it is expressive enough already and is better left pure and simple.

The basic tempo is ♩ = 52 but the movement is not to be too exact, the semiquavers in bars 1, 3, and 4 are unhurried. I went to some pains to show why, in my opinion, the semiquavers in the accompaniment of *Helft mir* should be made energetic; here the very reverse is the case, for now they ought to be languid.

Dynamic rises and falls are plentiful in the score (7–10 sees a *crescendo* marked in each bar) but these are sensitive nuances rather than swellings of tone, and never exceed a *mezzo forte*.

A compass of a fifth was wide enough for Schumann to unfold the utmost eloquence in these two verses. Bar 10 ('freudig') and 20 ('flüstern') are telling points where the singer enunciates with affectionate care but delicate tone. Indeed 'will ins Ohr dir flüstern alle meine Lust' (I will whisper in your ear) becomes a passage of touching beauty if the high note is taken *pianissimo*.

The pianoforte interlude (21–24) has a resolute air, as if the young wife summons up courage to divulge her secret.

The grace note before the voice's entry is a quaver in length.

Once again in this third verse Schumann's repeated quavers in the accompaniment are in evidence and give their pedalled *non-legato* an effect of hushed suspense; they are parenthetical. A different touch is needed in the bass when it responds to the voice's falling intervals; one thinks of the 'cello when playing here and makes it poignant with a keen edge; the dissonance between the alto E and bass F (26) must not be disguised.

It is all subdued, until quite suddenly, the pulse quickens (Lebhafter) to the words 'hold me closer'. Passion is recalled momentarily. It is in contrast to the rest of the song and makes the reversion to the main theme in the final verse more intimate and hushed with wonder, than before. The spread chord in the *Adagio* bar is played with tenderest expression.

7/AN MEINEM HERZEN

At my heart, at my breast, my child, my joy.
Happiness is love, love is happiness.
I once thought I was deliriously happy but
now I am happier than ever before. Only a
mother with a child at her breast can know
true love and happiness. A man is to be pitied
who cannot know such bliss.
You look at me, dear angel, and smile.
You, my child, my delight, my joy.

Considering he had written few songs since his student days, it is incredible that in one year – 1840 – Schumann enriched the world with so many masterpieces. Naturally enough, they are not, one and all, of the same high level. Who can explain why Schubert could devote the time and labour to write thirty pages of music to a Schiller ballad of interminable hyperbole called *Der Taucher* (The Diver) and two months later compose *Gretchen am Spinnrade* which will forever be a monument in the history of song writing? Schubert was human, after all, and had his shortcomings. So too had Schumann, and the penultimate song in *A woman's life and love* is one of them.

It becomes a challenge to the performers, who do not suffer the listener to be aware of its uninspired lack of depth. The singer's attack is immediate, she sweeps us along by her infectious enthusiasm; her pardonable gusto may impel her to exceed Schumann's recommended *piano*, and this is all to the good.

Half way through comes the direction *Quicker*, then only eight bars later, *Still Quicker*, so it is inadvisable to adopt a break-neck speed at the beginning. I suggest ♩. = 88 which may seem too sedate to some young artists, though it is a tempo that enables the singer to give some elasticity to a vocal line that is in danger of becoming wooden if one sticks rigorously to the printed score.

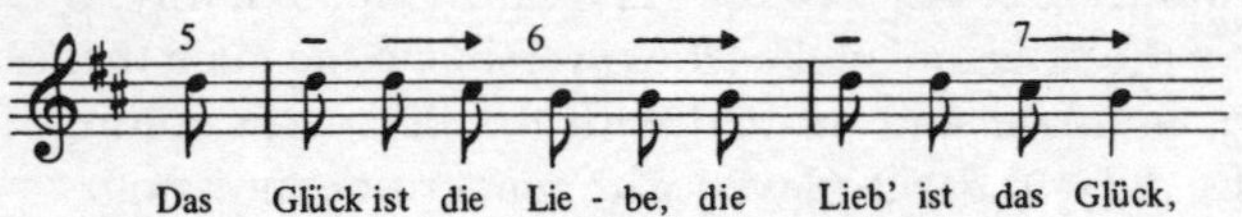

'Glück' and 'Lieb' are each stressed, not with a 'heave' of tone, but rhythmically, with a minute *tenuto*; it is a flexibility giving life to the phrase. Throughout the song this freedom should be discretely exercised.

The pianist with his arpeggios, rightly ignored by the singer, knows or hopes, that voice and pianoforte will meet half-way through each bar; they keep in touch with one another from time to time as it were. In fact the bright semiquavers are less important than the bass

The *Presto* (recommended tempo ♩.= 120 at the least) lasts only five bars, after which, with a *ritardando* the sentiment is truly heartfelt. To convey the rapture of 'My delight, my joy' the singer can take all the time she wants.

The postlude is quietly ecstatic – a relaxation after the boisterousness. Grace notes (so called) are played with repose and as leisurely as bar 57 in *Süsser Freund* to which it has an affinity.

8/NUN HAST DU MIR DEN ERSTEN SCHMERZ GETAN

Now for the first time you have hurt me, but
it is a hurt not to be borne. You sleep,
hard pitiless man, the sleep of death. Left all alone
I stare at an empty world. I have lived and loved
and now no life is left in me.
Numbed, I withdraw into my innermost soul; the
veil falls, there I have you and my last happiness,
you my whole world.

If the meaning of the words are to be truly expressed, the phrases, bars 1–4 and 4–7, cannot be sung in strict time but in recitative style with 'ersten Schmerz' the cruel high point of the first phrase. The second is shaped differently with 'Du schläfst' stressed and held. Grief is so bitterly manifested in the first half of the poem that to sing it in a restrained way would be out of character. Some sorrow is too deep for tears; 'Ersten Schmerz' (first hurt), 'traf' (cruel), 'harter unbarmherzger Mann' (hard, pitiless man) must be delivered with cutting articulation.

So despairing is the mood that the singer underlines it by allowing that harsh pianoforte chord to be well established before her entry. Rhetorical emphasis is not the only reason for her delay after that preliminary chord: she waits for the strident chord to decrease in volume.

This introductory triad to the saddest of songs is inflexibly hard and causes a shudder. Seldom do I suggest that the keys should be struck, but they are here, for a *sforzando*, so much more biting than an accent, is demanded. After impact, the tone should be reduced at once, and that is the problem.

Tone does not decrease sufficiently steeply if the chord is held or is sustained with the pedal. After impact, the hand springs off the keys and the sustaining pedal quickly catches the overtones. But, most important, the pedal is not depressed until after the hand is snatched away. If depressed too promptly the tone will be caught at its resounding strength; if too tardily, the player's efforts will be rewarded by silence. It must be judged to a fraction, perfectly timed. This naked triad is heard twice (bars 1 and 4) in all its anguish and the immediate *diminuendo* must be made, so that the voice, low in the stave is not covered. Instruments are not uniform in their co-ordination between keyboard and pedal: experiment is essential.

The greatest emphasis is reserved for "the world is empty"

The jarring dissonance in bar 10 must be made obvious, the singer holds her D flat tenaciously against the accompanist's clashing C natural; prolonging rather than curtailing it.

Without doubt Schumann knew *Die Winterreise* intimately for he uses the identical discord on 'leer' (bar 10) that Schubert has in *Wasserflut* on the word 'Weh' (bar 12), and again in *Der greise Kopf* on 'Bahre' (bar 26).

Bitterness has now reached its summit and gradually subsides to a subdued, but no less heart-broken, final phrase.

The chord on 22 is the dominant of the home key, D minor, and it is given a long *fermata* then melts with tenderness into the dominant seventh of B flat, the key with which the cycle began.

As a postlude, the theme of the first song is played in its entirety and we now realize, after experiencing the whole cycle, what a world of meaning is concealed beneath its simple and uncomplicated pattern. Why it should be so moving defeats us. We recognize at once that Schubert's *Der Neugierige* is a great song, but the saints and sages cannot explain why *Der du von den Himmel bist* is so magical and how it holds us under its spell. Franz Schubert bequeathed something to Robert Schumann and we sense it in the postlude to *Frauenliebe und Leben.*

LIEDERKREIS (Song Cycle)

(Eichendorf)

Opus 39. Edition Peters Volume I

1/IN DER FREMDE

Beyond the lightning the clouds drift in from my homeland. No one remembers me there, for my father and mother are long since dead. How soon will that quiet time come when I too shall rest, forgotten, under the murmuring trees of the forest!

It is pure coincidence that the first song in *Dichterliebe* and *In der Fremde* bear the same key signature and have accompaniments suggestive of rustling leaves. *Im wunderschönen Monat Mai* was flooded with sunshine and ardent desire, here the evening sky is overcast, fleeting clouds and forest murmurs induce thoughts of death. If one song was light and tender, here the singing and playing need more substance.

The vocal line is as smooth as the floating clouds, ominous too as they.

Legato is so much part and parcel of the sentiment that the singer gives the impression that he encompasses the entire phrase in an uninterrupted stream of sound, though at the essentially slow tempo (♩ = 54) he will need an imperceptible breath in bar 3 after 'rot'. Schumann's grace notes are again seen in this song and each time they are to be treated as semi-quavers.

The longest phrase of all:–

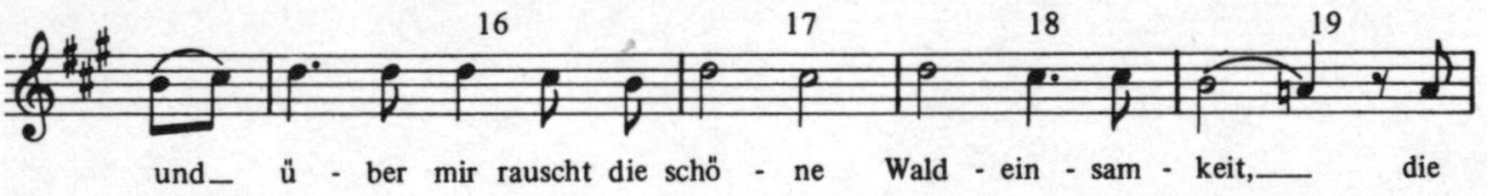

simply must be taken in one breath and it will be a pity if, in order to contain it, the singer is forced to hurry.

Smoothest playing is wanted with pianoforte on a slightly lower plane than the voice; the accents seen in the treble should not be taken too literally or become aggressively obvious. However, a singing response is made to the singer's 'How soon will that quiet time come?' (bars 10–15) and some reassurance is suggested by the sustained minims in the bass.

2/INTERMEZZO

A picture of your loveliness is always in my heart and it gazes at me smiling brightly without cease. My heart sings silently an old sweet song that takes wing and flies swiftly to you.

This little gem of a song falls blissfully on the ear. It is a ray of sunshine. Palpitating, inner excitement, is expressed by continual syncopation in the pianoforte bass. Not for a moment should its delectable charm, its animation, its blithe spirit, disguise the deep feeling which inspires every phrase.

Bearing in mind that we have two beats to a bar the sign *Langsam* is reasonable (♩ = 44 or 48), though if performers count it in four beats to a bar, it will lose its serenity and smoothness.

We should feel the connection between 'Dein Bildnis wunderselig' and (although there is a half-bar rest) 'hab'ich in Herzensgrund'. This gap in the vocal line, with no punctuation mark in the poem, comes several times. The singer does not 'go away' in these little silences for the voice, but 'thinks through them', always on his toes, metaphorically, ready to spring.

At all times in *Intermezzo* he establishes his tempo, whether this tempo is elastic is neither here nor there, the singer must lead with authority. Particularly is this essential from bars 10 to 17.

The first beat of the bar all through this example, and for several more bars, has a suspended chord in the accompaniment, only the voice pulls the strings, so to speak. It can be seen that the composer most decidedly wants the pace to be urged on even quicker. I have heard singers, confused by the syncopation, hang back waiting for some encouragement or prod from the accompanist on the first beat which he was unable to supply. It has happened to me more than once and when I have tried to urge the movement forward the machinery has become clogged, getting slower rather than quicker, as one partner waited for the other.

Great Chatham with his sabre drawn
Stood waiting for Sir Richard Strachan;
Sir Richard, longing to be at 'em,
Stood waiting for the Earl of Chatham.

The singer must lead boldly in these eight bars.

We sail into calmer waters at the return of the theme and the song ends with one of those heavenly postludes which seem to flow straight from Schumann's heart.

3/WALDESGESPRÄCH

'It is late, it is cold, why do you ride alone in
this great forest? Beauteous maiden let me lead you
home.'
'Man's deceitfulness has broken my heart. Hunting horns
are nearing; fly, for you know not who I am.'
'So richly arrayed are horse and rider, so entrancing
your fair figure. Ah! now I know you,
God help me! You are the witch Lorelei!'
'You know me well, and know my castle high above
the Rhine. It is late, it is cold. You will never
leave this forest. Nevermore!'

A woodland scene is portrayed, the presence of a huntsman announced by the sound of hunting horns in the introduction. The semiquaver's brazen 'ta-ra', though heard in the distance (*mf*), is repeated 'her und hin' (back and forth) in the course of the song.

With impetuosity the singer joins the theme of the introduction; animation and tone increase with a vigorous pianoforte trill – surely premonitory – up to the gallantry of 'du schöne Braut' and to the almost unearthly modulation into C major on 'heim'.

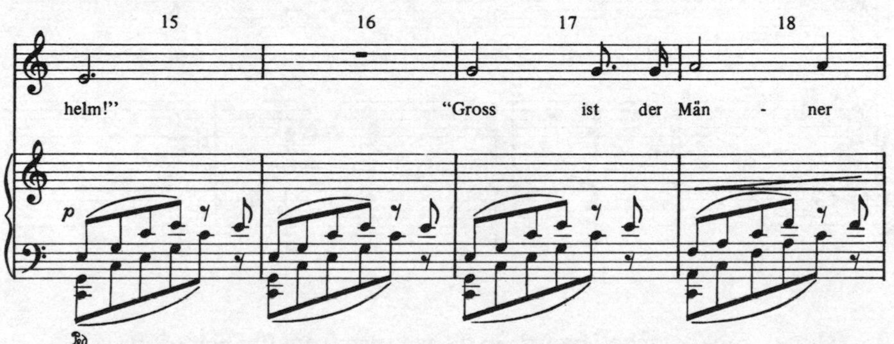

Not yet should the utterance of the sorceress be menacing (indeed she invites the man to flee) but it should be veiled and in complete contrast to the virile tones of the man. The pianist does his best in this most resonant register of his instrument to match the change of colour, for the accompaniment must not sound solid, and he would wisely use the sustaining pedal with economy. Quite suddenly, he emerges from this harp-like figure to draw attention to the horn calls in his left hand.

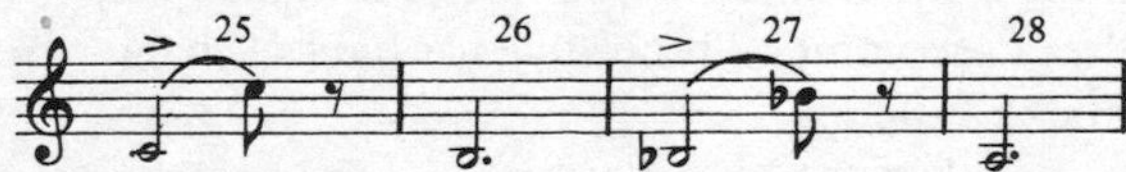

Self confidence brims over at the return of the theme, but crumbles at the moment of truth: 'Now I know you' (41).

It is marked *Im Tempo* but should be recitative. This shock almost deprives the man of speech; dramatic emphasis demands that a breath be taken after 'dich' (41) and again after 'bei' (42).

And now the menace of the Lorelei is undisguised, she becomes more and more shrill as she throws the hunter's own words back into his teeth with terrifying mockery.

She crushes her victim to her as she tells him he will never leave these woods. 'Nimmermehr' is heard three times with increasing triumph.

Those cruel detached chords in 59 are torn from the pianoforte.

The vision fades in the quiet postlude. Huntress and victim have vanished, evaporated into thin air, as if there were never a Lorelei, never a mettlesome gallant, never an evil spirit under the leafy shadow of the woods.

It has been observed previously, how Schumann often ignored the malignance he encountered in some of his poems; one thinks of *Erlkönig*, *Gruppe aus dem Tartarus*, *Herr Oluf*, *Edward* and wonders how Schubert and Loewe would have dealt with Eichendorff's *Waldesgespräch*. Schumann did not dwell on horrors; the ghastly realization that the huntsman has encountered the Lorelei and is a doomed man, takes only four bars. It is for this reason that I recommend recitative for bars 41 to 44 – the breaths allow time for a shocked silence.

The artists' problem, as I have attempted to express, is to transmute this (generally) bland music into a reflection of the drama of the story.

At all events these are my ideas when performing the song. Do I attempt to put more into it than the composer would have liked? This is for the reader to decide.

4/DIE STILLE

No one knows or can guess how happy I am!
It matters only to one person.
The snow outside is not so still, the stars above are not so silent as are my thoughts!
I would I were a bird flying over the sea, on and on until I reached heaven.

Schumann caught the blissful delicate spirit of this poem to perfection. It is all of a flutter, with the short utterances of the singer and the timorous *pizzicato* of the accompaniment, eloquent of shy trepidation. For the two artists the label 'Fragile' might serve as a guide; a sign which prescribes a sensitive treatment of the vocal line.

Quaver rest and 'rät' in the first bar have a rhythmical hesitancy not to be glossed over. The rise of tone on 3 is finespun, with an affectionate, almost unnoticeable, lingering on 'ist'; 'How happy, how happy I am' surely deserve this *rubato*.

Elasticity also prevails in the following:–

Not too much increase in tone is necessary on the *crescendo*, a filmy *portamento* on 'Einer' is substitute for it; again, as in bar 3, we make a very slight *tenuto* and slip smoothly down the descending slope in 7 with easy motion. The *portamento* on 'Einer' in the last verse is made more evident.

To compensate for my suggested waywardness of movement in the foregoing, bars 9 to 16 ('Snow and stars less mute than my thoughts') should be strict in tempo – precise and snug.

Only at *Etwas lebhafter* is happiness uninhibited, as if a window were opened.

It is still marked *piano* and should not become boisterous. For the first time in the song the accompanist uses his sustaining pedal in 17 and 19, but contributes to the feeling of freedom by the joyous *staccato* in 18 and 20.

Thereafter a return is made to the first verse. At the last, the phrase 'No one knows' is repeated and the voice leaps with the grace of a ballerina *prematurely* on to 'Kein', stays poised there (we savour the F natural in the accompanying chord) and takes the following bar (33) in tempo

If this is done, as I recommend, the *ritardando* as marked in the score, is redundant.

5/MONDNACHT

It was as if heaven had softly kissed the earth
so that earth with its shimmering blossom, dreamt
only of heaven.
The breeze gently swayed the corn, the woods rustled,
the night was bright with stars.
My soul, seeming to spread its wings, flew over the
silent land as if flying home.

In this magical composition the introduction begins with two single separate notes, the soft earth-bound B in the bass and its answer from the skies, the high C sharp. This separation between earth and the heavens will never again be so wide apart throughout the song; these two notes, one might say, symbolize the course of the song.

That first bass note must be established with certainty or it will be unnoticed, nor should there be haste to play the sparkling C sharp, which, by contrast to the deep low boom, can be as distant as you please. The semiquaver rest, in other words, is slightly prolonged, so that the starlit cluster of treble notes can glitter softly. Finger *legato* is necessary only in bars 2 and 4; for the others the sustaining pedal supplies a shimmering haze with the keys lightly touched.

The chords in 3 and 5, finishing each phrase, are played with composure; a slight pause enables the player, with help from the pedal, to move on smoothly; especially on 5 should the broken chord be unhurried. In this bar there are no 'beats' at all.

At the voice's entry, the pianoforte's repeated treble chords should be *sensed* rather than heard.

Our eyes have been on the singer all through this *Vorspiel* and we do not see any evidence of him having taken a breath, for he merges with the accompaniment as if he had been singing through those six bars – as indeed he has been in his imagination.

As if dematerialized, the voice floats up to 'Himmel' becoming more and more *piano*, until the top F sharp – in spell-bound wonder – becomes a whisper. (Far easier to make a *crescendo*, but how magical if it is *mezza voce*). Hearing this soft murmur stealing on the air, the partner at the pianoforte allows time for it to be relished, if he judges it to be of vintage quality. The singer lingers over his ascent in 8.

Up to this point we have been held in charmed suspense in the dominant key, but now, to the words 'softly kissed the earth' the music too embraces the home key of E major. (Composer and poet in felicitous accord.)

An awareness of the descent in the bass helps the singer to give an added vibration.

The 32nd notes of the 'turn' are taken with leisure. (Bar 12)

This music is repeated to cover the last two lines of the quatrain; the second verse is treated similarly.

More generosity of tone is needed for 'Und meine Seele spannte', with body to the accompaniment whose alto voice predominates. As marked, the *crescendo* is carried on through 49 to 55, making 'Flog durch die stillen Lande' the apex, with a shining F sharp.

All the time in the world can be taken over the postlude. It is important that the player should regard all those chords on the first of the bar (61 to 65) as points of rest; the whole passage is played as an improvisation, gradually fading away. There is no stir and the hands move unobtrusively. Finally the tenor voice murmurs a valediction:–

Freedom from the restriction of the bar line is essential in *Mondnacht*, without it the music is stiff and meaningless. The *rubato* in 5 and 6 is in truth exactly the same in shape as the introduction to 'Ich grolle nicht' (*Dichterliebe*); that the two songs are antipodes does not affect the issue. *Rubato* blesses one with grace and brings sinew to the other. *Rubato* ignores metronomic exactitude, and enables the music to take wing with glorious freedom. There is one proviso. The freedom is subject to good taste and form.

The voice's theme lasts for seven bars, a tune heard five times in this ephemeral composition; only for a short span (45–51) does the singer break away from this repeated tune. Why, then, is *Mondnacht* loved universally? It is loved because it is pure magic. Beyond that, there is no explanation. Once again Robert Schumann shows he could emulate Schubert occasionally, and create a perfect jewel with the simplest ingredients.

6/SCHÖNE FREMDE

The tree tops rustle and sigh as if the
old gods were making their rounds of these
ruined half-sunken walls. Here, under the
myrtles, what is your vague message to me,
fantastic night? All the stars sparkle
at me with love in their shining eyes, telling of
some great happiness in store.

Feverish excitement blazes itself all through this mysterious song and is exemplified by the harmonious friction between the middle voices.

Above this unflagging palpitation and continuous undercurrent, the melody moves ecstatically; now soaring and swooping with added animation, now more hushed and hesitant. No sooner is the basic tempo established when, in the fifth bar, the half-sunken walls and imagined gods are referred to with wonderment, and with a consequent and sudden retardation.

Almost immediately, with resumed verve, the melody wings like an eagle to the tree tops,

only to react to the words 'Was sprichts du wirr, phantastische Nacht?' 'Phantastische Nacht' is so much the crux of the situation that it should be uttered, or whispered, with impressive deliberation; every syllable distinct. These fluctuations of tempo, controlled by the singer with authority, are a feature of the song, part and parcel of the spirit of the words.

And now from bars 17 to 22 there is no holding back; with mounting excitement the voice flies joyously up to those resounding top notes until the climax is reached at 'great happiness to come'.

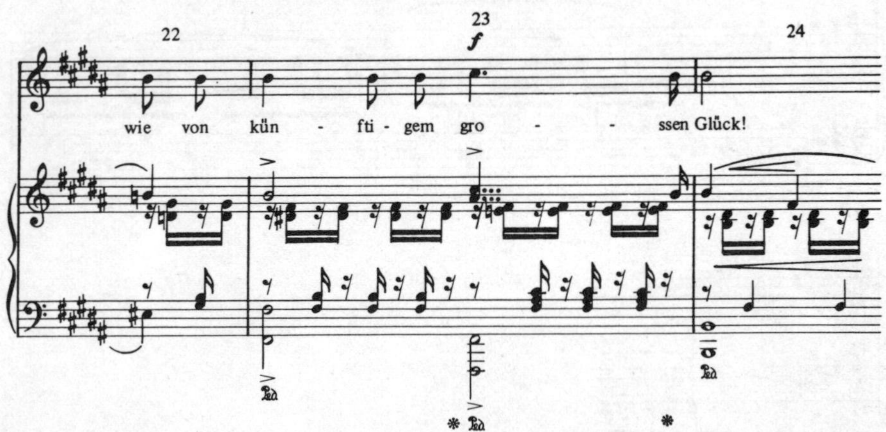

Certainly the above does not rise so steeply or picturesquely as 20 and 21, but it is the emotional high point of the song and is made so by the singer's rhythmic and verbal mastery: not only does he tighten rein on 'künftigen' but he allows 'grossen' much time, with special emphasis on the 'g-r' of the word. 'Glück' is afforded the same treatment.

The flurry of the inner voices is unabated in the postlude and the impetuous bass (25 and 27) is made evident, but through it all the pianist lets us hear the silvery line of lyricism.

7/AUF EINER BURG

The old knight sleeps at his look-out
undisturbed by rain or forest sounds.
Beard and hair grown into one,
breast and ruff turned to stone, for
centuries he has sat in his
silent cell up in that castle.
Outside all is quiet, everyone has gone
down the valley, only the woodbirds sing
in the empty window arches.
Far below in the sunshine a wedding party
floats by on the Rhine; musicians strike
up merrily – and the lovely bride weeps.

The statue of the old knight in the decaying castle brooding from his portcullis over the waters of the Rhine, dominates the song. His movelessness is reflected by the statuesque pace of the music, its tempo inevitable, measured and four square. (♩ = 40)

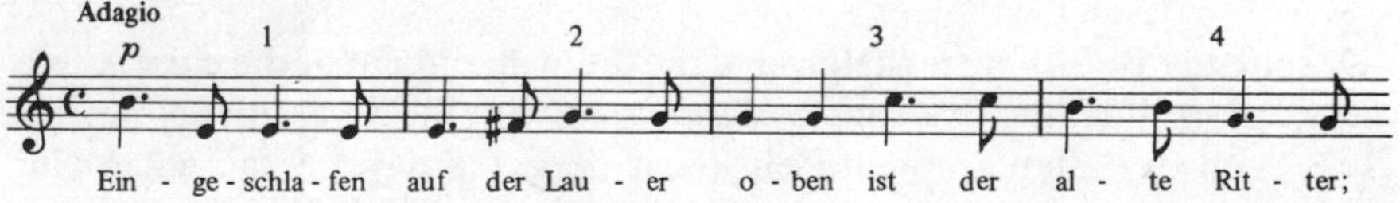

An unvarying *piano* must be maintained by the singer with tone as steady and smooth as marble. An ascent in the vocal line from 9–14 is so gradual and protracted that the *crescendo* ought to be minimal, though Schumann wants 'Jahre' to be given a sudden, but not exaggerated, emphasis.

The phrases at this slow pace seem very long, but, in general, punctuation marks in plenty, indicate where the singer can breathe. The two longest phrases are in the first and fourth systems (Peters Edition) and breaths should be taken after 'oben' (bars 3 and 15) and, in the second verse after 'singen' (27) and 'unten' (31).

A dynamic difference can be made when the wedding party is pictured, life and movement are subtly suggested by the syncopation; interest is quickened, and the singer responds with a gradual but very restrained *crescendo* from this moment (30) up to 'munter', where the musicians strike up merrily. In making this slight increase in tone the singer is anticipating the sudden and surprising turn in direction 'und die schöne Braut, die weinet,' and so is enabled to disclose the poet's bleak fancy with an appreciable break after 'munter' and a dramatic *pianissimo*.

This unexpected issue brings a chill to the summer day. The song ends in the dominant key; like the young bride's plight, it is unresolved.

8/IN DER FREMDE

The gushing brooklet and forest murmurs so
charm me that I know not where I am; the
nightingales too, call to me in the solitude, as
a reminder of dear bygone days. In the flickering
moonlight I seem to see a castle, which I know
is far from here. It is as if in a garden
of red and white roses, my darling were awaiting
me – yet she died long ago.

Despite the prevailing nostalgia and the disenchantment of the close, this is less forlorn than the first song of *Liederkreis* with the same title. Nevertheless 'Von der alten schönen Zeit' (dear departed days) is the underlying thought of the singer, even when telling us of nature's beauty. Rippling brook, chirruping birds, even capricious moonbeams are more graphically suggested in the lively accompaniment.

The phrases in the vocal line, though brisk in appearance, should be as smooth as possible, in contrast to the pianoforte's detached utterance in every alternate bar. Once again, the singer is reminded that it is not incumbent on him to take a breath every time he sees a rest.

In bar 3 the rests are observed, but a breath is quite unnecessary; the same injunction applies, for example, to bars 7, 11, and 15.

It will be seen that the pianoforte has a purling *legato* in every other bar (the odd numbered bars) and its neighbour is invariably detached. The grace note is 'crushed' against the following note, nearly simultaneous with it (but not quite!).

One could say that with its absorption in the *mise en scène* the accompaniment is impervious to the poet's repining, though the singer must be allowed freedom to indulge in the crucial phrase –

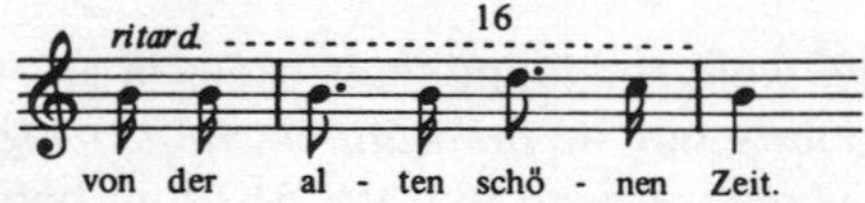

with the pianoforte gradually regaining tempo at 17.

Since the song is strophic, it only remains to add that in the last bars there is a slight extension; 'und ist doch lange tot' is heard three times: a *ritardando* is wanted for each, but the last is slowest and most expressive of all.

9/WEHMUT

Truly I can sometimes sing as if
I am happy, then tears will flow
to relieve my heavy heart. When
spring is in the air nightingales will
sing their song of longing and gladden us,
yet no one feels the pain and sadness
of their song.

This beautiful melodic line is contained, for the most part, within the compass of a fifth – F sharp to C sharp – and can easily develop into a surfeit of sweetness if the singer is heavy footed. Such is the repetitive nature of the sad tune that though marked 'Very slow' it should move forward lightly and on its toes.

The expressive, but restrictive tune, is heard often, with nuances that ought to be too delicate to be described as rises and falls. The continual ascent to that C sharp in 2 (as seen above) and in 4, 6, 8, 10, 12 becomes cloying if the singer makes heavy weather of it. Only at 'der Sehnsucht Lied erschallen' (their song of longing) should the stretch of the sixth be impressed on us,

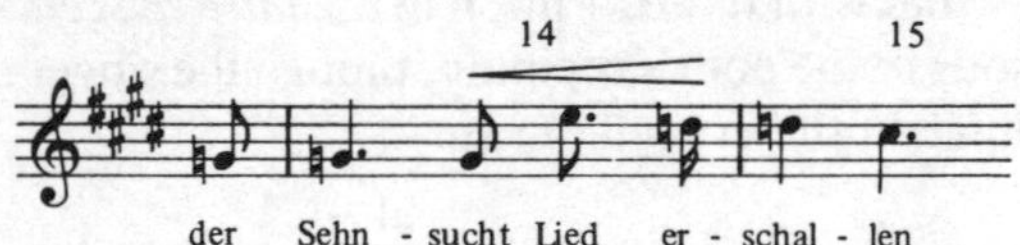

as if the nightingales were spreading their wings in an effort to escape.

Joan Chissell[1] points out in *Im wunderschönen Monat Mai* that 'the composer doubles voice and piano for the first four bars and then makes a gallant effort to break away, though he does not succeed in getting very far.'

In *Wehmut* the pianoforte treble sticks relentlessly to the voice and that, in my opinion, is an inherent weakness. It should be disguised, for the singing line only is of consequence, with the accompaniment rendered as unsubstantial as possible.

The postlude is enriched by the expressive descent to the deep bass.

It is suggested that *Wehmut* should take no longer than two and one half minutes to perform.

[1] Op. cit.

10/ZWIELICHT

Dusk begins to spread its wings, trees
shudder, clouds drift over like ill-omened dreams.
What does all this mean?
If you have a pet deer, let her not graze alone for
hunters range the woods calling and blowing their horns.
Do not trust a friend at twilight, he smiles with
eyes and lips but he is treacherous.
What goes wearily to rest now, will rise on the
morrow. Much can be lost in the darkness; be
wary, be on the alert.

Mystery shrouds several of the songs in this set, but in some respects *Zwielicht* is exceptional.

A three part accompaniment of restless quavers is heard in the introduction; the soprano voice is joined by the alto (2) and later (5) by the bass, whose entry deepens the twilight into night. The phrases, two – two- three bars in length each lower than the last, have more impact if individualized. Uneasiness is suggested by continual syncopation.

It is an evening overcast and foreboding yet, paradoxically, the punctuation as marked above corresponds closely to the clearly defined phrases of the limpid *Mondnacht* (No. 5). Both songs too have the direction *Piano*, but here the *Piano* is of Brahmsian quality; the atmosphere is heavy and humid.

The singer repeats the soprano melody of the introduction (1–4) but the onerous 'schwere Träume' is made more trenchant to meet the challenge of the pianoforte bass.

'What does all this mean?' is a question posed tremulously in recitative style. After the weight of the preceding bar the *subito pianissimo* is given greater penetration if the quarter note rest is prolonged.

Musically the second verse duplicates the first, but at 'Jäger zieh'n im Wald und blasen', the brassy quality of the verb 'blasen' should be noticed, though not exaggerated.

Bitterness reaches its peak at the third. 'Trust not a friend at this hour' (26) has a diminished seventh with a threatening *crescendo* in the accompaniment over which the singer rides with increasing vehemence. Now from 27 to 31 the voice is constantly at odds with the alto and bass of the pianoforte.

Distrust of others and inner wretchedness are ingrained there and the singer emerges from the clash with attenuated tone, as if weary. It is a change of pattern prepared by the diminished seventh arpeggio, which kindled the struggle with a *crescendo* in 26 but now, one tone lower, plays a different role and eases the crisis by maintaining its *pianissimo* level and making its ascent with calm deliberation.

In the Peters Edition *crescendi* are marked in each bar of the above example, it is only fair that I apprise the reader that I ignore them and compound the offence by suggesting a *diminuendo* in 32 and continuing the *pianissimo* to the end of the phrase.

After all the disquiet that has gone before, the outcome of the poet's moralizing is pronounced with singular impressiveness by being unruffled. It is all *legato* except for the final warning which is declaimed without increase of tone.

Muffled, *staccato* chords underline the portent of the words.

11/IM WALDE

A wedding party passed by the hillside; I heard the birds singing; then horsemen came flashing by, sounding their horns, a merry hunting party.
But before I realized it, night enveloped everything; the only sound to be heard was the sighing of the forest, and deep in my heart, I shuddered.

The pianist makes a brave attempt to set a spirited tempo in his short introduction, only to be pulled up by his partner at the sight of the wedding procession.

Do recollections of the weeping bride in the eighth song haunt the singer? Does he entertain some premonition? The latter possibility would have some justification, for once again Eichendorff closes the lyric on a bleak note.

When the bouncing rhythm is resumed, it is again stayed, but this time by the contented contemplation of bird song, so the suspicions that might have been entertained in the first instance are set at ease.

For the third time, with even more emphasis and enthusiasm, the accompanist forges ahead and at last the singer joins in whole-heartedly, with a swing. It was the hunt that cheered him, at least momentarily.

The step down to D–C sharp (21, 22) ('Before I realized it, night enveloped everything') at once darkens the mood and prepares us for the bitter end.

'My heart shudders within me' is sung twice. The basic tempo is not too quick; the note values are stretched to accord with the sombre sentiment and thus the phrase can be sustained in one breath. But its repeat is so extended and expressive that a breath after 'schauert's is necessary.

The low A, as seen above, should be taken rather than the higher alternative in the printed edition.

12/FRÜHLINGSNACHT

Over the garden I heard the migrant birds
returning; a sign that spring is in the air
and the time for blossoming.
I want to rejoice, I want to weep, for I cannot
believe what the moon and stars say, what the forest
whispers and the nightingales sing to me:_ "She is yours".

Such exuberance as this we have not met in the eleven previous songs. The whirring of wings and birdsong, the radiance of moon and stars flood the music. Brilliantly though it sparkles, it does not express joy unconfined, the peasant boy singing 'Mein' in *Die Schöne Müllerin* gives us that; this is more urbane and slender in texture, moreover the verse bespeaks a shade of scepticism 'ist mir's doch, als könnt's nicht sein' (I feel it cannot be) to which Schumann subscribes with subtlety.

The first nine bars indeed tingle with delight at the coming of spring. Excited triplets never cease.

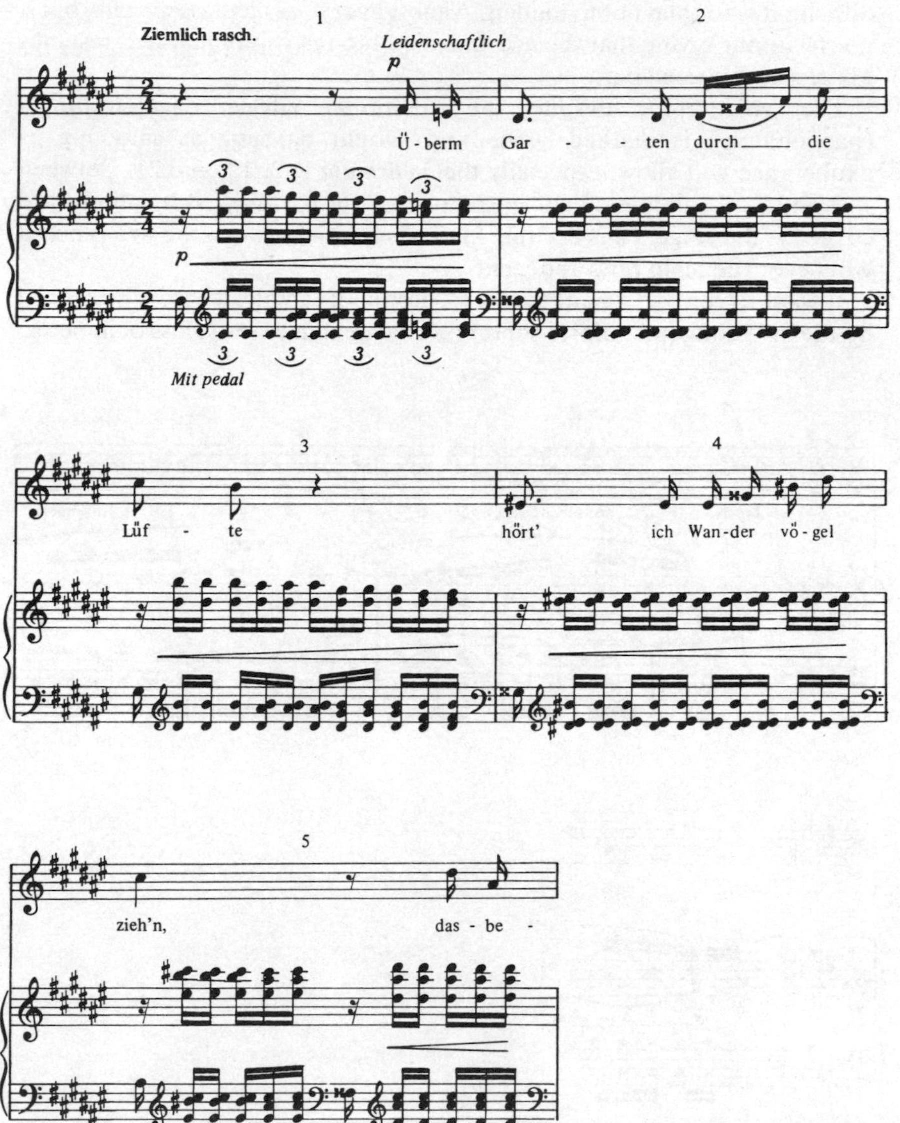

It is hoped the singer will observe the injunction *Moderately quick*, for if he adopts too hasty a tempo, he himself will be the sufferer in that the pianist, trying desperately to keep abreast of him, will be unable to temper his tone. It can be seen that the pianoforte treble is much higher than the vocal line and the player's problem (for the sustaining pedal must be used) is to abide by the prescribed *piano* , and the faster he is forced to play the more difficult it is for him not to louden. Almost every bar has a *crescendo* , but it goes without saying that the accompanist, though it is unmarked, resumes his *piano* with each bar.

The voice too, despite the additional advice *Leidenschaftlich* (passionately) is marked *piano* and should be sung as smoothly as exuberance will allow, especially the *melismata* in 2, 12, and 21. Between 1–2 and 3–4 a dipping flight in the pianoforte is answered by an upward curve for the singer; this exciting kind of see-saw between the two is heard whenever the main tune appears.

'I want to rejoice, I want to weep', despite its ambivalence, is heartened by the bird-song (pianoforte soprano) which ought to resist loss of impetus.

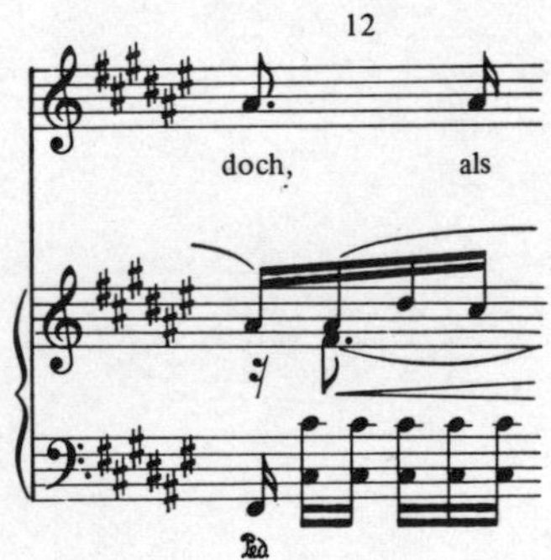

The happy little air in the accompaniment though but a thin sound, should be heard clearly and have some freedom; the singer will not be disturbed by the suspicion of a *tenuto* in the high note of each passage, the D sharp in 10, the A sharp in 11.

Should the singer be content to let the pianist lead the way from 10 to 13, he resumes charge for the rest of the song and soars with uninhibited joy up to 16 where he will reach a ringing *forte*, duly supported by his partner.

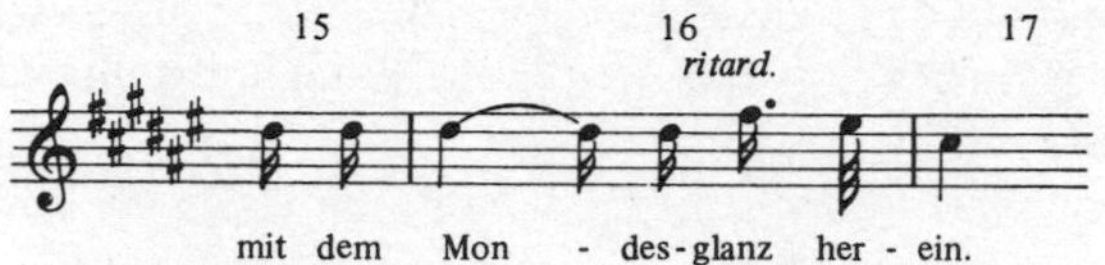

In point of fact the accompanist's first authentic *forte* does not appear until bar 22, though fortunately he has been permitted one or two *sforzandi*.

The above and 'Sie ist deine, sie ist dein' are naturally the two high points of the song.

An impression of misgiving, at the least a loss of zest, is suggested by the last few bars of the postlude; true the animation of the triplets is felt but this is parenthetical, the bass is the focal point as it recalls with ever deepening tones the once happy song of the birds.

SONGS FROM MYRTEN (Myrtles)

Op 25. Edition Peters Volume I

WIDMUNG

(Rückert)

Op. 25 No. 1

You are my soul and heart, my joy and pain,
the world in which I live, the heaven to which
I float. You are the grave where my sadness is
buried for ever.
Your love makes me what I am; one glance from
your eyes transfigures me.
You are my good angel, my better self.

The singer sweeps us off our feet with his ardour. In a series of rising phrases, the voice mounts higher and higher, first to 'Seele' next to 'Wonne' and then floating, or rather sailing up to the apex with a ringing G flat on 'schwebe'. It moves with speed (𝅗𝅥 = 72 or 76). As an accomplished batsman seems to be able to make his stroke unhurriedly against fast bowling, the singer takes plenty of time, so that 'Wonne' (Joy), 'Schmerz' (pain), 'schwebe' (float) are made clear. Consonants are distinct but in no way impede the splendid rhythmic sweep of it all. Above the active accompaniment the vocal line moves in a steady *legato* stream.

We are attacked at the outset by the accompaniment with its two handed arpeggio figure. The minimal wait on the quaver before the precipitate repeated note (semiquaver – quaver) in the above, is met also in 'Helft mir ihr Schwestern' (*Frauenliebe und Leben*) and is a 'figure of speech' often adopted by Schumann in a mood of elation. This invigorating device should be recognized and dashed off with *brio*.

It is a delusion to assume that a slower tempo is intended in the earnest middle section; admittedly a *ritardando* is wanted on the up-beat of 13 but the original tempo is resumed on 14

Where 'Du meine Seele du mein Herz' occupied scarcely more than one bar of music, the metrical line is now stretched to four, but the pulse is always made evident, or rather felt, by the soft triplet chords in the accompaniment.

On bar 20 a slow turn accords with the mood, it is deliberate (quavers on the fifth and sixth crotchets).

The tenderest moments come at the return to the home key 'You raise me above myself' etc.

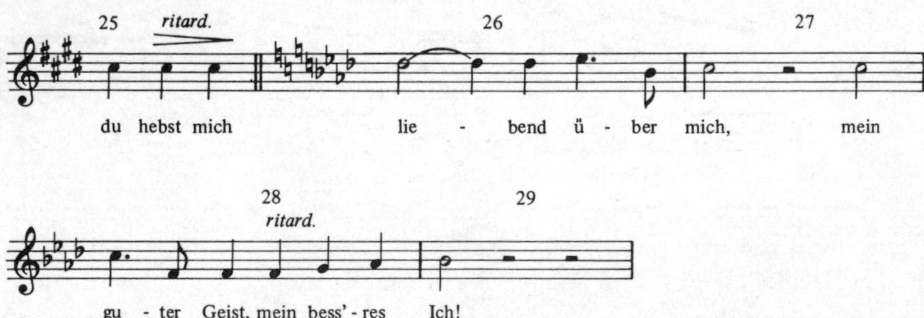

Wrung from the heart, these devoted sentiments would lose all semblance of sincerity were they not lovingly dwelt on, and most tenderly sung.

At 30 *tempo primo* and *forte* are resumed with a burst, as singer and pianist return to the opening theme.

The postlude is not fashioned to support the hot vein of passion but should surely be an echo of it. I feel the recommended *piano* is too subdued, and prefer a sonorous *mezzo forte*.

FREISINN

(Goethe)

Op. 25 No. 2

To be in the saddle is the only
life for me. Stay in huts and tent if you will
while I ride forth with
only the stars above my cap.
God has set them to guide you
over land and sea.
Take delight in them.

This four-square little affair, nearly all tonic and dominant, except for a moment in its relative C minor, is lusty and grateful to sing. It is full of the joy of life, and, as in *Widmung*, Schumann expresses this by means of his 'semiquaver – crotchet' on a repeated note; we see it thrice in the first phrase and often later.

If, in his gusto the singer is tempted to make a *portamento* on the climbing 'nur' (3) and 'euren' (7) it is all part of the picture.

The spasmodic (stop-go?) movement is positive in the accompaniment, with its numerous semi-quaver silences, with no tonal hang-over and no sustaining pedal.

Rhythm is steadied, reins tautened, by the singer's markedly even quavers at the verse's end 'über meiner Mütze nur die Sterne'.

DER NUSSBAUM

(Mosen)

Op. 25 No. 3

The leaves and blossom of an almond tree, softly rustling in the night breeze by the window of a sleeping maiden, are whispering to her. The maiden, loving and longing, cannot understand what they are saying until finally, after continual repetition, the meaning of the message becomes clear to her and she smiles in her dreams.

This little enigma is posed in the accompaniment and runs all through the song:–

It happens a score of times in different guises, but it tries most insistently to make itself understood when it appears thus, in the tonic key. The answer to this riddle is not supplied until near the end of the song when 'the leaves whisper of a bridegroom next year'. But the significance of this phrase lies in the fact that for the first and only time throughout the song, the singer sings the above figure in the same key in which her partner has been playing it so often; a subtle and charming way of letting us know that the message has been heard and understood.

It has all been beautifully and delicately conceived by the composer, but it is necessary that the singer and pianist should realize the import of this constantly recurring theme; being in the secret, knowing the solution, their singing and playing become tender and informed.

Every phrase of the singer and its echo in the accompaniment is shaped like the branch of a tree – it rises and then falls a little, and like the branch tapers off towards the tip.

It can be seen by the above example that if 'Haus' is held too long and too firmly it will create an unwelcome dissonance with the pianoforte's treble voice; if the singer tapers her D and then releases it with sensitivity this misfit can be avoided.

The branches, continually swaying, are not allowed to mar the over-all smoothness of singing and playing. Never should the voice rise above a *mezzo piano*. The following passage, for instance, loses all charm if a *crescendo* is tastelessly made up to the F sharp.

May I remind the singer that the word 'flüstern' (whisper) comes five times?

The final ten bars are different in character. Their promise 'vom nächsten Jahr' having been conveyed, the leaves cease their rustling, the tremulous undercurrent becomes more tranquil, lower in pitch, as 'the maiden hears and smiles in her dream.'

SITZ' ICH ALLEIN

(Goethe)

Op. 25 No. 5

Sitting alone, drinking my wine, who could be happier than I? With no one to disturb me, pursuing my own thoughts, where else could I be better off?

This miniature is the quintessence of snug satisfaction with the poet comfortably settled in his own armchair, a decanter of wine by his elbow. It is too elegant to be described as a drinking song which has a connotation of the taproom. I prefer to think we are sharing the thoughts of a connoisseur who raises the glass by its stem to the light so that the colour of the precious liquid may be appreciated before he savours the bouquet and the flavour.

So short is the song, only twenty-five bars, that it is refreshing how Schumann infuses variety into it without losing the tranquil pleasure of the mood. The little tune is in 2/4 time and in E major,

and only a few bars later we have an abrupt and delightful switch to C major, now in 6/8 time.

Opportunity to enjoy a taste is afforded now and again by the graceful pianoforte interludes. Only in the latter and in the 6/8 section is the accompaniment to be *legato*, elsewhere it is playfully detached.

One should not lose sight of the *Da Capo* sign on bar 2.

SETZE MIR NICHT

(Goethe)

Op. 25 No. 6

Don't bang the jug down under my nose
like that, you lout! Who serves wine
should behave affably or the wine will turn
acid.
But you, handsome lad standing in the doorway,
come in! You shall pour my wine and it
will taste all the better.

From the cosy cultivated atmosphere of the preceding song we are conscious at once of the Bierkeller: the very acoustics are different, the bare boards resound to the heavy footsteps of the clumsy serving-boy and to the careless thud as he thrusts the wine on the table.

Words and music are graphically matched in the opening bars. The singer does not merely sing *forte*, he makes no effort to produce an agreeable tone. The displeasure in his voice is answered in the accompaniment by the abrasive syncopation on the third and sixth beats and by the clatter going on in the bass.

A change comes o'er the scene at the mention of the likely lad who will become the wine-bearer; smiling address displaces lubberly haste.

Bars 2 to 5 are converted now to the major. Snapping *staccato*, growling syncopation suddenly evaporate, and the same tune is hardly recognisable when clothed with such grace and warmth.

The postlude could be written by no one but Schumann; he himself was sufficiently pleased with it to let us have it twice!

Simple, but brimming over with contentment. The broken octave intervals, slightly reminiscent of the interludes in the previous song, are a confirmation that good humour is restored.

Is it a little 'beschwipft'? Perhaps there is a suggestion that more than justice was done to the delicious wine.

DIE LOTOSBLUME

(Heine)

Op. 25 No. 7

The lotos flower fears the blazing sun and
with bowed head, dreaming, she awaits the night.
Her lover is the moon who wakes her with his
light and to him she unveils her innocent
face. She blooms and glows, gazing mutely at
the sky, and trembles with love and love's pain.

Innocence, and the depth of chaste love are so marvellously expressed in Heine's allegory that it took the genius of a Schumann to embrace the poet at this exalted level. *Die Lotosblume* is universally loved. It shares a virtue which many memorable creations have in common, utter simplicity. Also it is a mirror, exposing with a clarity that cannot be disguised, the stature of the singer. Beauty of voice is esential, but not enough in itself.

Die Lotosblume belongs to that order (*Du bist wie eine Blume* is in the same sphere) which can be read at sight. Let us not be deceived; the song must be approached with humility. It needs earnest thought.

The first and third phrases are typical of the consideration the song deserves.

It is natural for bar 2 to droop a little, not with a mannered *diminuendo* but in a sensitive decrease of tone as the passage falls. Though almost identical musically, the phrase (6, 7) 'with bowed head', should be shaped, one assumes, in the same manner, to do it otherwise seems illogical. On the contrary, with his eye on the *pianissimo* three bars ahead, the singer makes a very delicate *crescendo* to give 'Haupte' a well-supported lift (7), the two beats rest in the same bar become an expectant and hushed suspense made the more telling by the mounting F sharp octave in the pianoforte bass. The passage 'dreaming, she awaits the night' contrariwise, softens, becomes more distant with each ascending note, bar 8.

'Her lover is the moon' is the consummation to which all the preceding has conspired. With the voice high in the stave like a flower on a delicate stem, with the accompaniment lifted an octave higher, it is as if we are raised to the heavens.

The voice is a thread, the accompaniment unsubstantial. But with the following phrase 'unveiling her innocent face' the tone is released from its *mezza voce* as the flower-face loosens its petals. It is a restrained *crescendo*, for a bigger one lies in wait. We approach now the dynamic apex; 'blooming and glowing and trembling' palpitates with excitement; it is a *crescendo* indeed, and *accelerando*.

Tone grows freely when climbing and arrives at a *mezzo forte* on the high notes, and now 'Zittert' is held back to the old tempo after the hastening of the previous five bars. This check to the rhythmic urge is vital, for it smooths the way for the emotional high point of the song.

In the published score a *piano* is marked on the last beat of 23. It is too sudden, after the excited 'zittert', a *mezzo piano* is more fitting, for it enables the singer to make a continual and melting diminution to the very end. 'Vor Liebe und Liebesweh' is too momentous to be delivered in a whisper. In each phrase of *Die Lotosblume* the interval or distance from note to note is very close, but here for the first time the space is a wide one. 'Liebe' has a loving caressing interval of a sixth. The whole rapturous phrase is sung twice. I must warn the singer that a *portamento* on 'Liebe' or 'Liebesweh' would be in execrable taste. As for the accompaniment, in general it is subdued and *una corda*, though the warm double-bass in the first eight bars should be noticeable.

I plead guilty to having treated *Die Lotosblume* in a clinical manner, to having torn the lovely flower, petal by petal, to pieces. Alas, there seemed no other way of expressing my ideas on its performance.

TALISMANE

(Goethe)

Op. 25 No. 8

God is the East, God is the West, lands
to North and South rest peacefully in His
hands. He only, disposes justice and shows
man the path he must follow.
Of all His hundred names let this be glorified
above all. Amen.
I have erred and strayed, but thou canst
guide me aright in all my works.

The key of C major was chosen by Beethoven for '*Die Ehre Gottes aus der Natur*' (The glory of God in Nature).

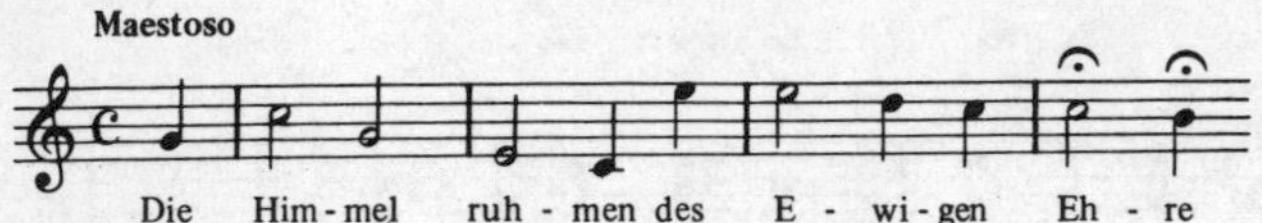

One can hear the awe-inspiring voice of Beethoven echoing through the great nave of a cathedral, with a multitude participating.

Schumann's nature precluded such a conception, his approach was more personal even at the cost of some grandeur.

It is an interesting coincidence that both composers used the common chord for their motto and that their choice of key was the same. C major is a resounding and historical trumpet for rejoicing and glorification.

Implicit obedience to the notation makes the singer's declaration very impressive; for instance the quaver on the second syllable of 'Gottes' and the three quavers in bar 3 stand up proudly against the semiquavers. However, the essential emphasis is in the pianoforte whose ponderous chords assert the inevitable forward march of the stately procession: this movement is maintained throughout the more restrained second verse.

'I have erred . . . etc' modulates to G major. Up to this point the mood has been festive, sung with energetic enunciation and attack; now, for the first time, the music craves to be sung and played smoothly.

Humility permeates this section, the vocal line's suppleness permits the rhythm to be more pliable. The accompaniment, in thirds, moves in little straying footsteps beneath the new lyricism. (Sheep may safely graze?)

The tremendous detached chord brings us back to the impressive main theme. This time the singer delays his attack, he extends the silence after the chord (30) and thus makes 'Gottes ist der Orient' more commanding than before.

Two 'Amens' bring the song to a conclusion. They are set fairly low in the voice, making a big tone inexpedient; much more devotion is expressed by Schumann's wish for a reverent *piano*.

LIED DER SULEIKA

(von Willemer)

Op. 25 No. 9

O, Song, I grasp your message. What joy you give me! You tell me I am ever in his thoughts and that he loves me.
Yes, my heart is the mirror in which you, my beloved, see yourself. Your poetry entwines itself rapturously round your love for me.

Rapturous is the melody with which this song of love is conceived.

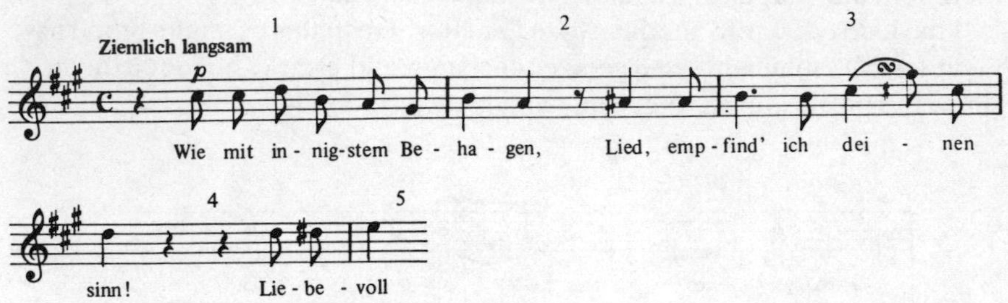

Even when it sinks momentarily as if from exhaustion (7) it is spurred on, or re-awakened, by the pianoforte which at this point ceases its smooth *legato* passages and has urging repeated chords, these in turn, reinforced by a bass (8, 9) refusing to be at rest.

The quavers 'innigstem Behagen' should sweep down with exciting freedom; the 'turn' on 'deinen' is unhurried, but passionate, without sacrificing the *legato* line.

There are only two verses, but Schumann repeats the main tune for six bars for good measure and then, reluctantly, and with an unexpected loss of conviction, brings the song to an end.

Ziemlich langsam in common time appears at the head of the score, but one cannot count four pedestrian beats to a bar in music whose flight is so unconstrained. My preference is for two beats to a bar at a basic tempo of 𝅗𝅥 = 48, though this is hastened at bar 11 (*nach und nach schneller*).

The poem is generally attributed, erroneously, to Goethe. Eric Sams (*The Songs of Robert Schumann*) explains that the 'song' alluded to in the lyric is Goethe's *Abglanz*, while the *Lied der Suleika* is Marianne von Willemer's response to his message of ardent love.

HOCHLÄNDERS ABSCHIED

(Burns)

Op. 25 No. 13

My heart's in the Highlands, my heart is not here;
My heart's in the Highlands, a‿chasing the deer;
Chasing the wild deer, and following the roe –
My heart's in the Highlands wherever I go.

Farewell to the Highlands, farewell to the North;
The birthplace of valour, the country of worth
Wherever I wander wherever I rove,
The hills of the Highlands for ever I love.

Farewell to the mountains high covered with snow!
Farewell to the straths and green valleys below!
Farewell to the forests and wild-hanging woods!
Farewell to the torrents and loud-pouring floods!

My heart's in the Highlands, my heart is not here;
My heart's in the Highlands, a-chasing the deer;
Chasing the wild deer and following the roe –
My heart's in the Highlands wherever I go.

After the energetic opening, the voice is marked *piano* and while we concede that this is a comparative *piano* it is well to bear in mind that the trend of the vocal line is a gradual climb to the end of the verse: at least it serves as a warning that honest enthusiasm be tempered, so that there is power in hand to cope with the last foot of the verse 'My heart's in the Highlands wherever I go.'

Vigour loses its edge and becomes bombast if the rhythm is not handled with musicianship.

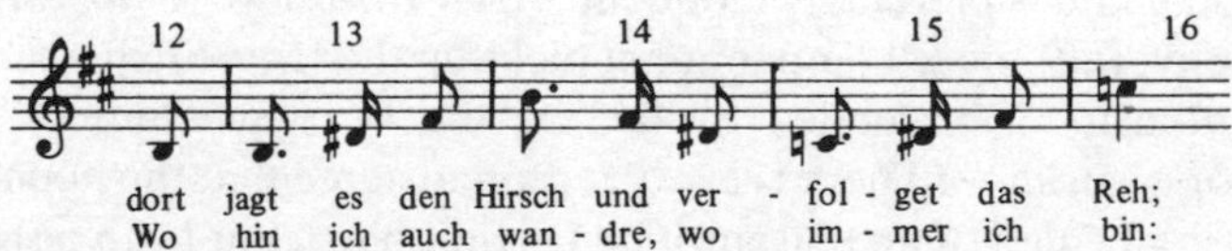

In the above example the pianoforte is in octave unison with the voice (a figure repeatedly heard) and the semiquavers are given less weight; one bounds off them as lightly as a deer. It is an instance where rhythmical authority gives zest to the passage.

AUS DEN HEBRÄISCHEN GESÄNGEN

(Byron. Trans. Körner)

Op. 25 No. 15

My soul is dark – Oh! quickly string
The harp I yet can brook to hear;
And let thy gentle fingers fling
Its melting murmers o'er mine ear.
If in this heart a hope be dear,
That sound shall charm it forth again:
If in these eyes there lurk a tear,
'T will flow, and cease to burn my brain.

But bid the strain be wild and deep,
Nor let thy notes of joy be first:
I tell thee, minstrel, I must weep,
Or else this heavy heart will burst;
For it hath been by sorrow nursed,
And ach'd in sleepless silence long;
And now 'tis doom'd to know the worst,
And break at once – or yield to song.

The melodic line is piercingly eloquent. After the retarded opening phrase, quietly delivered, the accompaniment picks up the tempo expectantly (8); it has an intensity transcended by far, by the heart-swelling 'Auf' of the soprano or contralto. (There is every reason to agree that the poem suggests Saul is being healed of an evil spirit by David's harp, but I can only hear the ringing tone of a woman; no other voice can bring the thrilling quality those cutting F sharps deserve.)

In those few bars, the keen augmented interval (7) occurs four times: though it comes at the end of a phrase, it is too poignant to justify the tapering off in tone which I sometimes advocate. (As seen in the sixth song of *Frauenliebe und Leben* this interval is used by Schumann in moments of deep emotion.) This is not a miniature as songs go and should be treated unsparingly, not painted with too delicate a brush.

Much as one loves the harp we are grateful that Schumann did not carry verisimilitude too far but called on the pianoforte for this accompaniment; the voice needs the support of the sostenuto pedal, the music needs the dynamic contrast that, with respect, the pearly harp could not provide. The introduction sighs in wave after wave of ever mounting aspiration and those chromatic passages are much too urgent to be played with reserve.

At the voice's entry the pianoforte initiates, with keen sonority, the apex of each passage, before the downward curve; the voice follows in its path but with more pungency than the player can achieve.

The major section is contemplative, the vocal line therefore keeps to a more even tenor and the accompaniment has that tender syncopation which Schumann loved.

A repeat of the introduction serves as an interlude leading to the second stanza, but now emerges into an unexpected C major.

'But bid the strain be wild and deep' from Byron, is not wild from Schumann, but it is deep. A singer would be advised to follow the composer and not try to infuse the music with an element that is absent. She should sing it calmly and quietly. It brings us to the second subject previously heard in E major, but now in the minor, and the voice ends with a reiteration of that aching interval with which it began.

As a postscript may I make it clear that in expressing a preference for the female voice in this particular song, I am only speaking personally and have no intention of discouraging a tenor or baritone from singing it.

VENETIANISCHES LIED I

(Thomas Moore)

Op. 25 No. 17

> The first of the two Venetian songs tells of the shadowy passenger in the gondola urging his gondolier, at dead of night, to make no noise with his oar as they glide over the lagoon. None must perceive them save the inamorata towards whom they hasten. 'Ah', says the lover, as they approach the lady's balcony, 'if only we took as much trouble to please the gracious heavens above as we take to please a woman, what angels we would be.'

Although we have no reason for supposing that the gondolier's interest in the matter is other than professional, it is he who is the recipient of the lover's confidences, it is he who waits and keeps watch below, after the young man has disappeared through the window to hold converse with his lady. The song ends without the young lover emerging, but we can picture him in the cold grey light of dawn, being rowed back to his wife and family by the ever patient gondolier. How fitting that the role of the gondolier, in the song, should be given to the accompanist, that monument of unselfish discretion.

The accompanist must bear in mind that the singer keeps to *piano* and *pianissimo* throughout the song and his piano part is just background. The swaying figure is sensed rather than heard, the *crescendo* on bars 8 and 40 and 48 applies to the singer only. The charm of this song will be realized if the performers obey Schumann's instructions to the letter, 'Heimlich streng im Takt' (secretly, strictly in time). Here in the accompaniment is the gentle rocking of the boat and the rhythmical swing of the oar.

The rocking rhythm is not that of a berceuse and is on no account to be sung indolently. While the tone remains very soft, the words are projected with energy. Energy and stridence are not synonymous, and the singer must be seething with suppressed excitement and urge, for our gallant, be it remembered, never allows his tone to rise above a whisper.

The effect of a sibilant whisper can be obtained by making the 's' and 't' sounds, very clearly. In the line 'die Flut vom Ruder sprüh'n so leise lass, dass sie uns nur vernimmt, zu der wir zieh'n.' there are no fewer than nine sibilants and these should predominate, for they suggest at once the stage whisper of the lover. The song abounds with such examples; here is another; 'er spräche vieles wohl von dem, was Nachts die Sterne schau'n'.

The word 'leis' (*leis* – softly) is an onomatopaeic word, the 's' sound in it, if lingered on (like the 'sh' in the English word 'hush') imposes silence. In bars 10 and 11 Schumann has made *staccato* signs, as seen in the following example. The notes, however, are long minims not crotchets. What, then, did Schumann mean? Possibly that a portion of the minim should be occupied by the softly hissing consonant; written out it would appear to be something like this;

so that the 'sss' takes up the second beat of bars 10 and 11.

'Leis' is a word with an implied diphthong; since it occurs eight times in the first verse, the singer does his best to avoid the intrusive diphthong 'e-e' which converts the vowel into two syllables and becomes irritating.

On bars 20 to 30 the voice and accompaniment become, if possible, softer than before. The writing looks square-cut and ugly, but in fact it is delightfully impudent and charming if performed according to Schumann's markings.

The accompanist uses the soft but not the sustaining pedal; his chords should be feathery – they should bounce in perfect time with the singer. The gondolier no longer swings his oar in this little section – he is pausing, either for a breather or out of politeness to his patron's confidences. The *ritardando* applies to bar 24, but I make a preliminary *ritenuto* on the first beat of bar 20, and it seems instinctive for me to make this – finishing off the old rhythm with a curve, before starting the new.

The close of each verse is so charming that I reproduce it here.

Each set up, on the part of the singer and accompanist becomes lighter and lighter. The singer's last note is *pianissimo* in the extreme, in fact in the second verse his final 'sacht' is barely audible.

VENETIANISCHES LIED II

(Thomas Moore)

Op. 25 No. 18

I like Schumann's two Venetian songs sung as a pair, with no applause between them. Of course they can be sung separately – Mendelssohn, in fact, composed a setting to 'Wenn durch die Piazzeta' without touching 'Leis' rudern hier'. It is only by a stretch of the imagination that we can call the second song a continuation of the first, but its lively confidence makes an admirable foil after the clandestine nervousness of the other. Again, the final 'sacht' of 'Leis rudern hier' leaves us more or less suspended in mid-air, halfway between the balcony and the boat, while the second song brings us into the presence of the lady, whose charms, let us say, have drawn the enthusiastic serenader out into the night and prevented the gondolier from going home to his bed.

If we expect to see an abduction or elopment we shall be disappointed. All our hero says in effect is that at night he will come for his dearest Ninette and together – she in her mask, he clad as a gondolier – they will float away over the silent lagoon. It is all very proper and inconclusive. Mendelssohn's setting, sentimental and earnest, with its soft pleading, suggests that the singer is really in love, but Schumann on the other hand, gives us a young man more concerned with his own posturings than with the lady of his supposed passion; a lover full of *joie de vivre*, full of gusto rather than ardour, enjoying adventure for adventure's sake.

Scintillating with vivacity and gaiety, the introduction is marked 'Munter' (lively) and 'zart' (sensitive). The syncopated left hand gives impetuosity, while the right with its gay impudence and curvets suggests great play with a cloak; a plumed hat brushing the floor in the most elaborate of bows.

The singer must be impatient for his entry at bar 8. It is better for him to anticipate his up beat on 'Wenn' than to be a fraction late, and the accompanist makes no slackening in the tempo leading to the vocal entry.

In bar 9 the semiquaver is as brisk and snappy as possible. Bars 9 to 16 are lively in the extreme and the accompaniment should be energetic. The hands do not fall on to the notes, they spring up into the air from the keys, as if the latter were red hot. No sustaining pedal is wanted.

Becoming quite sentimental at 21 to 24 of each verse, the singer makes full use of the *ritardando* mark, and sings the phrase *legato*.

He can make a *portamento* from the F sharp to the B on the first syllable of 'Venus', while in the second verse he makes the *portamento* on 'leben' almost heavy with sentimentality. It is too good to be true and should be overdone.

The piano postlude, at the end of each verse, is in the same style as the introduction; after the *ritardando* (22 to 24) it does not strike the old lively tempo until the first beat (left hand) of 25.

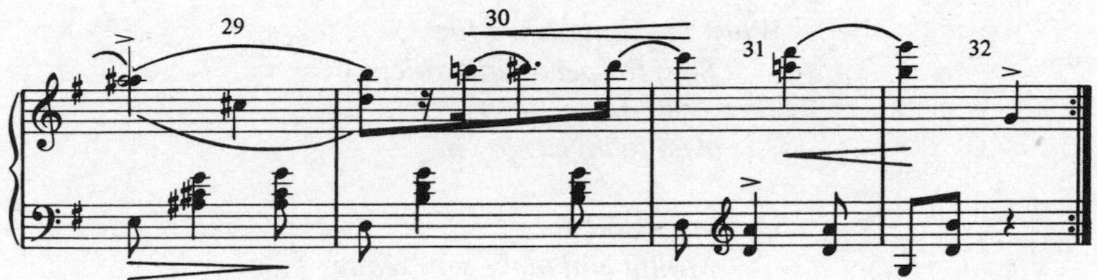

I like a *fermata* on the last quaver of 24 and a quaver rest in the left hand (Schumann's marking gives the bass chord a minim's length) for it is charming to hear the suspended A in the treble ringing by itself, before the bouncing rhythm is resumed at 25.

In the interlude there should be no semblance of a *rallentando*. In the postlude a slight *accelerando* can be made on the two final bars; this has a devil-may-care effect, which is justified, if my idea of Schumann's setting is acceptable.

It is a delightful song but Thomas Moore would probably have found Mendelssohn's romanticism more to his taste.

HAUPTMANNS WEIB

(Burns)

Op. 25 No. 19

O, Mount and go,
Mount and make you ready;
O, mount and go,
And be the Captain's lady.

When the drums do beat,
And the cannons rattle,
Thou shalt sit in state,
And see thy love in battle.

When the vanquished foe
Sues for peace and quiet,
To the shades we'll go,
And in love enjoy it.

O, mount and go'
Mount and make you ready;
O' mount and go,
And be the Captain's lady.

Undoubtedly the lady Burns depicts is suitably clad for riding but the breast-plate, helmet and sword are figments on the part of the translator, Wilhelm Gerhard. After all she is invited to sit in state and see her captain in action; possibly in her equipment will be found a pretty dress and hat and a parasol, she will look worthy to be ca captain's lady and thus enabled in comfort to 'see the soldiers, how they die!'

It is really a grim picture and Schumann gives it the necessary brazen touch.

The key to the tempo is in the pianoforte interlude bars 9 and 10; the bass

played in a resonant *legato* against the detached treble chords, is a feature of the song.

Keck (bold) is the advice in the score, and to follow this, a measured tempo is recommended; I like ♩ = 80. This is a personal preference and I warn the reader that some singers are happier with it quicker. Taken at a higher speed the vein of iron in its soul (which I read in the song) is disguised, but if the singer feels bravado is the be-all and end-all, then it may be taken considerably faster.

DU BIST WIE EINE BLUME

(Heine)

Op. 25 No. 24

You are like a flower, so sweet and pure and fair.
I look at you and melancholy steals into my heart.
I feel I ought to place my hands on your head and
pray that God may keep you pure and fair and sweet.

Like *Die Lotosblume* this is an imperishable song. Schumann's sublime music catches the heart with exquisite ache as surely as Heine's moving verses. 'There is a kindly mood of melancholy that wings the soul' and it is enshrined in this blest act of dedication.

One cannot think of *Die Lotosblume* in the same breath; both are inspired by profound love and piercingly express this ardent emotion in simple soft-spoken terms.

In *Die Lotosblume* I suggested that the voice should rise freely to a *mezzoforte* at the dynamic climax, also in the penultimate phrase that a *mezzo piano* was more expedient than the printed *piano*. *Du bist wie eine Blume* is not proof against such freedom, for in the last resort – comparison is inevitable – it just misses the chaste simplicity of the other song. In performance, its thicker texture and, by comparison, its rich colouring, particularly in the last eight bars, verge on the rhetorical.

Lovers of Hugo Wolf deplore Schubert's and Schumann's seemingly perfunctory disposition of prepositions, conjunctions, articles (definite and indefinite) on the strong beat of a bar, or on an eloquent turn in the melody, or on the highest note in the vocal line. We find examples of this in the first two phrases.

Music and words are at odds on 'eine Blume'. 'Blume' is unquestionably the goal of the poem's first line, but the music's significant moment is the triplet and if it is made parenthetical out of deference to verbal meter, it will sound mannered and insincere to those who know and love the song. Therefore the triplet is unfolded tenderly and deliberately, given as much weight as 'Blume'.

'So' on the other hand, should be lighter than 'hold'; here, musical and verbal stress correspond, despite the high F; Wolf would not have set it differently. Should the parallel phrase in the second verse 'aufs Haupt' – etc. be treated similarly? No, this time the 'laying on of hands' is a blessing. Not only is 'aufs' given as much tone as 'Haupt' but a slight *tenuto* is made on it, and thereby the whole passage becomes more radiant.

The demi-semiquavers (32nd notes) on 'schön' and 'legen' (4 and 12) are shown as grace notes in the published score, but it is certain they were intended to be sung slowly and with significance.

As I have intimated, the close of this lovely song should be conveyed with restraint.

The *crescendo* on 14 will happen naturally, without special pleading on the singer's part. More often the pianist can be the offender; bar 15 gives him his first chance to emerge and he is tempted to leap into the breach with uncalled-for vigour. Let the soprano voice of the octaves sing gently, let his spread chord in the bass match the singer's grace notes in 4 and 12 in their easy, unhurried flow. This ukase applies to the postlude, in which we do not 'keep time' for it is recititative. There should be no awareness of bar lines and the player has all the time in the world. Grace notes though very soft are not parenthetical.

AUS DEN ÖSTLICHEN ROSEN

(Rückert)

Op. 25 No. 25

My greeting is like the scent of roses,
I send it to one whose cheeks are like a rose.
My greeting is like love in springtime,
I send it to one whose eyes are as the
light of spring.
My heart is torn with sadness but when you
think of me, my darkness is turned to light.

Melisma (the stringing together of two or more notes on one syllable) was used sparingly by Schumann but it is found here in almost every passage of the vocal line; it might be said that the part *melisma* plays in the shaping of a melody is insignificant, but if we expunge it in the following example we have:-

which has nothing like the same warmth or elegance of

appearing, even as it does, on the indefinate article!

It is used in every sentence to the beloved, as though, on the very words 'I send' the message is wafted away on a puff of airy *melisma*. If this reiteration conveys a suggestion of hesitancy or uncertainty, these are dispelled at the final 'you turn my darkness to light'.

There is a family likeness between this and '*Hör'ich das Liedchen klingen* and *Am leuchtenden Sommermorgen* (numbers 10 and 12 respectively in the *Dichterliebe*). In the accompaniment to these three we find the same captivating, almost apologetic syncopation so often used by this composer when singing of love.

For all the resemblance, *Aus dem östlichen Rosen* cannot claim a place beside the Heine songs, Rückert was not of that stature, and yet the music has a perfume and thistle-down lightness that are characteristic of Schumann.

ZUM SCHLUSS

(Rückert)

Op. 25 No. 26

Here in this world of sorrow, I have fashioned an unworthy garland for you my sister-bride. When, together, we are received above in the radiance of heaven, our love will bloom into a perfect wreath.

For the *finale* to this gathering of miscellaneous poems which he entitled *Myrten* (Myrtles) Schumann chose a nebulous lyric by Rückert 'At the last'. No one ever accused this master musician of ostentation and he concludes this garland for his beloved Clara with a singularly modest, even undistinguished song.

It is not unlike a hymn for the first ten bars; the accompaniment always in block harmony, its soprano voice faithfully doubles the vocal line. Only on bars 11 and 12 'Gottes Sonn' entgegenschaut' (the light of God's sun) by a change of note values from crotchets to minims in the pianoforte giving the voice of independence of movement for the first time, promising that the four-square nature of the music is now shed, do we come to the consummation.

We have said elsewhere that, like his beloved Schubert, Schumann had moments of magic that were inexplicable. This is one of them for it is strangely beautiful and moving.

The influence of the *melisma* in 13 and 14 transforms the phrase, pulling our heart strings, and the accompaniment's F flat in 15 makes its contribution. The song is lifted on to a higher plane by this passage as indeed Schumann intended. Felicitously, these four bars are repeated as a postlude.

SONGS FROM AUSGEWÄHLTE LIEDER

Volume I Edition Peters

WANDERLIED

(Kerner)

Op. 35 No. 3

Come friends, one more glass of wine, and
I must be off; its time for me to say farewell
to my father's house and the country-side I love.
The sun does not stand still, the waves, the
clouds are ever moving; so is a young man
urged to roam.
Overseas he is greeted by birds who know his
bithplace, he sees flowers that have the same
perfume as those he made into a bouquet
for his sweetheart. He feels at home in a distant
land.

Sehr lebhaft is the direction and the tempo should be ♩ = 126: I prefer to think it in *alla breve* at 𝅗𝅥 = 60. A slower rate, with such prosaic material would be pedestrian, nay more, would be insupportable. The singer carries us along on the wings of his enthusiasm.

Therefore those vigorous flights are taken with *brio*; the quavers must be on tip-toe for the take-off on to the top notes. A slight impatience here is human and what is more, provides the voice with a moment's expansion on 'Wein' and 'sein'. Semiquavers crackle with physical energy.

Not content with letting us hear this eight-bar pattern three times in succession, the composer, for good measure, lets us have it a fourth time, when he repeats the first verse. Fortunately, before this final appearance there is a slow section in D flat, contemplative and more relaxed, as the young man is reminded of sights and scents of home. It is a change of mood, a relief, which is conveyed by colour of voice rather than by too much slowing down.

In the postlude, slurred quavers followed by snappy *staccato* chords are marked meticulously. The player will look in vain for a *ritardando* sign at the finish, nor should he make one: the two final chords are brisk with no lagging but much *sostenuto* pedal (which embraces the last chord of 70).

ERSTES GRÜN

(Kerner)

Op. 35 No. 4

Oh young fresh green grass, how many
a heart you have revived that was sickened
by winter's snow and oh, how I long for you.
My eyes light up when you spring from earth's
wintry night, I press you to my heart and sink
my lips in your greenery. My urge to avoid
my fellow-men who cannot ease my sorrow is only
eased by you, fresh green grass. You calm
my heart.

The depression the human heart suffers after a long and gloomy winter is understandable, but Kerner's last verse wherein he expresses a wish to retreat from all human contact, with no one to whom he can appeal to heal his misery, comes as a surprise if we are to take him literally. Fortunately Schumann did not. True, he puts this strophic song in the minor, though the music is anything but sad; sprightly, yes, whimsical and capricious, but eager air breathes all through it. As for the major postlude to each verse, it is alive with such zest and playfulness that the song's title could easily be *Frühlingsglaube*.

The basic tempo should be around ♩ = 63 but it fluctuates continually. I like slight pauses on the first two beats of bar 1, 'Frisches Gras' are words to be enunciated with gladness. For two bars only 'das von des Winters Schnee erkrankt' the tempo slows down and the accompaniment soberly joins the voice in rhythmic unison and ceases its off-beat semiquavers.

For the accompanist, the playing of the interlude which now follows, is unalloyd pleasure. (How thankful he should be that the composer did not take the poet too too seriously!

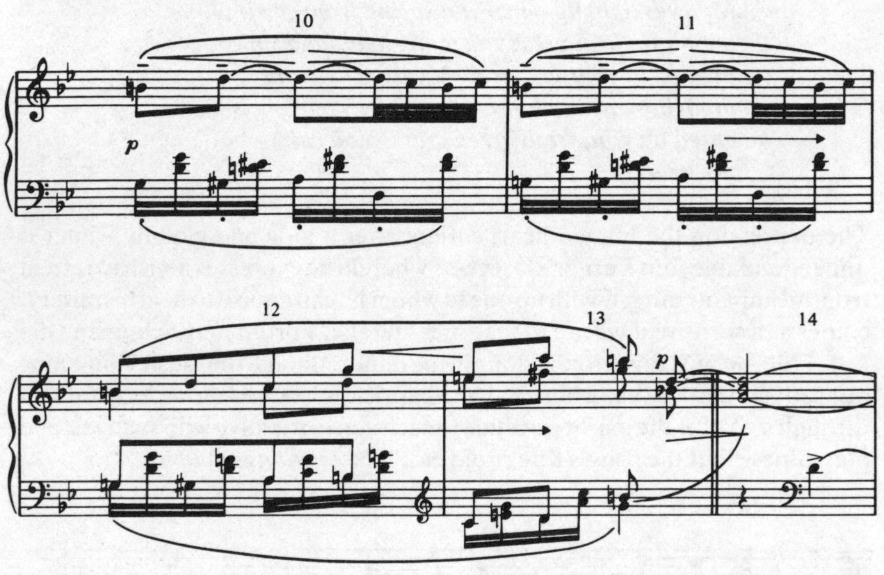

Elasticity is essential. The hesitation on the first two quavers of 10 is pointed, but 11 less so, and then the scamper up to the top of 13 must be full of joy of life. One must believe in Spring.

Frederic Mompou of Barcelona wrote a pianoforte suite *Scènes d'Enfants*, and one of the most charming pieces entitled *Jeunes filles au jardin* is headed with the words 'Chantez avec la fraicheur de l'herbe humide' and I cannot help thinking some such though is applicable to this fascinating song.

DIE BEIDEN GRENADIERE

(Heine)

Op. 49 No. 1

Two grenadiers, after long captivity in Russia, were making their way across Germany when they heard news that made them hang their heads in shame; Napoleon had been defeated and captured.

They wept on learning these tidings, and one said 'I feel my old wounds burning, I shall die'.

'I would gladly die with you' said the other, 'but my wife and child will perish without me'.

'Wife and child can beg, if they are hungry. What matter they, when my Emperor is taken? Oh my brother, take my body and bury it in French soil, lay my cross of honour and its red ribbon on my breast, gird my sword about me and put my musket in my hand and I will lie there listening like a sentinel. Then, when the cannons roar, amid the thunder of horses' hooves the Emperor will ride over my grave, and armed as of old, I shall rise up from the grave to defend him, my Emperor!'

Naturally, the music is in march rhythm, but not in brisk time. Schumann's instruction is *Mässig* (*Moderato*) and this should be appreciated, for the men are veterans, wounded and tired. Their weariness is suggested by the dragging triplets in bars 3 and 7; the fall of every phrase adds to this impression.

The tempo I prefer is ♩ = 88 though I am aware it is often taken at 104, or quicker.

Despair injects the muttered colloquy as the men hang their heads in shame and is mirrored by the low tessitura in the vocal line and by the subdued, now stable, accompaniment (11 to 17).

Weeping and resigned stupefaction do not prevail over one man, for his companion's compassionate, almost apologetic allusion to wife and child is impatiently brushed aside by patriotic fire, or fanatical devotion, and the contrast between the two characters is clearly delineated in the music. The contemptuous 'What care I for wife and child' etc. is indeed hot-headed but it must have only a suggestion of haste, so that the outcry 'Mein Kaiser, mein Kaiser gefangen' can have its full meed of desperation.

A difference of pattern in the music, marked 'nach und nach bewegter' has a more urgent accompaniment for 'My brother, grant me one last wish'.

And now we see the rationality of Schumann's recommended *Mässig* at the song's beginning, which it is hoped, has been upheld until this moment. It is a passage leading us to eight bars (53 to 60) of breathless expectation and marked *Schneller* (suddenly quicker not an *accelerando*).

This two-bar phrase in the dominant seventh is repeated four times with growing passion, a passion engendered by the restless accompaniment with its trenchant and ever-loudening bass. A pent up pressure that culminates in the mighty 'So will I lie like a sentinel' and it is sung to the tune of *La Marseillaise*.

A *rallentando* on 60 is mandatory if the grandeur of these moments is to be realized, it also enables the *moderato* tempo to be resumed. I go further and am convinced it should be sung majestically at ♩= 80, which is slower than *tempo primo*. At the words 'armed as of old . . . etc' the pianoforte's thundering bass octave quavers drag the movement back still more and overpoweringly to ♩= 66.

With his last breath the stricken man sinks into the arms of his fellow-soldier and the postlude depicts him being lowered gently to the ground.

Bar 75 has a *fortissimo* which is not curbed until 78 by a small *diminuendo*. Each long drawn-out chord should unmistakably decrease in weight but to a noble *piano*, no less. One thinks, when playing this postlude of the brass rather than strings.

The 'Chant de guerre' *La Marseillaise* by Rouget de Lisle has on the printed score 'Temps de marche animé' and when we hear it, a lively pace is expected, say ♩= 120. In the context of Heine's poem, which should be the main consideration, such a speed would be inconsistent.

VOLKSLIEDCHEN

(Rückert)

Op. 51 No. 2

When I take my morning walk in the garden
in my green bonnet, I think first of my sweetheart
and wonder what he is doing. There's no star in
the sky I would not give him; if I could, I would
give him the heart out of my bosom.

This delicious miniature typifies the genius of Schumann when grace, humour, and femininity are his theme.

One can picture this damsel through his music more easily than through the verse: she is elegant and of course attractive, which is why she can afford to laugh at herself in her floppy bonnet, since she is usually *bien soignée*.

It is the green hat with its laughing *melisma* that attracts our attention when we catch sight of her. And then we see how daintily she walks with those little *staccato* steps in the accompaniment.

But that she has that spark of self-assertion, the prerogative of beautiful women, is shown in her next phrase.

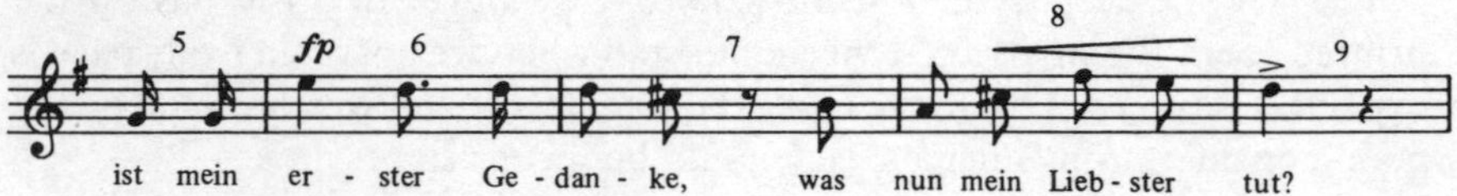

The fitful interruption (7) is admonitory; in a playful way it admits suspicion, showing a sweet lack of reason (which is what makes her so intriguing).

Softer thoughts of her own true love follow and the tour of the flower beds is arrested, the vocal line is no longer jaunty.

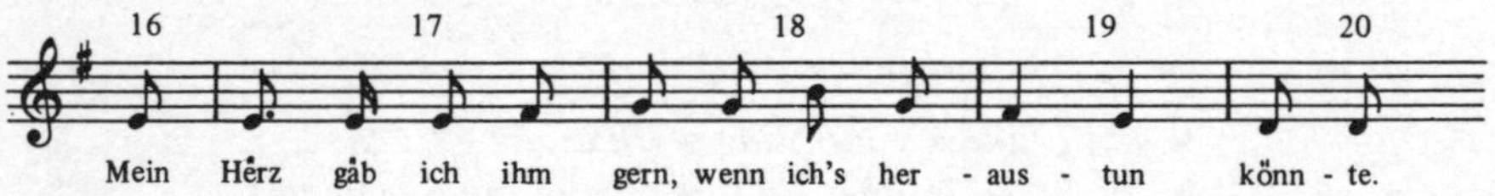

This section of eight bars beginning at 13 should be made distinctive from the rest of the song, not by slowing the tempo, not by increasing the tone, but by the seriousness with which the singer keeps to her *legato* line.

And then, with bewitching change of mood, we are taken back to the green hat and 'what is he doing?'. This time, however, there is a slight variation with two top and quite exhilarating G's and a little extra playful *melisma*.

DER ARME PETER

(Heine)

Op. 53 No. 3

I

Hans and Grete are dancing together and revelling with their friends. Peter watches motionless and dumb, with his face white as chalk. Hans and Grete are newly wed, resplendent in their wedding attire, but poor Peter outside gnawing his nails, is in his working clothes. He says, eyeing the couple despairingly, 'It's a good thing I'm a sensible chap or I'd do something mad.'

It is inevitable that we compare poor Peter's plight with that of the lover in *Es ist ein Flöten und Geigen* for both are watching the wedding festivities of the girl they adore. The *Dichterliebe* song, though heart-rending, with agony rife in every bar, sees the sufferer at the cycle's end surmounting his woe with a philosophical gleam of hope.

Here, paradoxically, the music is jovial (even though its gaiety can be read as superficial) yet we know the *dénouement* will be lamentable. Perhaps it can be explained by suggesting that we are among the merry-makers looking out at that scruffy fellow with the white face and feeling little concern for him, while in the *Dichterliebe* we were outside looking in, sharing the jilted man's suffering. This is what the music says to me.

Above, the adjective 'jovial' was used to describe the spirit of the occasion; the dancers are country-folk and the waltz is in the *Ländler* style. Although the texture is light-weight, the dancers take large strides, as suggested by the broken octave intervals in the pianoforte treble and do not move on tip-toe (see the accented third beat). Schumann's instruction is *Nicht schnell* and I suggest ♩.= 48 as the approximate tempo.

The singer should feel one beat to the bar in a steady slow swing, undisturbed by the false accents in the pianoforte.

For seven bars (19–25) the mood is more robust with a sturdy bass; the canon in the accompaniment treble may make the pianist ambitious but it is the voice – now *forte* – which dominates. In this tiny section the singer allows himself to impart some bias on the first beat of each bar.

Peter's morbid reflections 'I might do myself some harm' are not reflected in the music, and as if to underline this, the postlude is impervious, for the dancers are happy.

II

There's a pain in my breast which tears me in half;
it drives me now here, now there, I cannot stay still.

Above all it drives me to be near Grete, but when I look into her eyes I cannot bear it and hurry away. Only in the hills can I be alone and standing quietly there, I weep and weep.

The inner tumult which racks the breast is evident in that vocal line. There is one note that acts as a needle in those bars, it is the B natural, heard no fewer than fourteen times, and it should be made piercingly audible; for this reason I like it stressed every time it comes. (A violinist, for argument's sake, would take a separate bow for each note in that cluster of quavers and would plan a down-bow for the proscribed B.) The tempo is marked 'somewhat quickly' – perhaps 𝅗𝅥 = 80 or 88 – and possibly my suggestion may make these passages sound laboured; this is all to the good, for facile authority is unwanted. The singer can throw off the shackles I impose on the high point in 9–10 'wills mich von hinnen drängen.'

In fact this agitation is short lived for now (*Etwas ruhiger*) 'I am driven to be near her' is *legato* and its effect is greater in contrast to the hectic nature of the first nine bars.

Still more sustained and now marked *langsamer* 'I make for the hills' is recitative in style and only on the final word 'weine' is the needling motif resumed in the pianoforte.

There is spirit in the accompaniment. The introductory chord is parallel to the harshness of the preliminary of *Nun hast du mir den ersten Schmerz getan* (*Frauenliebe und Leben*). Care is taken to differentiate between the spiteful stabbing chords and the compassionate *legato*.

The postlude is all *agitato*, only on the penultimate bar should there be a *rallentando*.

III

Poor Peter goes tottering down the street, ghastly pale, unmanned. People stop still at the

sight of him, and stare. Girls mutter to one another
'He must have risen from the grave!'
'Not so, dear young ladies, he is making his way
to the grave.'
He has lost his love and the grave
is the best place for him; let him lie there
and sleep till the Day of Judgement.

There should be no appreciable break before starting the third song.

One is tempted to try to match the words by singing in a pale colourless tone, but the rather thick accompaniment hinders this. It can be repaired by remaining persistently *piano* and by making the triplets in bar 1 and the quavers in 3 (and similarly thereafter) extremely deliberate.

In the accompaniment a lower dynamic level than the voice is wanted, but there is a profundity in the bass octaves.

The voice vibrates with a shared sorrow when answering the young women.

But at 17 'he is going to his grave' should have an air of inexorability, that grips the heart with a cold hand.

The voice grows in volume, steadily and dispassionately, and the funereal drums in the bass mark the inevitable course towards the grave.

DIE SOLDATENBRAUT

(Mörike)

Op. 64 No. 1

Oh, if only the king knew how brave my
sweetheart is! He would lay down his life
for the king and he'd do it just as willingly
for me. My young man has not, like
the noblemen, won any ribbon, stars or
military cross, nor has he, so far, become a general.
But over yonder church, where we are to be married
there are brightly shining stars, there will be a
ribbon to tie our wedding knot. As for a cross –
he will have this to bear at home!

This amusing song, in a similar vein to Hugo Wolf's *Der Tambour*, is a typical example of Mörike's wit and playfulness, well caught by Schumann.

Springing, youthful rhythm is the fulcrum. The girl's vivacity is expressed in her laughing lightness of touch and by the physical energy of her semiquavers.

The roguish contrast in the pianoforte's paired chords, alternately *legato* and *staccato* cannot be exaggerated, and they positively chuckle when they echo the voice, as seen in bar 4 (and in 6, 15, 17).

This variation in colour is very evident in the vocal line. It cannot be doubted (at least by the maiden) that her hero would lay down his life for the king, but this ringing passage is followed, now *piano*, by a vastly more important 'he'd do it for me too' and there is an unmistakable twinkle in her eye as she repeats the confidential aside.

Schumann wants the third verse at a somewhat slower tempo. The block harmony for 'dort über Marienkapell' should be played very lightly for it is not to be taken seriously (no suggestion of a church-organ accompaniment!) for this section shows that this charming creature is as saucy as they come; she makes this abundantly clear by her play on words in regard to the stars, the ribbon and 'the cross he will have to bear' when he is married.

Brisk march tempo is resumed when the first theme is repeated and is heralded by the rattling kettle drums and the martial *staccato* chords.

In my opinion *tempo primo* should start immediately with the drum beat on 32, but the score does not mark it till the last beat of 36, meaning that the example seen above should be in the *etwas langsamer* tempo imposed in 24. To play these bars slowly, however, is illogical and this becomes obvious if such an experiment is made. Furthermore the rat-a-tat-a-tat of the drums should invariably be noisy and the intervening chords *piano*. It is much more fun this way.

MARIENWÜRMCHEN

(Anon.)

Op. 79 No. 14

Ladybird, come, settle on my hand, I'll
do you no harm, I only want to see your
pretty wings.
Ladybird, fly off home, your house is burning,
your little ones are crying, for the spider is spinning
his web around them.
Ladybird, fly next door, the children there won't
hurt you, for they too want to see your pretty wings.

Seventeen bars, heard thrice, are the sum total of this little affair; one cannot imagine a happier or more deft setting for the song the child is singing. It is at once ingenuous and clever. The cleverness is Schumann's in spinning such an innocent and delicious web. George Bernard Shaw was wont to declare that most of his plays were 'actor proof' and although we take this with a grain of salt, we could say that the composer of *Marienwürmchen* has made, with some adroitness, a song that is fool-proof.

One cannot go wrong, provided the few instructions are obeyed; for instance:–

It may not be necessary for breaths to be taken in the first six bars but it is much more true to nature to take them or at least, to break the flow of the vocal line, by observing the commas.

To make the 'grace' note in bar 5 truly graceful it is advisable to take it before the beat, robbing the end of 'dir'.

It is the singer who determines the length of the pianoforte's *tenuti* in 6 and 7, for the accompanist cannot release it until he hears her preparing to sing 'nichts'. The pianist is very alert in bar 12 to ensure that his semiquaver passage is twin with the voice; this is one of those occasions (very rare occasions, dear reader) when the accompaniment should not be noticed.

DEIN ANGESICHT

(Heine)

Op. 127 No. 2

Last night in a dream I saw your face
so sweet and fair, angelic, but pale
as death and oh, so sad. Only your
lips are red, but death will kiss them white
and the shining light from your eyes will
be no more.

Schuman's gift for tracing a smooth silky melody is seen in this melancholy and moving setting. The poetic significance of the repeated note which Hugo Wolf was to exploit so tellingly some years later in his *Italienisches Liederbuch*, is to be noticed. Its seeming uneventfulness throws up the high point of the musical and vocal line (bar 3) so that the latter stands out with eloquence without the singer having to bring any extraneous interpretative pressure to bear upon it.

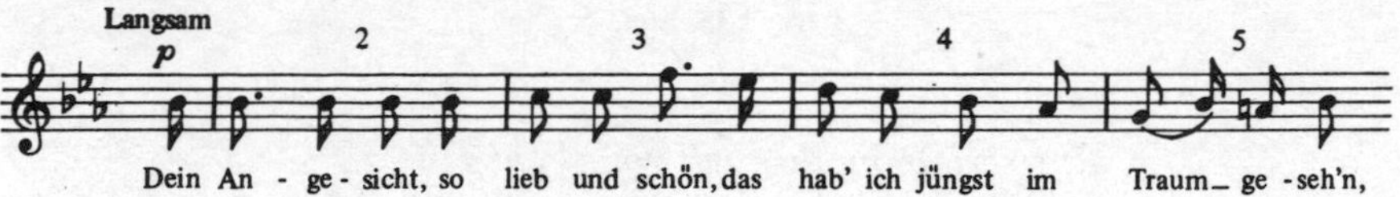

Indeed we are grateful to the artist who can unfold this tribute to beauty with purity and simplicity. But 'so sad, deathly pale' brings a shadow, expressed by a gentle syncopation,

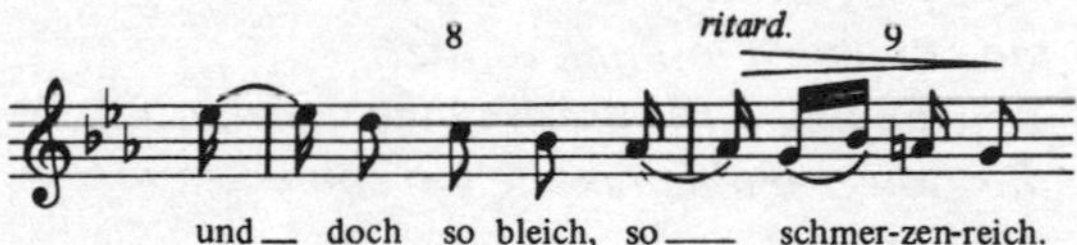

as if a thought, hesitant and unwelcome, possessed the heart of the poet.

Melismata are used tenderly in arches of parallel shape in 5 and 9, as seen above, and in 13 too, where a modulation to G flat for 'Himmelslicht' (heavenly light) leads to a repetition of the first verse.

The pessimism of the lyric is endorsed by the chromatic friction between the middle voices of the postlude – bars 26 and 27.

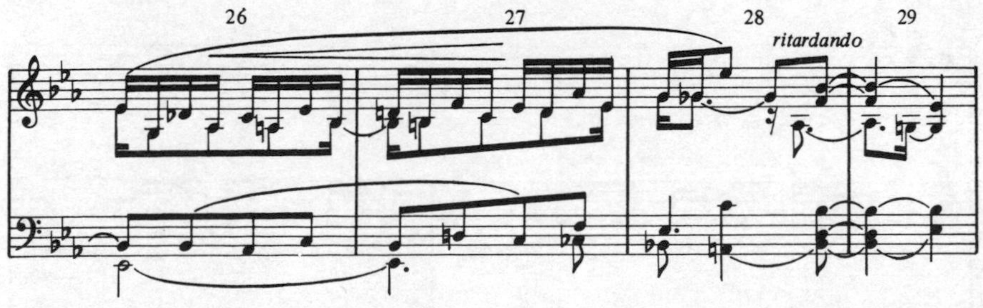

FLUTENREICHE EBRO

(trans. Geibel)

Op. 138 No. 5

Ebro, rippling through your banks of
wild flower, does my beloved think of me?
Green pastures ask this of her too. Forest
glades when she rests in your shade, ask
if she is too contented to think of me?
When she breathes the early morning air,
ask her, pearls of dew, as she walks
bare-foot through the wet grass, is she
too contented to think of me?
You singing birds greeting the dawn, ask
this flower maiden is she too contented to
think of me?

The poet, as in the Rellstab-Schubert *Liebesbotschaft* is confident that the river will take his message to the beloved one, the poplars and the birds will all join in the happy chorus.

A guitar accompaniment quietly murmers all through the song and provides the softest cushion for one of Schumann's loveliest melodies. No answer comes to the questioner but we can assume he has no qualms, for the music is not merely serene, it is enraptured and has a spell-binding symmetry.

These four bars are an intimation, not only of the lyricism and curves of the vocal line, but of its rhythmic play. It is not a melody which 'sings itself', nor is it enough for the singer to 'flute' nonchalantly, even in a pleasing *legato*. Colour is needed. A rise and fall in tone is indicated in bar 4 following the shape of the line. Similarly, though unmarked in the printed score, the climb on 2 and the fall on 3 ought to be observed by the singer with warmth, so that his pleasure is at once communicated to the listener. It is no problem to make the rising semiquavers in 2 as smooth as may be, but the semiquavers in 4 might be disturbing and are to be sung with gentle composure. The triplets in 3 float unhurriedly.

The pianist plays his guitar-like semiquavers detached, with the sustaining pedel in active participation and there is no difficulty until he finds he has two voices in the treble clef to contend with. A circus performer is no good in the sawdust ring unless he can ride two horses simultaneously, and this, in some degree is asked of the pianist here. The fourth and fifth fingers of his right hand sing melodiously and with smooth relaxation, while the other fingers cope with their *non-legato* and inconspicuous plucking. This is seen above on the last beats of 2 and 3 especially in bar 4.

It cannot be denied that a feeling of freedom is to be enjoyed by the player when he is able to sing out with less restraint.

There are several moments such as this where the guitarist takes a short rest.

The four verses are largely repetitive and (deserve to be, so lovely are they) though a playful variation in the fourth demands a word. The other verses have an interlude of one bar, here this bar is dispensed with and the pianoforte plays the motif (bar 2) ahead of time, upon which the voice, as if taken by surprise, repeats the theme in amiable pursuit. This verse is extended by three bars with a tiny coda: 'Ob in ihrem Glücke sie meiner gedenket' (if in her contentment she thinks of me) has been reiterated each time it appears, but in this verse, even more than previously. It is by no means tedious, for just as we were anticipating a full close, Schumann deceives us with an interrupted cadence, one of the most engaging moments of the song:-

The singer's graceful sweep is more affectionate than ever, but the accompaniment tells us that the end is not yet reached and the top notes of his octaves sing sweetly. As can be seen the C natural in the deep bass appears as a grace note but it is of great importance and wants sonority. Schumann was fond of the interval of the ninth; we see it in *Dichterliebe* (bars 57, 58, 61, 62 in the fifteenth song).

LIEDERKREIS

(Heine)

Op. 24. Edition Peters Volume II.

* Volume I Peters.

MORGENS STEH ICH AUF UND FRAGE

(Heine)

Op. 24 No. 1

When I awaken I ask myself, will my darling come to-day? By sundown I am utterly dejected for another day she stayed away. At night I am sleepless, and I wander throughout the day in a half-waking dream.

The short phrases of the singer and the detached chords in the accompaniment (which should continue throughout) are a reflection of nervous uncertainty. Only where a *ritardando* is marked on bars 9, 10 is there a momentary hope that the dear one might come

but the faint hope is quickly disillusioned by the false accents in 11 & 12.

'A half-waking dream' is the clue to the singer's colour, when the vocal line rises at 'träumend wie im halben Schlummer' he makes no *crescendo*, it would be contradictory to do so. If anything, this arch suggests physical fatigue and it is accomplished purely by vocal means.

Though keeping to a *mezza voce* there is always an underlying feeling of anxiety.

The false accents are heard in the postlude and the final chords seem to ask a question.

I play the grace notes as *appoggiaturi* with a leisurely spread chord and the C sharp coming on the beat, but this is a personal preference.

ES TREIBT MICH HIN

Op. 24 No. 2

I'm driven this way and that, quivering
with impatience, knowing in a few hours
I shall see the fairest of maidens.
How hard my poor heart is beating! These
wretched hours dawdle, they crawl!
Get a move on, you laggards, you can never
have loved, you enjoy watching a lover's torment.

Fierce attack should startle one from the beginning. Where the first song was sung with some constraint, this one rants and roars: where the accompaniment was played with quietly detached chords, this one is *staccato* and violent. These terms 'roar' and 'violent' are used metaphorically but there should be no mistaking the biting difference between this mood and the other. It is a wayward vigour, 'driven here and there' as the poet says, for by the eighth bar there is already a slackening of temper leading to 'the fairest maiden'.

Here tender singing is wanted. Alternative notes are to be seen (also in 34, 35, 38) but the lower notes should be taken if possible. Bar 17 is long and sung in recitative style with the 'small' notes lingered on and a pronounced *fermata* on the F sharp. Before the pianist plunges into his forcible interlude he waits until the singer's note has been released – even allowing a momentary silence.

The drive to whip up the lagging hours is exemplified by the combat between voice and pianoforte, bars 30 to 40.

Before the end of the affray, shown above, they have been tugging at one another in canon style. Here we can see why the lower notes in the vocal line are essential, they set the pianist the course he must pursue two bars later (the lagging hours). The higher alternative notes mean nothing.

Raging haste consumes the singer in his final phrase; it is marked *a tempo* but he takes the bit between his teeth and storms to the very end; shooting out every word savagely.

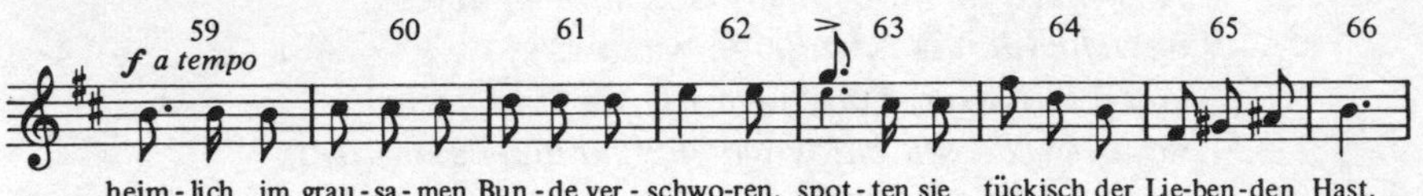

This impetuosity seizes the pianist by the hair in a superb postlude and he tries to match the rage of the singer.

It can be seen there is an alternative to the high G on 63. Having previously shown a preference for the lower notes wherever there was an option, there is no doubt what the decision should be here. At the risk of being accused of oscillation or being 'driven this way and that' I say categorically that the top note must be taken.

ICH WANDELTE UNTER DEN BÄUMEN

Op. 24 No. 3

Alone, with only my grief, I roamed under the
trees, and old dreams stole into my heart.
Birds, high in the sky, who taught you that
word so dear?
"That word we learned from a maiden, the tune
came from her lips and we seized upon it."
It is not for you to tell me. You birds are trying
to soothe me but I do not trust you.

Of all the songs in the cycle this is the least excited, has least restlessness; its melancholy is resigned and is a mood so real to the composer that he wrings our hearts.

What could be more eloquent or fore-shadow sadness more surely than the prelude?

There is much here to give the player thought: the shape of the arch rising to a G sharp then descending chromatically and despondently to E natural; the nuances to be suggested rather than underlined; not least there is the smooth syncopation, the life-blood of the passage even though muted. It is a reverie and if performed in this tenor will be of great help to the singer. Only four bars, and once heard never alluded to again, until they are used as a postlude.

Ideally the first four bars of the vocal line should be covered in one breath; the smooth concentrated stream of tone grips the attention of the hearer, but it is not feasible with this slow tempo (♩ = 55 to 60) and long stretch to contain it without breathing in the middle. A quiet breath can be taken after Bäumen' (bar 6). The second phrase, given below, has the same question and a breath is taken after 'Träumen' (10).

Unfulfilled longing awakened by 'old dreams' is the emotional high point, expressed by triplets for the voice, doubly emphasized in the accompaniment.

It is far easier for the singer to make it a climax by a *crescendo* in 11 up to his high note, but it is more faithful to the meaning of the poet if he allows the music to speak for itself. He is following a train of thought, not making a proclamation.

The song is strophic except for the third verse. This section with its magical transference to G major has, seemingly, the voice strung on a higher level. Actually, the *tessitura* is largely as before, but the repetitive B natural round which the vocal line weaves, induces this impression. No doubt the singer's *mezza voce* as he tells of the birds' message and the accompaniment placed entirely in the treble and played with airy lightness, add to the illusion. A comma in the text after 'hübsche' (29) enables the singer to carry through to this point where he may snatch a breath.

The return to the tonic key and main motif is in a more decisive vein, for the birds are not to be believed. Gradually, however, the voice sinks lower in tone and pitch as the lover declares he trusts no one.

LIEB LIEBCHEN, LEG'S HÄNDCHEN

Op. 24 No. 4

My dearest, lay your hand on my heart; can
you hear it hammering? Living inside there
is an evil carpenter fashioning a coffin for me.
This banging goes on all day and all night
and I get no rest: O, master carpenter,
hurry up and finish your job that I soon may
sleep in peace.

Heine's sinister lyric is wonderfully matched by the music. The voice starts by itself with no preamble and, like the carpenter in the lyric the singer refuses to be hurried, and ignores the impatient off beats in the pianoforte. The sensitive artist, in an eloquent song such as the previous one, makes delicate nuances with the rise and fall of the vocal line, but here he eschews such practice; the knock-knock of the beating heart is relentless, so that 'ach hörst du' is of a quality which I can only describe as husky; it is neither *forte* nor a dainty *piano*, in any case there is no swelling of tone to be made on the ascent up to it.

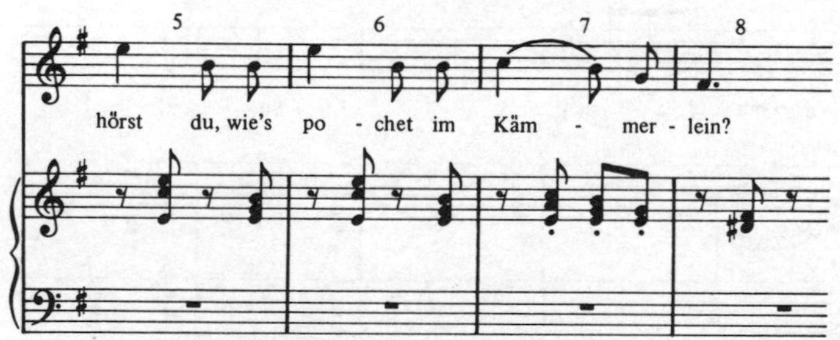

The 'sympathetic' accompanist would be a deplorable impediment; indeed he should be the reverse, always with the proviso (a paradox perhaps) that he listens carefully to the voice and does not cover it, for he plays the role of the carpenter whose hammer blows never cease. Although the pianoforte is marked *piano* the player must contrive to get a hard sound by letting his hand drop with a degree of stiffness on to the keys.

It is at the mention of the carpenter that the voice takes on an extra dimension. This is the point of the poem and here Schumann manifests it with three strokes. First he makes 'Zimmermann' an abrasive triplet against the accompaniment's steady two beats; he makes a modulation – charged with fate – to E flat; and lastly he brings the pianist's left hand into play for the first time, sounding an accented C flat. The cross rhythm of

'Zimmermann' is sung with obstinate indifference to the regularity of the pianoforte and, for the first time, with a tone of intensity (as apart from the 'husky' quality previously suggested).

That C flat in the pianoforte bass rings in the ear like the knell of doom. But the shocking moment is still in store.

"He's making me a" and the voice breaks off abruptly with a bar of silence, as if the singer were unable to continue – and then – "coffin".

The end of the song is even more ghastly, again with the singer silent as in 15, but with his final notes 'schlafen kann' naked, unaccompanied, stranded in mid-air like a wraith.

And yet, when all is said and done, the *staccato* 'schlafen kann' must make an impact. To this end the singer does not reduce his tone and render his words – charged with fate – less audible. Again, and unlike the pianist who keeps meticulously to the regularity of the tapping hammer, 'schlafen kann' is uttered at a portentous and slightly slower tempo. We shudder on hearing it.

SCHÖNE WIEGE MEINER LEIDEN

Op. 24 No. 5

Cradle of my sorrows, tomb of my contentment,
beautiful town I leave you. Farewell.
Farewell to the place where my beloved dwells
and where I first saw her.
How much happier had I been, never to have seen
you, my heart's queen.
I never craved for your love, only asked to
breathe the same air you breathed.
But my mind reels at the cruelty of your words
and, sick and sore at heart, I will drag myself
away and seek rest in a distant grave.

This song is *Rondo* in form though the description can only be loosely applied so varied is the compound of patterns and shapes. Homogeneity is provided much of the time by the accompaniment with its pulsating quavers alternating between the hands; here all the agitation and motive power of the song frequently reside. But the pianoforte remains an undercurrent, only occasionally coming to the surface with a significant comment; it is the melodic line that holds the listener's attention.

The voice's main subject is a sweeping melody of ever mounting arches and is eighteen bars long. Keeping to a firm *legato* the singer invests the melody with a timbre of noble proportion; by this I infer that the voice should be sonorous and with a Brahmsian quality of *piano*. The term 'noble' is suggested because vexation of spirit is concealed beneath the surface, and the burning, palpitating heart is portrayed by the accompaniment.

At the words 'Lebe wohl' (Farewell) the flowing movement abruptly ceases for a painful moment, as the fugitive looks back at the 'beautiful town' he is leaving. There are three *ritardandi*, certain indication that the singer may feel free to take his own time, (*a piacere*). How vital is the pianoforte's affirmation of smart (17) with the chromatic cluster and accented B sharp in the bass!

If the lover, so far, has drawn a veil over his suffering, in the third verse, he makes known the depth of his bitterness.

A rejected man's spleen cursing the day he met his 'heart's queen' is in the minor; the phrases are shorter with more vehement accents.

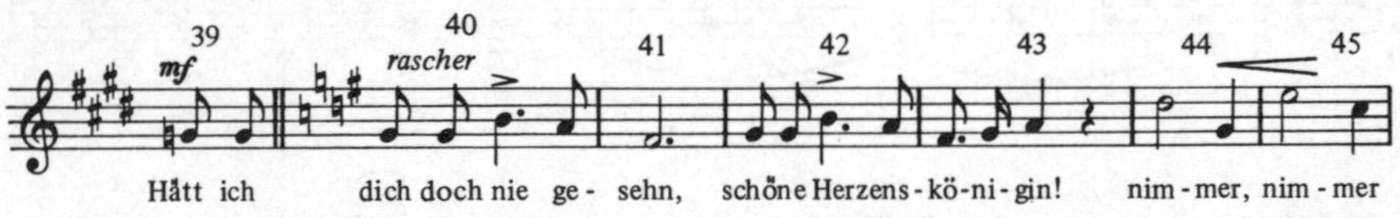

'Nimmer, nimmer' grows in desperation, a desperation goaded by the rasping false accents in voice and accompaniment (40 and 42).

But it is the fifth verse 'Wahnsinn wühlt in meinen Sinnen' when madness threatens to overturn his reason, that he momentarily seems to lose all control in an explosion.

This hectic syncopation in broken octaves, a seventeen bar stretch, is a test for the accompanist. While it is an expression of utter abandonment, paradoxically it needs absolute rhythmic control, for the syncopation must be precise. Nice perception is necessary too, so that the opening of the floodgates does not drown the singer.

Heine's poem ends at this point, but Schumann repeats the first verse with its fine melody.

After the final 'Lebe wohl' there is a postlude of some dozen bars. That it is quite different thematically and stylistically from anything we have met earlier in the song, is of no matter, for it is impressive. The first half is manly in spirit with a melody for the inner voices which sings of courage; the remainder is more melting and feminine and can be played, as Schumann so often liked, in an improvisatory fashion.

The tempo is marked *Bewegt* (with movement) but it is allowed to fluctuate very frequently.

WARTE, WARTE, WILDER SCHIFFMANN

Op. 24 No. 6

Wait, wait, wild ferryman, I'll embark
anon, but first I must say good-bye to
two loves, Europe and her.
Let me write down my sorrows in blood that
streams from my eyes and my body.
Why, my love, do you shudder to see me thus
when you have witnessed my pallor and my
bleeding heart for so long?
Remember the ancient fable of the serpent
in paradise, whose gift of an apple damned
for ever our ancestor.
Evil began with that apple, Eve brought death
with it, Eris put Troy to the torch with it.
You, you have brought forth both – fire
and death.

'Sehr rasch' is the recommendation, and the metronome speed should be approximately 66 with one beat to the bar; anything quicker than this trivializes it, denudes it of violence. Only occasionally and for cynical effect does the singer have recourse to a *legato* line. Schumann is at pains even with the minims on bar 4, to show that the two syllabuses on 'Schiffmann' are to be detached. Above all, articulation must be distinct; too often one has heard this song roared through without being able to make out a word – full of sound and fury – signifying nothing.

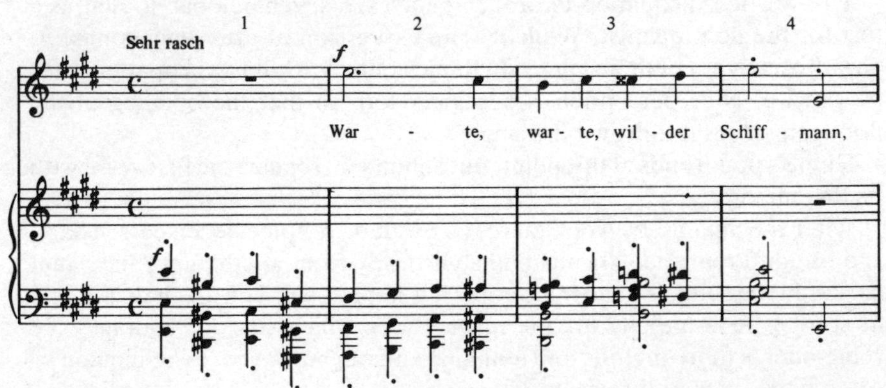

Each chord or octave in the accompaniment is a separate world in itself, always percussive and, more often than not, marked *staccato*; the bass minims, for instance, seen in 3 and 4.

The *piano* phrase at the allusion to 'zwei Jungfrau' (12–16) to whom the jilted lover wishes to say farewell, is not to be taken as a fleeting moment of tenderness, for there is an acid thread in it and the tone is thin and no longer robust.

'Why shudder at the sight of my blood?' is lurid in the extreme and more to the taste of Loewe, but Schumann makes it the occasion, and a valid one, for unlovely intervals (37–40) and for ungainly syncopation (41–43).

These four bars of diminished fifth intervals, prompt an immediate response with like intervals inverted (45–48). Suggested alternative notes to these latter are to be seen in the score, higher in the stave, but quite unacceptable. Equally pointless too are the high substitute notes of 49–52, they lose sight of the syncopation (41–43) to which they are supposed to make reply.

Reference was made above to the irony in bars 12–16: now the same phrase is heard again as we are told of the serpent in paradise, but now the cynicism is unmistakable and delivered in a tone suggesting the curved lip of contempt.

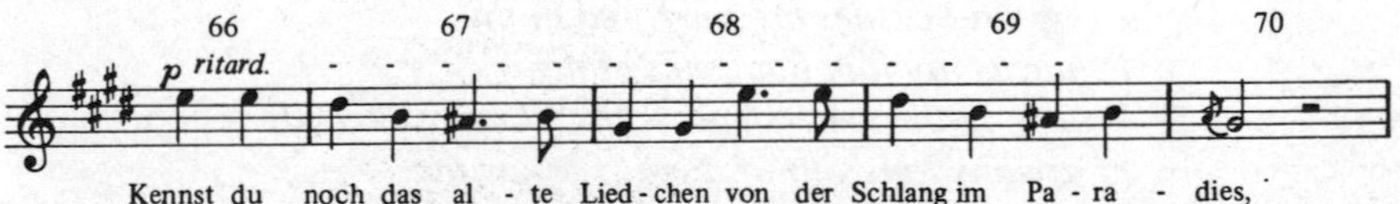

The smooth veneer with which this phrase is sung after so much bluster, makes the barb all the more penetrating.

A tremendous climax for the singer, who reverts to his belligerent mould, gives him a mighty top A for his final word.

All the postlude is played without sustaining pedal in strict tempo and with relentless pugnacity. At bar 107 a gradual *diminuendo* comes, but there is no *ritardando* to be made until 115.

Tone has already been reduced before the above is heard but a suggestion of steeliness should be evident. This is made manifest if the last three chords (120–121) are played in the basic tempo of the song. This is in accordance with Schumann's custom of marking; it can be seen on the score that the *ritardando* ends at 119.

BERG' UND BURGEN SCHAUN HERUNTER

Op. 24 No. 7

Crags and castles are mirrored in the
Rhine as my tiny boat sails along.
Watching the waters' gentle flow I am wakened
to dreams long out of mind. I know that
beneath the river's placid murmuring, death
is lurking: it resembles you, my beloved one,
with your sweet smile and treacherous heart.

A charming picture is evoked by the limpid eddies of the accompaniment and the graceful tune for the voice floating on its surface. The mood is peaceful, the melody nostalgic but there is no suggestion in the music whatsoever of the envenomed parallel that Heine creates. It is another instance of Schumann's unwillingness to see what he did not wish to see, unless the bitterness was purposely ignored after the *Sturm und Drang* of the earlier songs. Possibly the composer was too happy at the time he was at work on this *Liederkreis* to change the strophic pattern he had decided on for *Berg' und Burgen*. A peaceful song at this juncture is not unwelcome.

The singer would be well advised to sing this as a lovely piece of music and not to endeavour to bring Heine's nightmare too vividly to our notice.

ANFANGS WOLLT' ICH FAST VERZAGEN

Op. 24 No. 8

At first I was almost in despair
and thought I could never endure it.
Yet borne it I have, do not ask me how.

This song, or rather chorale (reminiscent, perhaps intentionally, of the Chopin Prelude in C minor Op. 18 no. 20) is nearly the shortest song ever, being eleven bars in length. Yet *Xenion* (Epigram) by Richard Strauss is even shorter, for it consists of only six bars.

The brevity of these songs is of little matter, but it is interesting to compare Heine's verse with Goethe's in the Strauss song. To some extent the two poets had the same philosophy, for the first lines of the Goethe quatrain are:–

Let us not dwell on the past
no matter what happened.

Strauss's fragment says little musically, whereas Schumann's is serious and acts as a link with the final song in the cycle, ending, as it does, in the dominant A major.

MIT MYRTEN UND ROSEN

Op. 24 No. 9

With myrtle and roses sweet and fair,
with perfumed cypress and leaf of gold,
I would bedeck this book as if it were
a shrine to enclose my songs. If only my
love for her could be buried with it! On love's
grave the flower of peace blossoms and
it will bloom there for me. These songs which
I inter burst from the depths of my being
like a stream of lava from Etna. Cold they are now
and dead, but if love's spirit hovers over them
they will revive. And in my heart I feel that
spirit will restore them by this book when it reaches
you, beloved, so far away. Then shall the
pallid letters look up imploringly into your
dear eyes and whisper of love.

Only a cursory glance at that splendid rising sweep tells us that bitterness of heart has been dissipated; heard first in the introduction this impression is strengthened by the voice. Much depends on the singer. One has heard the adjoining quavers in triplet and duple rhythm and the 'interrupting' crotchet, conspiring – and succeeding – in breaking up what should be a steady flow. A creamy smoothness of continuity is needed. Naturally, there is an increase of tone up to 'hold' but the singer makes no accent on the first and third beats, he gives the so-called unimportant notes (the quavers) the same sonority that he gives the crotchets; the triplets are unhurried and yet made distinctive from the duple quavers. If the lover in his distraction suffered from a lack of mental poise in one or two of the earlier songs, there is no hint of it here. A dignity, presaged by the previous little chorale (number 8) now takes possession, and the singer preserves this by the firmness of his line and tone. He does not, therefore, indulge in snatched breaths anywhere, but takes calm breaths after 'hold' (6) 'Flittergold' (8) 'Totenschrein' (10). The latter is the apex of the vocal line followed by *staccato* chords in the accompaniment against which it is essential for the singer to keep steadfast to his *legato*.

And now the voice is marked *piano*. Being the first time the singer has been asked to reduce his volume, my partiality for a full-bodied tone heretofore, is supported.

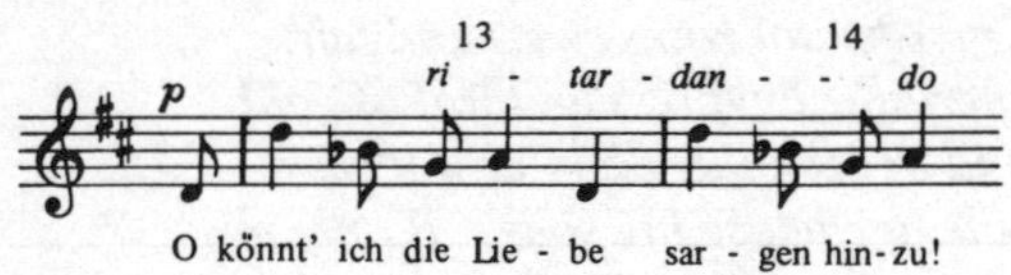

The addition of a *ritardando* makes clear that the phrase is to be sung with intense seriousness; it is of great moment, which is the reason for singing it softly.

Schumann's *penchant* for syncopation in the accompaniment is noticeable in the development: light and airy (the flower of peace blossoming) it leads us to the third verse.

Always portended by the heavy smoothness of movement, the lava stream and its fire now inflame the singer in a passionate outburst.

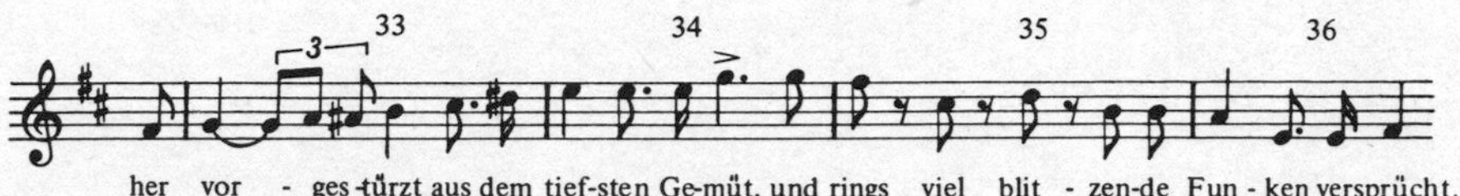

For once the perennial *legato* line is broken and the accompaniment shares the ruffle with *staccato* chords.

The last two verses are the most telling of all and are preceded by the sign *Schneller*: Contradictorily, on the entry of the voice the pace quite suddenly slackens, the mood is calmer, reflects the more sanguine temper of the poem. In fact the faster tempo instruction only applies to the short pianoforte interlude, for the singer immediately pulls back the tempo. His line bears some resemblance in shape to the opening theme but is more flexible, less insistently *legato*. (The view that every note should be the same weight as proposed at the beginning of this homily is to be discarded now.)

The lightness of texture is most noticeable in the accompaniment, with its slim chords alternating between the hands. It contributes, with the syncopation, to the voice's most moving moment.

From here the movement becomes slower and slower until it reaches a final *Adagio*.

A MISCELLANY OF SONGS

Edition Peters Volume II

JASMINENSTRAUCH

(Rückert)

Op. 27 No. 4

In the evening the jasmin bush was green
but morning's sunlight revealed that while
it slumbered in the night, it turned to
snowy whiteness.
'What changed me in the night?'
If you dream in springtime this is what
happens to trees.

This song has only sixteen bar of singing, divided into four phrases.

With utmost simplicity Schumann begins each phrase (except for the last group 14–17) identically, but develops each one with a delightful variation. Bar 2 is heard thrice but at the crucial 'What changed me?' the repeated C sharp sinks to a *pianissimo* C natural, while the accompaniment has a dominant seventh *arpeggio* dropping down into the deep bass.

Such pleasant words as 'Jasminenstrauch' and 'Morgens Hauch' (morning breeze) are savoured; all is to be sung with an airy lightness. It floats along with gentle sway and a feeling of two beats to the bar until we come to the perplexed and *pianissimo* 'What changed me?' which slows down and has a long pause on 'Nacht'. The smiling answer is marked *mezzo forte* but should be sung with such tenderness that a *mezzo piano* is more than adequate.

As can be seen in the example, the little pianoforte clusters in the treble are cut short by the accompanying chord, as if they were unsure of themselves; a pattern which is consistent until the postlude.

This tiny appendage bears no resemblance in shape to the preceding seventeen bars, it is charming:

The leap from the *staccato* on to its point of rest is performed with the ease and grace of a ballerina and is as light as thistledown.

DER KNABE MIT DEN WUNDERHORN

(Geibel)

Op. 30 No. 1

Nobody could be so full of good cheer as I.
I sound my silver horn as I gallop along
and it resounds through hill and forest.
Is there a fête for dancing and sport,
then I dismount, invited by the melting
glances of the girls. I kiss and dance with them
to the sound of the guitar, I drink the
wine. But as soon as the sun starts to
sink, I make my adieux, and gallop away.

The spirit of youth, its zest for life and unquenchable exuberance, are the ingredients here. 6/4 time is clearly announced by horn calls in the two bar introduction. Even by maintaining this rhythm, however, it becomes unconvincing and spiritless if its mien, in the slightest degree, is too square and solid. This point is made clear in the opening phrase.

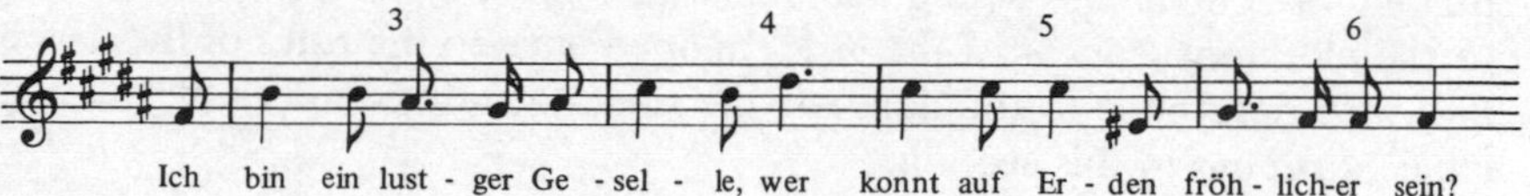

He is far too lusty a lad to need a breath after 'Geselle', what is more, he makes this obvious by sailing quickly up to 'wer' and arrives on it fractionally ahead of time. The accompanist anticipates this but his revenge comes in a moment.

Are the last three quavers in 8 and in 10 to be played in strict time? No, they must be precipitate and sail up, as the singer's did, with abandon. The singer in his turn anticipates this, furthermore he continues this pliant shaping with his 'trägt mich mit Windesschnelle' and is able to compensate by giving the top G sharp a little more space.

All this is done to give muscle to the music, and the listener, while excited by it, is unaware of the secret battery which charges it, provided the artists are governed by taste. At bars 21 to 24 a similar position arises.

Without losing its self-assertion, the vocal line becomes less angular and is made more chivalrous with graceful falls and rises, when reference is made to the eloquent glances of the girls. In obedience to the rules of the dance and with deference to the dancers, the singer kindly complies by steering clear of *rubato* in this section.

A reminder of his earlier gusto is heard as the jolly fellow makes his 'Ade'. His silvery horn is heard 'trara' etc. but he still finds breath to assure us repeatedly that his horn is blowing its final salutation, getting more and more distant, each time. A *rallentando* is marked at the end, but if this were obeyed the music would lose its gaiety. The sounds recede but the pace of Pegasus never slackens.

DER PAGE

(Geibel)

Op. 30 No. 2

Since my love for you is hopeless, let me kiss the ground where you trod. I can never be your knight but let me be your page when you attend mass. I will be ever faithful ever discreet. Each morning I will greet you with roses and each evening I will take my guitar and sing to you. When it is your pleasure to hunt I will carry your spear and falcon. I will light your steps for the meetings with your lover and stand guard whilst you are with him. My reward for all this will be but a glance and a smile from you my shining star.

To deprive this song of its youthful lilt out of compassion for the young adorer's hopeless love would be a pity. Such sympathy is misplaced, for this Octavian will forget his Marschallin as soon as he sets eyes on Sophie.

Accordingly, the singer trips over the first page (the page of music, not the attendant!) quite happily and the page 'follows' with modest detached chords. Always the accompaniment is lighter in weight than the voice, especially when the two set forward together.

The *ritardandi* in 7 and 15, the duple quavers in 8, 16 and elsewhere are indications that the composer wished the vocal line to be treated with elasticity. As in the previous song the voice moves in springing *arpeggio* passages when the hunt is envisaged (41–44).

Not a suspicion of sadness clouds the close. Schumann, admittedly seems to think otherwise. His peroration consists of the phrase 'einen einzgen Strahl mir schenket' sung thrice, but each time with a *ritardando*. It is too much: at first appearance, yes, (bars 70 to 72) but thereafter though sung with affection and the slightest caress on 'Strahl', the passage should sound free from care.

The tiny postlude is delightful and need not be hastened, and the grace notes in the bass in the final bar are played with deliberation.

In the previous song we met *Der Knabe mit dem Wunderhorn* who, with his egomania, admits he is desirable to the girls and quaffs their wine as if it were his due. Now we have *Der Page* who has the submissive self-effacement that was expected of a Victorian accompanist. What two songs could be in greater contrast? In one way, paradoxically, they are very much alike, both being in a lilting 6/8 rhythm: the fact that one moves at a much brisker tempo than the other does not hide this resemblance. For this reason it would be unwise to place them as next-door neighbours in a recital programme.

DER HIDALGO

(Geibel)

Op. 30 No. 3

To make sport with songs, with hearts,
with quarrels, is my delight. When I roam
under the light of the moon I am equally
ready for love-making or fighting. I carry
with me my mandoline and my blade
of Toledo steel; the one to serenade the beauties
of Seville, the other to welcome my rivals.
Off then for adventure! In the morning I'll
bear home flowers or wounds.

One bar suffices for introduction but it merits a paragraph on its own, for it is the rationale of the composition and proclaims with its few notes the devil-may-care character of a veritable Don Juan. The direction is *kokett* and one imagines an arrogant and flamboyant cavalier ready to take offence at the merest hint. This proscribed bar comes half a dozen times or more in the pianoforte and in the vocal line, and should never lose its swagger. There can be no swagger if it is performed in strict time. The octave leap in the treble to the top A is a brave gesture – cloak flung defiantly over shoulder – but this high note is not so insolent and assertive as the accented F sharp minor chord at the end of the bar which is held for a tantalizing moment before condescending to plunge into the tonic key. Having dissected this introductory figure, it must be understood that these details, full of meaning as hopefully they may be, do not prejudice the over-all sweep of the bolero, whose insistent rhythm is asserted by the muscular energy of the semiquavers, symptomatic of the bolero.

The singer will adopt a tempo consistent with the dashing fellow he portrays, yet not so quick that it runs away with him. That Schumann wanted vigour in the semiquavers 'zu scherzen' is indicated by the spicy rest after the third beat. It is more difficult for the singer than the pianist, especially with the convergence of sybilants as in the above example, but he will find 'wie zum Gefecht bereit' (16–17) slips easily off the tongue. He shapes bar 25, a duplication of bar 1, exactly as it was played; failure to do this evinces insensibility, and should he not exult in his top note?

Quite different in character is the middle section (the song is in A B A form) where the pulse of the bolero is not altogether relinquished but allowed, here and there, to lapse into smoother strains, more becoming to the beauties of Seville. Even so, hints of the motto (bar 1) are heard from voice and pianoforte, suggestive of the flashing eye of the knight-errant.

The song ends on a note of defiance

He would be weak-kneed who shirked the top A, (an alternative is in the printed score) the high note is mandatory. Let the singer brandish it but, having enjoyed it, let him sing 'nach Haus' with dash.

The basic tempo is ♩ = 95 approximately.

DIE LÖWENBRAUT

(Chamisso)

Op. 31 No. 3

In her wedding dress the keeper's pretty daughter goes into the lion's cage. The great beast lies down before her as she fondles him. With tears in her eyes she says 'Once you were a playful

baby and I was child, we both grew up together,
you became a king with your mighty mane and
I became a woman. If only we were young again.
But I am forced to marry a man who will take
me far from here'.

As the girl stooped to kiss him, the cage shook,
the lion lashed his tail and roared, crouching
menacingly before the opening. She implores him
to let her pass but he will not move.

Screams of panic are heard in the grounds, the
bridegroom cries 'Bring a gun quickly, I'll
put an end to him'. The lion, further excited by
the shouting rears up made with rage, and strikes
the sweet girl to the dust.

Then, shattered by sorrow, the lion prostrates
himself before the torn and bleeding body until
the fatal bullet enters his heart.

It is matter for speculation why Schumann found a fascination in setting this unlikely story. It is possible the composer saw in the lion a comparison with his prospective and hateful father-in-law, Friedrich Wieck, who bitterly opposed his courtship of Clara. The slaughter of the rosy-cheeked bride is naturally a horrible and shocking affair but Schumann does not deny altogether a certain sympathy for the dumb animal, who, in fact, is the central figure of the story.

That bass octave passage beginning the short introduction is the motif depicting the cat-like tread, soft but heavy, of the lion. Singer and pianist must have perfect agreement regarding tempo, for at the singer's (and maiden's) entry, the lightsome gait should accord with the pace established by the pianoforte in the above example. It is marked *Langsam* but the music has an inner movement, lithe and muscular, ♩ = 52 is suggested, not one whit slower.

Under this vocal line the pianoforte, in wide contrast to the introduction, has chords so detached that the voice sounds unaccompanied. The girl looks radiant, her utterance should be tripping and graceful, not until bar 7 where a *ritardando* is wanted should it be *legato*.

Forty-one bars in which the bride recalls happy times when the two of them played together, are put into 3/2 time and are mostly in the major. This section is marked *Etwas Langsamer* but in my opinion it should not be noticeably slower, (I confess I wish it were *Etwas schneller*). These reminiscences of childish days inevitably lack the underlying sinew of the minor mode and they can become, by contrast, insipid, if the singer allows the movement to sag. Interest lies entirely in the voice part with an uninspired *ostinato* pattern shared with pianoforte. Without our being aware of it, the singer smiling happily at these recollections and keeping a soft *legato* line, sings with intense concentration and may carry us along with her.

The drama grips us at the return of the leonine motif, (56) this dormant power becomes manifest after the maid's lips touch the giant beast in farewell, its angry deep-throated growls (62, 63) swell to terrifying roars.

I give the interlude (67–68) not because it is the climax, *fortissimo* comes later, but to expose a pitfall which sometimes shows up in the execution of the passage.

In 67, the second beat's F in the bass, the fourth beat's octave B natural (similarly in 68) are sometimes inaudible after the false accentuations that precede them. If these resolutions are unheard there is no evidence of syncopation and the passage assumes a nondescript rhythmic shape to the listener.

Attention is paid to ensemble between 65 and 76 so that singer's and player's semiquavers are thunderously exact – 'gebietend und drohend begehrt hinaus' in 65 is an instance.

The final scene where the remorseful creature lies down beside his adored victim is sung to the theme (4–5) with the final bar delivered slowly and painfully. The last note for the singer 'Herz' ('hit in the heart') is in the dominant seventh and, most vital, Schumann expressly desires a long silence after it, a dramatic and tearful silence after which the bass creeps sadly in with the same colour and pace as the song began. Only the last three chords of the postlude are *adagio* and dry.

DIE KARTENLEGERIN

(Chamisso)

Op. 31 No. 2

Has mother fallen to sleep at last over her book of sermons? Good, no more sewing. I shall read the cards and see what fortune has in store for me.

First I want to see my lover; here he is, the knave of hearts. But what is this? A rich widow! My sweetheart woos her, the rascal. After much vexation I read here a school with confining walls, then a king of diamonds! He delivers me and makes me rich and happy. Hallo, here's an enemy who wishes me evil, unveils a dread secret and I have to flee.

And now the cards show an old woman coming to shatter my dreams and disturb me; sure enough it's my mother who is waking up and will scold me: the cards never lie.

The fluctuating fortunes of the girl as her spirits soar and plunge irrationally on the turn of a card are interpreted in masterly fashion. It is one of our composer's happiest compositions. There are a hundred deft touches; impatience to put the sewing away (11 – 12); hesitant trepidation as to 'what is in store? (17–19); excitement as the knave of hearts is exposed; a cry of woe at the entry of the rich widow, almost every bar provides a descriptive commentary on the girl's emotions. One imagines the cards being flicked by the fingers in bar 1, followed by the paper-weight *staccato* as they are dealt.

Movement is constantly interrupted as the cards' meaning is pondered over; 'what awaits me?' (13–19) is typical of eagerness tempered by uncertainty.

It would be a misrepresentation to sing the above at the same tempo as before, not only is it slower but is sung without worrying about the metronome. The *ritardando* coming on 17 appears too late and should be felt already at 16. After the long wait on 19 we suddenly scamper off with renewed curiosity.

More uneventfully (or we should say taken with happy nonchalance) comes a whole page marked *Schneller* where school-confinement is skipped over and mostly occupied by the king of diamonds who brings with him visions of gold and the promise of luxurious delights. 'Stop-go' moments of meditation lead us back to the old pattern until this in turn brings tidings of an enemy and some guilty secret. Drooping passages (97 to 112) sinking lower and lower at a slower tempo, corroborated by chromatic slumps in the pianoforte bass, reflect this gloomy turn of events.

A pianoforte interlude as the girl ponders on the purport of the cards' messages, is wonderfully descriptive.

All the above are two-bar phrases and the comma between them (the demisemiquaver rest) is made longer each time as perplexity grows. Movement too gets slower with 128 and 129, the slowest and most uncertain bars of all. The *fermata* after 129 enjoins a silence which seems interminable. It is broken as the girl (130) seeing that mamma is stirring, bursts forth with her former liveliness.

For postlude the girl is seen scrambling the pack together hurriedly. We have seen children, with the palms of their hands sweeping cards together and this is what Schumann depicts with genius. It is played as it if were a scramble (though we must hear every note, please) and the final chords continue the acceleration. A *diminuendo*, is not to be considered.

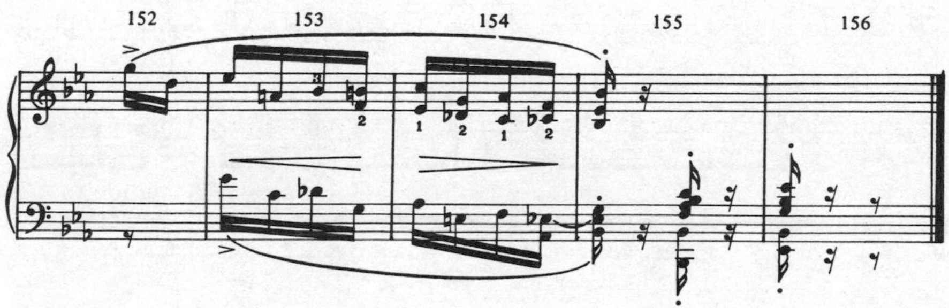

LUST DER STURMNACHT

(Kerner)

Op. 35 No. 1

When rains stream, winds howl, windows rattle and wayfarers are lost in the gloom, how blissful to be within doors with one's loved one. O, merciful life, hold me fast in gentle arms until the flowers spring up and the birds sing. Meanwhile rage on storm, rattle on windows, I am locked in delectable embrace.

Wind and rain assail us with the fury of a cavalry charge. In a superb sweep the singer rides the stormy accompaniment in a thrilling arch, startling to the unprepared listener.

How largely the accompaniment contributes to this turbulence can be seen by the unremitting argument between left hand and right. They never synchronize from beginning to end and their *sforzandi* in 2, 4, 6 etc. coming on the sixth beat where one would least expect them are, as intended, disturbing.

The splendid range of his line should induce the singer to give us a steady stream of sound and the agitation of the accompaniment (where the sustaining pedal is used) should not persuade him otherwise.

When the pianoforte floats up to the treble, it cools the air with the major key preparing for 'ruht es sich so süss hier innen' (rest is blissful within). According to the score there is a *crescendo* on 9 and 10 to which there is no end, presupposing a *forte* (at least!) on the succeeding bars. If this instruction is followed it will make that peaceful phrase sound very very angry. No, this mark is incongruous, bars 9 and 10 demand a *diminuendo* and the singer meets it with repose.

'Rage on storm' sees a return to the fury of the opening motifs. Trills for the voice on the D natural appear in 41 and 43 but at a recommended speed of ♩.= 66; these may be found to be impracticable and I suggest they are given the same shape as bars 18 and 20.

The postlude should be rhetorical, especially the second half of 46 which wants playing of great authority.

STIRB LIEB' UND FREUD!

(Kerner)

Op. 35 No. 2

In Augsburg, near the cathedral, stands
a tall house and from it, one sunlit morning,
emerges a lovely pious maid. Amid loud hymns
of praise she enters the House of God, kneels before
the image of the Blessed Virgin and prays,
'O Mary, grant that I may be yours alone.'
To the peal of muffled bells, the dear maid
moves up the nave heedless of the crown of
white lilies shining with heavenly light in her
hair. At the high altar she again sinks to her
knees, 'Make me, unworthy as I am, a nun.
Die, love and joy!'

God grant she may wear her crown in peace
for she is my true love and shall be till Judgement
Day. My heart breaks for the love of her.
Die, love and light!

We sympathise with the spiritual exaltation of the aspiring novice, her dedication to the vows she intends to uphold till her latest breath, her sacrifice of a life lost to the world, yet our hearts are with the devout lover whose life is blighted, whose suffering will be without the solace that she, it must be hoped, will find.

Schumann inspires this response in most of us, but whatever one's reaction the song remains an impressive creation.

In *Im Rhein im heiligen Strome* we heard the diapason in Cologne Cathedral, here we listen to an organ with a more tranquil and persuasive tone. Its soft persistence is the foundation on which the song is constructed, moving undeviatingly with eight crotchets to a bar to the ancient signature of CC.

The vocal line cannot be sung too smoothly. As the tenor sings he envies the organ accompanying him which does not need to breathe at all and has one long unbroken flow. He tries to contain bars 1 to 5 in a single breath, but if necessity compels, can break at the comma after 'Haus'. (𝅗𝅥 = 60). He should not be too hushed and can sing with some resonance, reserving his quietest tone for the whispered prayer.

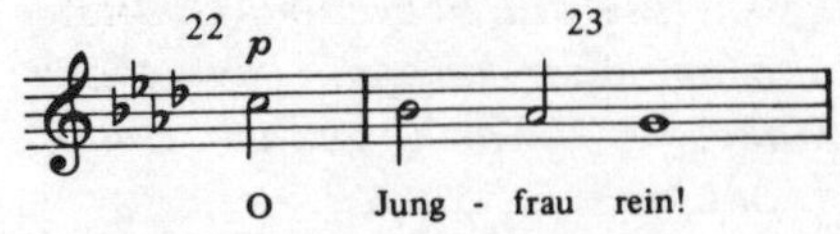

It is a pitiful, lonely entreaty, inaudible in the vast cathedral, smothered by the chanting congregation; only in the soul of the desolate lover does her prayer resound.

The Bach-like *passacaglia* is abandoned for these six bars (22 – 27) and is now block harmony, a chorale. Peace seems to take root in the mind of the supplicant, yet apprehension, gentle and persistent, is suggested by the syncopated alto in the accompaniment. When the *passacaglia* motif is resumed it holds sway generally, until the maid sinks to her knees before the high altar. Now her prayer is pitched one fifth higher.

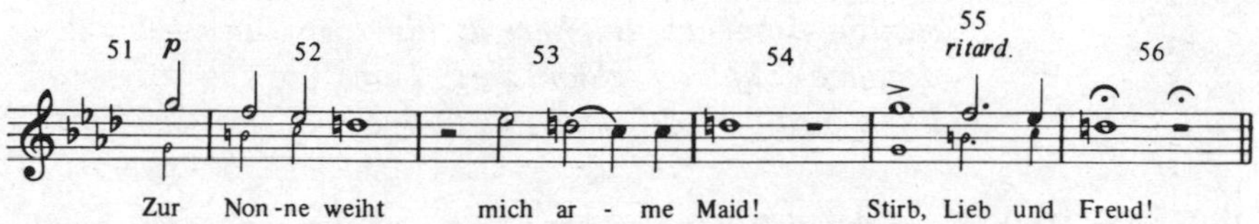

Sung even more tenuosly than the first invocation, it can be heart-rending. It is as if the maid were already in another world. (Alternative notes for this passage seen in the printed score are meaningless).

As she moves away we are brought back to the world, back to the poor youth. At once the music becomes more substantial

'She knows not that my heart is broken. Die Love and Light'. We hear again the same motif as in the maiden's prayers, these are groans from the heart's core, tragic and crushing.

SEHNSUCHT NACH DER WALDGEGEND

(Kerner)

Op. 35 No. 5

Would that I had never gone from
you, dear friendly forest! Standing in
your shade I heard birds sing and
springs murmur; I was awakened to song.
Yes, song sprang from my heart
aroused by the constant music of your
rustling branches. But here in this
desolate country I seldom sing. I am
like a bird parted from its leafy trees.

Johannes Brahms might well have written some of these phrases, small wonder that he is said to have expressed a liking for the song. The melodic line in the first two bars seems particularly to bear his stamp with the quick quaver after the third and sixth beats, in fact the rhythmic pattern here is identical with the Brahms *Alte Liebe* Op. 72 No. 1 and, moreover is conceived in the same key.

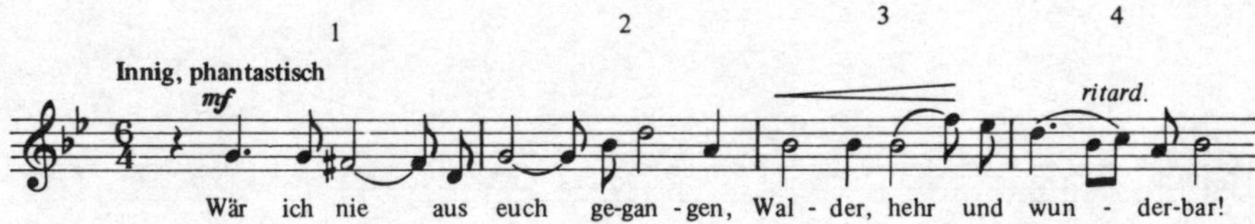

Since the instruction is 'phantastisch', the singer does not hasten too punctually off those short notes, they should be given more time but not more weight. The above example seems instrumental rather than vocal; an observation not intended to be disparaging, for the restlessness of bars 1 and 2 speaks unmistakably of nostalgia, as do the arch in 3 and the ache in 'many a long year'. (6).

Only a one bar interlude (7) suffices to chasten the singer's mood, for we are taken reassuringly from minor to major key with happy recollection of bird song and forest stream. The thought of this stream takes possession and, to a quicker tempo, it is heard flowing blithely under the voice.

With its fusion of serene vocal line, gladsome triplets and fluid semiquaver accompaniment, this is a section to transport the singer to happier days.

The pianoforte at this *bewegter* tempo can easily become ponderous if over-pedalled, Schumann has duly marked it *pianissimo*.

A return to the minor nd unquiet pattern says, sure enough, that the day-dreamer has come down to earth. The postlude dwindles away to nothing. Its mere two bars are enough to apprise us that the friendly forest is far away.

AUF DAS TRINKGLAS EINES VERSTORBENEN FREUNDES

(Kerner)

Op. 35 No. 6

Noble glass you are empty; raised so often
to his lips, you now have a spider's web round
your rim. Now I shall fill you with golden
Rhine wine. I gaze into your lucent depths and
know full well that death cannot sever true friends.

So, sacred glass, I drain you with exaltation and
from your heart the shining stars are reflected.
The midnight hour solemnly tolls.
The glass stands empty but those grave chimes
echo in its crystal depths.

Harry Plunket Greene liked to recall Heraclitus when discussing this song:-

I wept as I remembered how often you and I
Had tired the sun with talking and sent him down the sky.

Kerner did not quite succeed in catching the magic of William Cory but Schumann did. He penetrates to the heart of the mood so surely and feels so keenly that we are held in awe as, on the anniversary of the friend's death, this appointed rite is enacted.

The song is written in sequences of four bars and with a sustained note at the end of each group. This *fermata* and the bare octaves accompanying the voice in unison, seem to rivet the eyes on the wine glass, fix the thoughts on the departed comrade.

Seriousness of utterance, absorbed concentration do not connote a heaviness of tone; the *mezzo forte* sign if taken too literally might prompt the singer, with his *crescendo* on bar 1 and another on 4, to become too expansive. The accompaniment too is light in tone and the chords in 1 and 2 though marked *staccato* should be connected by the sustaining pedal. We approach the coming moments with care; the music is handled as respectfully as we grasp the stem of a goblet of precious wine.

But it is from 17 to 28 with voice and pianoforte moving almost uninterruptedly in octave unison that we are held in awe.

Chromatic descents (17 – 18 and 21 – 22) are a hushed affirmation of belief that his friend is with him in spirit.

It is then that the glass is drained (25 – 32) to the opening theme, and now we see the wisdom of saving our true *forte* for the exaltation that this dynamic apex demands. It is not short lived, and full value is accorded the *ritardandi* and the long held notes at the end of each passage.

And now silence.

Whispered words succeed the *forte* as the singer is lost in meditation and sings as if in a dream.

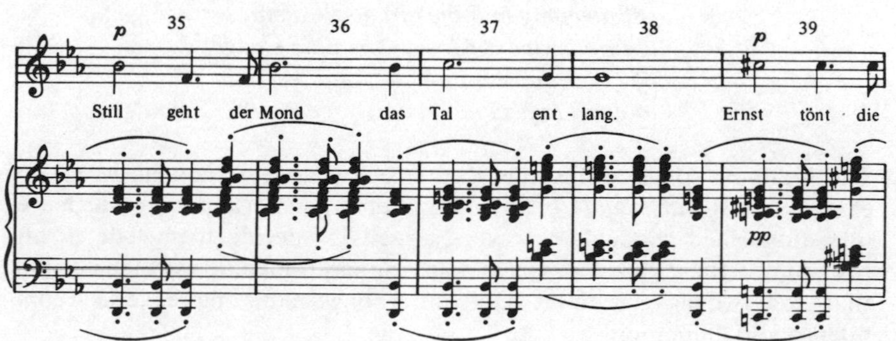

These are moments of magical stillness. The enharmonic modulation on 39 is marked *pp* in the accompaniment and the singer should reduce his tone to a thread. 'Leer steht das Glas' cannot be uttered too slowly for though the rite is concluded, the singer is still absorbed in deep, not to say reverential, reflection.

WANDERUNG

(Kerner)

Op. 35 No. 7

Many a loving tie is severed as I set off on my wanderings. You, dear shrines before whom I prayed, you, woods and hills, give me your blessing. Though the world is still sleeping and the birds still silent, I am not alone for I wear the little pledge of my dear one. I touch it and feel akin to earth and sky.

The Opus 35 songs of Justinus Kerner are vintage Schumann with two exceptions, *Wanderlied* (Vol. 1 Edition Peters) and *Wanderung* which are undistinguished. Should, however, a recitalist decide to include in his programme these twelve songs as a group (and I hope he will) he will find that these two play a useful part. No other songs in this opus have such confidence and animation.

So the pianist sets the tempo immediately – he is off like a shot – with not too strict a regard for the precautionary *piano*. The singer is impatient to attack.

Neither vocal line or words suggest *legato* treatment; energetic enunciation is more important and the frisky *staccato* can be left to the player.

The 'rough places' are made plain at 'Ihr heimatlichen Kreuze' for the boisterous rythmic shape changes to a smooth *piano*, and a warm *legato* is welcome. We are on the brink of a modulation – having arrived at the dominant seventh of D flat – when Schumann turns away from this pleasing prospect and balks us by a return to the tonic B flat. Disappointing! However, the singer revives us by shooting up to several rewarding and resounding top notes.

The pianoforte's springy figure seen in bar 3 is always delivered with vigour, even when it is less than *forte*.

STILLE LIEBE

(Kerner)

Op. 35 No. 8

If only I could extol you in song,
the singing would never be done. Alas,
it is my troubled heart that mutely sings
the burden of my love.
Thus, through this agony I am forced to
sing this little song, which, to my bitter
regret, is utterly unworthy.

In *Pause (Die schöne Müllerin)* there is a paradox when the young miller complains he cannot sing but proceeds to do so in the most poignant and sublime manner. Schumann's *Stille Liebe* is trivial compared to a song which can be described as one of Schubert's masterpieces for it is, by comparison, diminutive and shallow. But it has an endearing melodic line, grateful for the singer and charming to the listener.

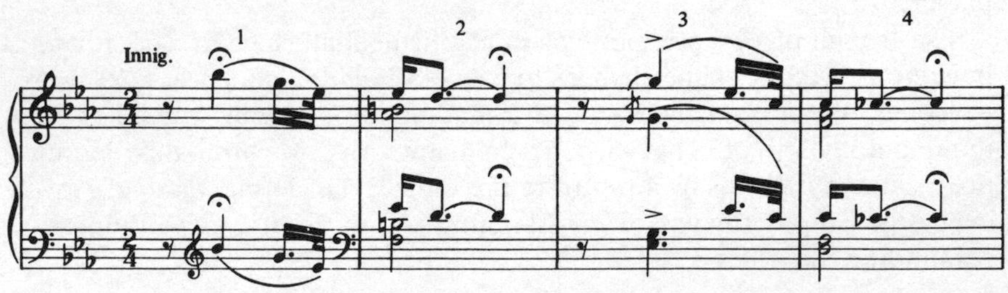

In these bars reside the most melting nuances which the singer is denied; the long-held and acute B flat octave, the step down with decreasing tone to the diminished seventh, silence, a renewed urge on to the keen-voiced C minor chord with the soprano voice predominating. It is *recitative* and an over-all diminuendo is felt throughout.

Not until the singer's entry is the basic tempo of the song established.

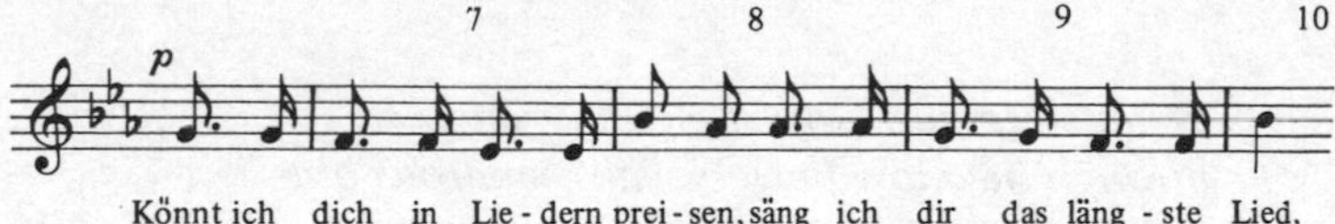

The humble, almost shame-faced sentiment of the lyric is well reflected in the vocal line which modestly declines in shallow intervals. Sentimentality is inhibited. Only in bar 11 (and bars 23 and 36) is there a wide interval and the singer takes care to deal with it smoothly and quietly. It would be a mistake to make much of the *crescendo* which is marked on this bar.

In the accompaniment the 'off-beat' chords in the treble of the first two verses should not be obtrusive, yet their nevousness contributes to the pleader's timidity.

FRAGE

(Kerner)

Op. 35 No. 9

But for you, illumined night, and
your blessed evening star; but for you,
scented flowers, leafy woods, mountains
and birdsong; but for you and the
melodious call of the man on the hill;
without all these, what joy could the
heart find in its hour of trouble?

Frage can be regarded as a continuation of *Stille Liebe*, it is in the same key and the melodic line bears the closest resemblance. Here, however, though ending on a note of interrogation, the springing intervals denote a spirit in striking contrast to the rueful modesty of the previous Lied. It starts in E flat but finishes in G major the dominant of *Stille Tränen* which follows. Although this acts as a link, it is quite beautiful in itself and is infused with that quiet haunting charm Schumann seemed able to kindle without effort.

STILLE TRÄNEN

(Kerner)

Op. 35 No. 10

From sleep you have risen and wandered
through meadow flowers with wondrous blue
skies over your head. While you slumbered
free from care, that same sky poured with tears.
So it is with many a man; on silent nights
he weeps, but in the morning you think he is cheerful.

So massive is the texture of the song and so noble the music that if there were no words and the melody were played by a violin or violoncello one could feel it as an expression of ecstasy. The accompaniment has an orchestral texture with resounding depths for the double-basses from first bar to last; it has an urge too that acts as a spur to the singer.

The vocal line is superb. *Sehr langsam* and six crotchets to the bar are deceptive symbols, and the singer would be wise to feel two beats to the bar rather than six, at a speed of 𝅗𝅥. = 40. Not, I concede, a very slow tempo. How is the singer to compromise between spaciousness and urge? By elasticity. The splendid arches must disdain the metronome.

Thus, in the above, it is the crotchets, the unimportant weak beats, which are made to hinder the momentum, so that while the motion is ever on its toes there are moments of retardation, cutting in their expressiveness. This stress on an unimportant beat or syllable is not designed to belittle the long and chief note which follows; on the contrary, it underlines and heralds the sustained note's significance. These wide arches continually expand making 12 and 13 the most imposing of the three and allowing the second syllable of 'allen' to reverberate with as much splendour as 'Landen'.

It means that the repeated crotchet chords in the accompaniment, far from being square, are imperceptibly hastened up to the sixth crotchet which is perceptibly held. Obviously this pliant treatment will not be needed in bars 1, 5, 9, 13. The playing must be sensitive, also bold so that the deep bass semibreves resound, especially in their descent from 5 to 8.

According to the score, *piano* is the norm for this first section of eighteen bars, but the singer should not restrain 'durch die Au' and still more 'ob allen Landen', (with the proviso that he remembers the huge climax ahead of him) each needs a heart-swelling *crescendo* which will inevitably bloom into a noble *forte*.

The gradients are more gradual when we modulate to A flat (19), curves take the place of arches and can be made in one's stride, without the arbitrary long up-beat becoming uniform. Only on the mighty climax beginning its build-up on 35 do we resort again to the spring-board for the glorious leap to the top B flat. It is the culmination of a huge *crescendo*.

By the very nature of things the top B flat becomes the mightiest note in the song. (There is an alternative G in the score, one third lower, but the high note is mandatory. A tenor who finds the B flat troublesome or unreliable should sing the song in a transposed key.) Once again those deep bass semibreves in the pianoforte bass form the plinth of this towering edifice of tone:

the cymbals' *fortissimo* on the low octave E flat can be heard!

(When accompanying this song I became so excited for the singer's B flat that I gave everything I had in support. Now, even in writing about it my blood tingles and in consequence I have called it 'the mightiest note' of all. While this description may be true in fact, it should be added in deference to Schumann that a *fortissimo* is not demanded until bar 61).

From 49 to 55 the interlude puts the pianist on his mettle for he tries with all his might to continue with the fervour of the human voice. His tune – the main theme – is set forth with a stoutness of tone (French horn!) that cannot be denied. It must have declamatory freedom so that the grace notes preceding the trill in 54, are deliberate quavers in triplet form.

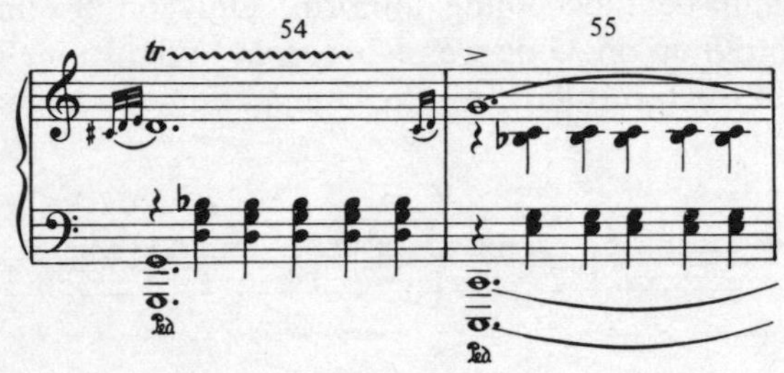

Thus the trill begins on the second crotchet: the turn at the trill's end becomes two quavers on the sixth crotchet.

The player should dream through the postlude; even so, he does not start too softly, there must be room for a *diminuendo* through its eight eloquent bars. He does not bound up gymnastically to the F natural in 65 but takes all the time he wants after the preliminary chord (it synchronizes with the bass G); he makes his quintuplets in the four final bars expressive. These bars have to accomodate more than six crotchets, Bar lines are ignored.

Justinus Kerner might find that the music is not a reflection of his current of thought. This may be so but, in the opinion of the writer, it is an opulent and soul-stirring creation.

WER MACHTE DICH SO KRANK

(Kerner)

Op. 35 No. 11

What has made you so ill?
No chill wind from the north is the cause,
nor heat of the sun, or day-dreaming
in the valley's shade.
If I bear mortal wounds, it is man who
has inflicted them. Nature will restore me.

This fragment, its phrases so short that they seem to lack sufficient strength or breath to sustain them further, expresses undeniable debility.

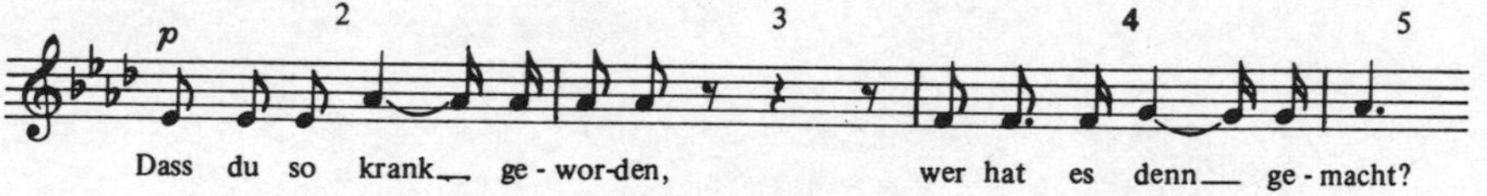

The pianoforte too droops inevitably with a compassionate discord on 'krank' (ill). The voice climbs, but not without effort, (9–10; 11–12; 13 to 15) to its highest point at 'Kein Schlummern, and then sinks down gradually and exhaustedly to the end.

No attempt should be made to curtail the rests, (3, 5 and elsewhere) only the held chords in the accompaniment connect one thought with another.

ALTE LAUTE

(Kerner)

Op. 35 No. 12

Old sounds of a bird singing; from the distant past
the voice of a lad who had faith and hope.
These are dreams and only an angel
can wake me from them.

Schumann has strung two separate poems together to make one single strophic two-verse song and has treated *Alte Laute* as an answer to *Wer machte dich so krank?*

When urging the artist to sing these twelve Kerner songs as a group, I feel there is nothing to prevent him presenting them in any order he pleases. He might find this last pair too limp for a finale. They could be inserted after *Frage* (no. 9) thus making the noble music of *Stille Tränen* bring the group to a conclusion. The fact that these songs are under one opus does not make them a *Liederkreis* as is the Heine Op 24 where I found it necessary to pluck *Mit Myrten und Rosen* from Volume I (Edition Peters) and put it in its proper place in this book. For this reason I left *Erstes Grün* and *Wanderlied* undisturbed in Volume I though they should, of course, be included in a performance of the Op. 35 songs.

STÄNDCHEN

(Reinick)

Op. 36 No. 2

Come to me in the silent night, beloved,
Why do you tarry? The sun has long since
gone to rest, the world's eyes are closed.
Love alone keeps watch. Already the stars
are bright, but they, like the moon, speed
fast, so you must make haste too, my darling.
Hark to the nightingale, listen to my pleading.
Come, oh come, while all is still.

This dear little serenade may lack the wit and sparkle of Schubert's *An die Laute* but its slender texture is a reminder of it. Here the serenader is of a more earnest turn of mind. Are you ardent, then the more serious and clandestine your approach. The proof of this precept is seen in *Der Hidalgo* who, far from being secretive, sings very raucously indeed beneath the balconies of Seville. The gentle and steadfast simplicity in this *Ständchen* speak convincingly of a continent and loving heart.

The strophic first two verses are very simple with each phrase two bars in length uniformly, but spice is found in the accompaniment with its eager triplet in the bass

Unfortunately the plucked chord sequence in the treble has too short a spell but there are compensations in the delightful confidences exchanged between voice and pianoforte. (Bars 9 to 12, and 13 to 16).

Is it the nightingale's song that now gives more verve to the appeal? Certainly the serenader has renewed eagerness in the third verse.

The chromatic ascent in the bass acts as a spur and the smiling high notes come as a cooling current of air.

DER HIMMEL HAT EINE TRÄNE GEWEINT

(Rückert)

Op. 37 No. 1

Heaven shed a tear that would have been
lost forever in the sea had not a mussel
closed on it.
'My pearl you shall be from now on. Have no
fear, you are safe in my care.'

Oh, you my pain, my joy, heaven's tear-drop
in my breast, God grant that I may
be pure in heart to preserve the purest
of your sad tears.

One can accept Mahler's *Rheinlegendchen* (from *Des Knaben Wunderhorn*) where the little gold ring is hurled in the river, is swallowed by a fish, which in turn arrives on the supper table of the king. The mussel and the tear take much more swallowing and what possessed the composer to set it is one of those quirks that is difficult to explain.

These were my reactions when I first met the song. I found after studying it and hearing it sung that it haunted me. It is beautiful and we can be grateful to Schumann.

Einfach (simple) seems a contradictory sign but one finds, after examination, that it counteracts the solidity of the texture and prompts a more forward movement. The resonant vocal line, earnest to a degree and well-supported, need not be heavy, even though the depths of the sea might have been in the composer's mind.

At the entry of the mussel everything is lightened, the music rises to the surface (8) with a charming change of tonality and a floating *mezza voce* for the singer.

'You my pain' sees the opening motif repeated, but now more solemnly than before: a noble arch (displacing the key change of bar '8) with growing weight of tone reaches its summit with the prayer 'that I may be pure in heart' and subsides peacefully.

The postlude is poetry. The player takes as long as he likes over it, loving every note, particularly the eloquent semiquavers.

O IHR HERREN

(Rückert)

Op. 37 No. 3

Oh, you great and wealthy nobles, do you
not want a nightingale in your lovely gardens?
Here is one who has searched the world for a
quiet resting place. Let me stay and I
will repay you with my singing.

For fifteen bars out of the song's twenty, the little bird addresses his audience, not until the remaining five (when the singer has ceased) does he burst into song. So delicious and spontaneous is the postlude that it steals the show.

Schumann lovers are familiar with *O ihr Herren* and like it, for it is not so lack-lustre as it appears.

It can be chirpy and amusing and should be performed with smiling animation. The singer disguises the square-cut pattern whenever she has a chance; the gliding semiquavers in 3, 7, 15 for instance. A difference is made between the (comparatively) bold and the softer pleading section.

The pianoforte all through, is featherweight, its doubling of the vocal line should not be manifest; the *mezzo forte* sign is for the singer. Chords are detached and not lumpishly bound together. A semiquaver ripple in the alto voice of the accompaniment (8 to 12) is a welcome change, but the pianoforte should not really be noticed until the postlude is reached and then it sings out with freedom, flexibility and gladness.

MÄRZVEILCHEN

(Andersen)

Op. 40 No. 1

A lad stands and wonderingly examines the flower picture that frost has drawn on a window pane. As he speculates, he sees two laughing eyes meeting his own through the glass; they are as clear and blue as the skies above him. Violets! Warm breath, he thinks excitedly, will melt that frosty veil.
God be with you, young man.

Though the vocal line does not seem remarkable, it is in keeping with the puzzlement of the boy and is a continuation of the treble in the introduction. In fact the pianoforte treble all through, is questioning; first the pictures on the frosted glass and lastly the message of those eyes smiling out at him. The semiquaver rests are tokens of his perplexity; they are hints which the singer adopts; he does not attempt to sing *legato* and since, unlike the accompaniment, there are no semiquaver rests, he makes full use of the punctuation marks.

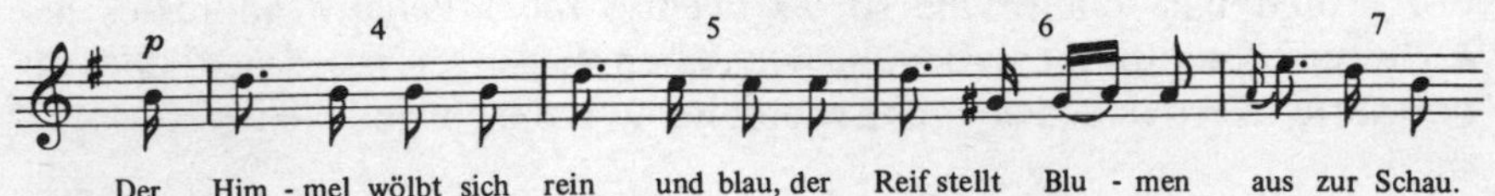

For example, he breathes after 'blau' and 'Schau', not because he needs to, but because it reveals the boy's state of mind. Naturally only a light tone is necessary.

Contrast comes when, behind the flowers, those smiling eyes are detected (13 to 16). This is the time when a *legato* line is wanted; a warming *crescendo* is marked as well.

The treatment of the second verse asks for a return to the questioning nature of the first but now, surely, with a little more animation, for the blue eyes are decidedly more provocative than the icy window panes. This excitement declares itself by more tone, but no more than a light *mezzo forte.*

God's blessing on the youngster is affectionately sung with benevolent smoothness.

And the dénouement? The happiest imaginable. One only has to hear that blissful, endearing postlude to be certain that all will be well.

MUTTERTRAUM

(Andersen)

Op. 40 No. 2

The mother rocks her little boy to sleep,
he is her angel, she looks at him in his
cradle with pride and joy. She kisses
him and prays for God's blessing on
the babe who gives life a new meaning
to her.
But outside, the ravens overhearing
her prayers, caw 'Your angel indeed! –
This robber will make a
good meal for us when he hangs from
the scaffold.'

Zwielicht springs immediately to mind, not only in the first bar of the introduction, but in the alto voice of the two following bars. Eichendorff's lyric is ominous but it pales beside the horror of *Muttertraum*. Set in the minor key with its syncopated and continually descending passages in the bass, the music is premonitory from the start. We are told that the fond mother forgets her troubles as she kisses and hugs her baby but this is disputable if we are to believe Schumann. Hugo Wolf would not have allowed us a hint of the ghastly death-blow at the end.

What is the singer to do? She must persuade us that she, like the mother, is unconscious of the future and is lost in the bliss of the present. Therefore she wants a tempo that is not too static, gives credence to the rocking *arpeggiandi* in the accompaniment, and uses as buoyant a tone as possible so that there is an uplift on to the high point of 'Wiege'.

'Sanft' and 'traut' are sung with convincing warmth.

It is the raven who shakes us out of our peace of mind, 'Dein Engel' (28) is uttered with startling venom. The singer is not expected to croak but the quality of voice must not be dulcet, at the least it should be hard and unfeeling; the more guileless her lullaby has been, the wider the change of colour will seem here. In the phrase 'Dein Engel, dein Engel wird unser sein' the consonant *N* comes six times and if this is stressed at the expense of the vowels it tends to produce a nasal sound, the reverse of pleasant. In any case it places the tone in an unaccustomed position and can be endured there for another four bars which sees the voice through.

The accompaniment's rocking figure which had been abandoned at the raven's croaking, is now resumed in the postlude, but our morbid attention is held by the bass with a passage that drops and drops with sinister intent and staggering gait until it stretches down to the very edge of purgatory.

DER SOLDAT

(Andersen)

Op. 40 No. 3

We march with full band to the sound of the muffled drum, it is a long way to the place of execution. He was my friend, my heart will break, and I am detailed to be one of the firing party. He looks for the last time towards the sun before being blindfolded. May God give him eternal rest.
The nine of us took aim, eight bullets went wide, so shaken with grief was each man. But I, I shot him clean through the heart.

This grim procession is nominally a slow march, but the instruction is *Not too slowly* and if this is not borne in mind the accompaniment's rhythmical design becomes irksome. It is not a procession so protracted as to torture the delinquent. I suggest ♩ = 88 as a reasonable tempo.

Drum-rolls, not convincingly simulated, are marked without pedal in the printed edition but the player may feel that the muffled effect is better achieved *with* sustaining pedal and is defeated if each note of the semiquaver group is rapped out with scrupulous clarity. The voice is marked *piano* against the *forte* chords of the accompaniment, chords obviously intended to symbolize the boom of the bass drum, it is also the moment of the singer's entry; in order that he may be heard, the emphasis should be confined to the bass and not the treble chords.

Although the working of the soldier's mind is inaudible to his comrades, he is in torment and his thoughts must be made audible to us. Under these circumstances it is a mistake for the singer to be subdued. He can conceive the entire first verse as an ascent, mounting to 'my heart will break'; with the second verse beginning the descent. Bars 11 to 14 are the apex of this wide arch. The full band does not rise and fall with the vocal line but keeps, apart from the painful accents, below the dynamic level of the voice.

In the thunderous interludes (21 to 27 and 36 to 39) the pianist throws off all restraint.

At 'the nine of us took aim' the music palpitates, as the shaking soldiers raise their guns, and there is a temptation to quicken the movement; this is unnecessary for the treble triplets in the pianoforte reinforced by the doom-laden bass octaves, are agitation enough. The agony of the protagonist is best conveyed by a strong tone and firm line from the singer in marked contrast to the ferment in the accompaniment. It is an agony which reaches its almost unbearable summit at 'ich' (bar 46)

'Ich' on the minim is not only the longest note in the song it is the most piercing and the singer allows the *tremolo* underneath him to be well established, before he releases it. Then a dramatic pause from him, (the accompaniment still quaking) and very slowly he takes a breath. 'Aber ich traf' (46, 47) is uttered desperately, rather than in measured accents, but he makes the final phrase as tearful and prolonged as he feels able.

This man will never forget what he has done, will never return to normality. The postlude ends pitifully in the unresolved dominant.

DER SPIELMANN

(Andersen)

Op. 40 No. 4

In the little town there is a wedding with revelry and dancing. The groom is flushed with happiness but his bride is

as white as death. She is indeed dead to one man though she cannot forget him, and he is there among the guests playing the fiddle. To all appearances the player seems to have no care in the world, but listen to him! His tone is piercing as he crushes his violin into him. Look at him! His hair turns grey.
O, do not stare at me for it is cruel for one so full of life to die of grief. God save me from madness, I am only a poor woe-begone musician.

Schumann was intrigued by the wedding party's veneer of merriment, boisterous dancing and drinking, with tragedy lurking below the surface. *Das ist ein Flöten und Geigen* obviously springs to mind, but the theme is also the central purpose of *Der arme Peter*. In Eichendorff's *Liederkreis* it occurs twice if *Auf einer Burg* is admitted to the sombre circle with its 'Far below on the Rhine a wedding group floats by to the strains of happy music, but the bride is weeping.' However *Im Walde* has the stronger claim to candidacy for its main tune closely resembles that of *Der Spielmann* though the latter is far less reticent.

It might seem that a suggested speed of 𝅗𝅥. = 72 is too slow but the *Presto* is qualified by *Quasi*. If the singer counts three beats to the bar at this speed he will find the tempo very quick indeed, not to say uncomfortably rushed. One beat to the bar is the solution and will enable him to sing the quavers in 7 with a little latitude and clear articulation; the pianist too can give full value to the dotted quaver in 9.

The vocal line is liberal with dramatic outbursts of tone for the joyous throng, for the frenzied attack of the violinist, alternating with the subdued misery of the bride and the fiddler's fear of madness.

Schumann is generous with his instructions but too literal an observance of them might be injudicious: it is safe to sing *piano* 'the bride is as white as death' (25 to 28) for the voice will carry over the pianoforte but at the next phrase 'she is dead to one man she cannot banish from her mind' the singer must raise his dynamic level, for the voice lies low in the stave over a vigorous accompaniment (34 to 44). 'He plays on happily enough' (55 to 58) must again be projected. Even at the *Langsamer* now three beats to the bar (♩ = 112) and marked *pianissimo* 'God preserve me' is less poignant if whispered though the accompaniment should be as soft as possible. The final *Adagio* can be treated with freedom.

As in *'Es ist ein Flöten und Geigen'* the pianist, after his uninhibited introduction, lets us hear the thud in the bass at the beginning of each bar when *forte* is wanted, but his *staccato* chords are comparatively light. The high treble imitation of the voice in 9 and 15 should be a smooth echo, but such interludes as 21 to 23 and 31 to 34 do not ask for beauty of sound.

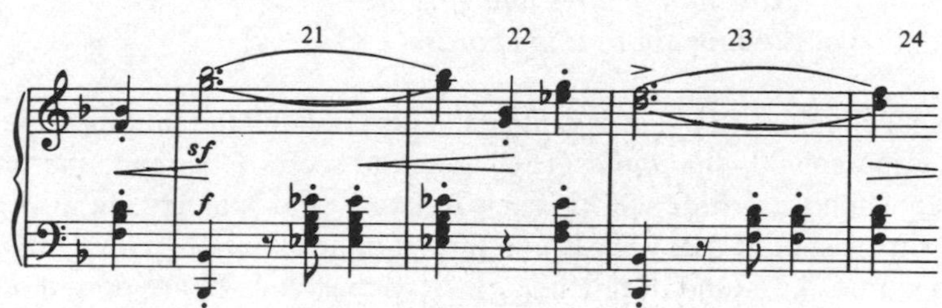

Here the tone is harsh and piercing, the bow is slashing across the strings, the fingers of the violinist's left hand are straining with the double-stopping. These outbreaks are confined to the interludes and are invariably succeeded by a *piano* on the entry of the voice.

After the singer's final phrase, the postlude resumes the tempo ♩ = 112 at the end of bar 134. The final and expressive groan is lost, however, if it is too subdued.

The upper chord, long held, can absorb those sepulchral notes like blotting paper if they are played without purpose; they must have meaning and, though soft, are sonorous.

VERRATENE LIEBE

(Chamisso)

Op. 40 No. 5

That night when we kissed, only
the stars saw us and we were
sure they would not reveal our
secret. But one star dropped into
the sea and told the sea who told
the oar who told the fisherman who
told his sweetheart who told everybody.
Now all the boys and girls are
singing about it in chorus.

How perfectly this little posy is realized! A soft kiss and the smiling hope that it was unperceived, the smile growing as the secret is spread, the happy laughter when the whole world seems to know, and is merry about it.

The singer should feel pleasure in the art of articulation. The words 'Da Nachts wir uns küssten O Mädchen', light as thistledown, are poised on the lips and sung at a tempo which enables him to utter them with utmost clarity and delicacy. This lightness of touch extends as far as the tell-tale star and fisherman's oar. Not till the fisher tells the news to his sweetheart does tone increase, but when the rumour is sung in the streets and market-place, all restraint is cast off as who would say 'Let the whole world know'!

Only at bar 23 'Nun singen's auf Strassen und Märkten' should we notice there is an accompaniment; here, there is a tangible *forte*. But in the postlude the pianist has a field day; it is a riot of laughter with the last three bars vanishing, with no suspicion of loitering. It disappears as does the girl in the Mörike-Wolf *Begegnung*.

DER SCHATZGRÄBER

(Eichendorff)

Op. 45 No. 1

When all was still, he started digging
for treasure in the mountain gorge.
Madly and tirelessly he worked as
God's angels sang. At last the glint
of precious metal, like eyes, shone from
the depths. 'You are mine, all mine'
he shouts wildly. Deeper and deeper
he plunged his pick, until to the
sound of savage mocking laughter,
the shaft caved in on the unfortunate
fool. The song of the angels died
sadly away.

The impact of the first note in the pianoforte is earth-shattering, as the pick-axe is swung with demoniacal fury: each of the introductory bars mounts as if the man were a grave-digger piling up the earth higher and higher. A sense of effort is expressed by taking time – a huge swing – before each *sforzando* crash. Minor key and the dark descent of the vocal line are ill-omened, for the treasure hunter is, in all truth, digging his own grave.

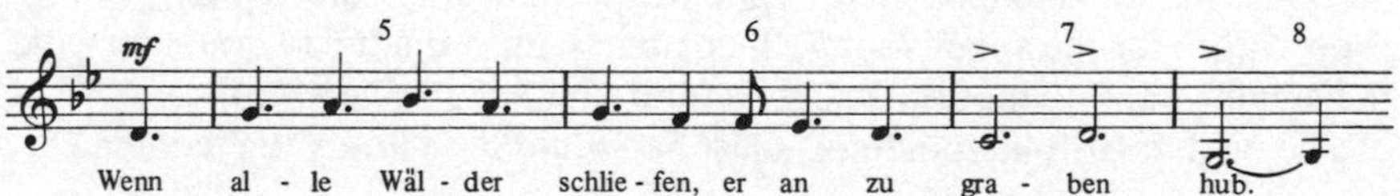

A voice of wide range is required, for the low G's want strength and as can be seen above, vigorous accents are demanded in 7 and 8. Effort is evident in each bar, therefore a smooth line would be out of place, yet the notes should not be detached. Each note is given a distinct and individual attack as a violinist, with intention and for effect, would change bow and give a slightly aggressive accentuation at the start of each bow. Though the vocal line descends, the voice should louden to 'hub'. A breath can be taken after 'schliefen'.

From bars 1 to 16 the pianist has passages that are allusive as we have tried to indicate, but he must temper his *sforzandi* in 8, 15 and 42 otherwise the voice will be covered. A bass singer, with a big voice, cannot compete on a low note against a heavy *fortissimo* from the pianoforte. There is still another instance where the composer's instructions must, of necessity, be disregarded.

No greater contrast can be imagined than the transformation from the clangour of the ruthless digger to the strains we now hear from the heavenly choir. With gentle *legato* waves in the accompaniment (as unsubstantial as possible) the voice floats easily up to the top of the stave.

Advantage is taken of the *ritardando* and *fermata.* The seraphic murmurs from on high are brief enough and we make the most of them. The *crescendo-diminuendo* 'hairpin' is hardly perceptible.

Though the pianist should take his 'digging' motif in the interludes at a more laboured pace, the basic tempo for the singer is ♩. = 66.

But now at 'Und wirst doch mein' the man goes berserk and a faster tempo is essential ♩.= 88. Falling rocks (39, 40) will be taken precipitately by the singer, nor will he feel inclined to decrease his tone at 43 and 45 (though he is marked *mezzo forte*) if he expects to be heard above the clattering rocks and mocking laughter so violently illustrated in the pianoforte. The tempo here cannot be slackened: this means that 46 is very significant; in this one bar the accompaniment makes a steep *diminuendo* and drags the tempo back in preparation for the angel's song. 'Der Engelsang verhallte' (47) is sung with the similar floating motion as before, but now sung so very sadly.

The octave G in the postlude's last bars should be firmly played

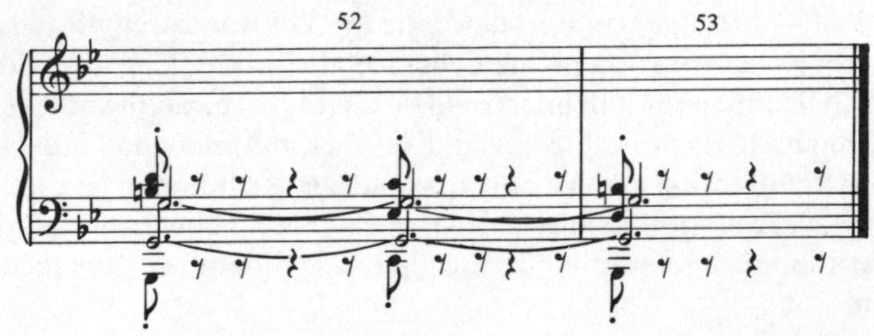

No pedal is used, so that the dry chords do not interfere with the sustained octave.

ABENDS AM STRAND

(Heine)

Op. 45 No. 3

We sat by the fisherman's house
and looked out to sea. Through the
gathering mist, lights shone in the
lighthouse and one ship could still
be seen. We talked of storms and
the strange customs of the people he
meets. We spoke of the sparkling Ganges
and its giant trees and quiet people
who kneel to lotus flowers, and then
of Lapland where dirty flat-headed
people squat over their fires, fry
fish, grunt and squeal.
Then silence fell. The ship we had
watched was not to be seen, it was
far too dark.

The quiet lapping of the sea, the dim eye of the lighthouse glinting through the mist, cast a calming spell on the small group sitting by the shore. A ship in the distance seems motionless. Therefore the composer's instruction *Ruhig* is followed by a *legato* line.

The pianist, once he is joined by the singer, disguises the fact that the figuration in the right hand cleaves to the vocal line by giving prominence to the lowest passing notes in each quaver group. In pursuance of this laudable practice, it is the left hand from 13 to 16 that is more pronounced and suggestive of the tranquil heave of the deep sea.

I omitted to give notice that the *Ruhig* injunction is followed by 'nach und nach bewegter' (more and more animation) and this omission was intentional for there is to be no suggestion of liveliness in the first twenty bars. On the other hand 'we talked of storms' at 21, is taken suddenly at a faster tempo and should be marked *piu mosso*, the singer fearlessly leaps ahead, aided by the restless accompaniment.

After a turbulent interlude we seem to burst into blue skies and sunshine in the unexpected key of E major when told, in warm tones, of the magic of India. This loses its oriental serenity if the tempo is not calmed down.

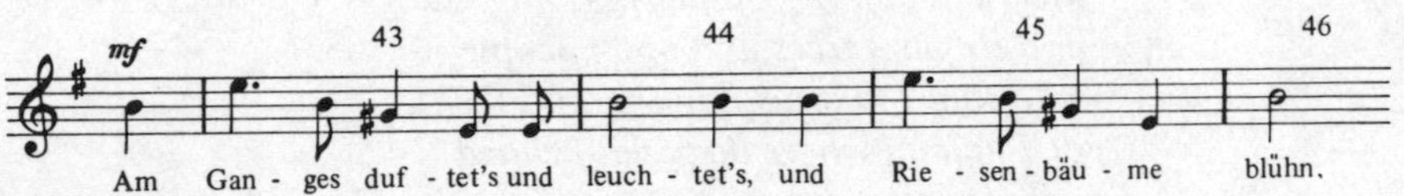

In view of the unlovely visit to Lapland, our next point of call, the singer imparts his most scrupulous *legato* to the worshippers of the lotus; repeated chords in the accompaniment are joined unpercussively.

For the Laplanders we revert to the quicker tempo and Schumann has matched the poet's fancy by angular raucous *staccato* phrases and thereby made it extremely funny, especially the long 'Schrein' (scream) on the high G.

In the gathering darkness the rhythmic murmur of the sea holds the listeners and they fall silent. The scene is impressively described by very hushed singing and a sense of awe. One must be made aware of the deep bass notes in the accompaniment.

Am I being hypersensitive? Do I detect a veiled suggestion of disparagement on Heine's part where the natives of the icy territory to the north are concerned? Be that as it may, the singer is advised not to include the song in his repertoire if engaged for a recital tour in Lapland.

DIE FEINDLICHEN BRÜDER

(Heine)

Op. 49 No. 2

High on the summit of the hill stands the castle shrouded in darkest night, but below in the valley lightning flashes from the clash of arms as broadswords are measured, hand to hand. Brothers aflame with hatred, are fighting a duel to the death. How can such things be? The eyes of the Countess Laura had set each of them aflame, but which of the two will win her, only the sword can decide. Bravely they fight, blow upon blow. Alas fierce warriors! Alas, for the blood-stained valley! Each brother is felled by the other's steel. Many centuries pass and sadly, desolate, the castle looks down. All is quiet in the valley below until, at the first stroke of midnight, the brothers appear sword in hand, and fight.

From the first note the singer acquaints us that trouble is afoot, his line throbs with convulsive energy and his tempo is exact.

The quavers in the above, should render any idea of a smooth line impossible, they jolt uncomfortably. It is a rhythmic shape that has been adopted to reflect physical effort and the sanguinary hatred of the brothers. Similarly, the accompanying right hand quavers must on no account be parenthetical, they contribute with their energetic *staccato* to the violence.

A change of scene to the beauteous Countess Laura, though sudden, is not to be anticipated by a conventional and conciliatory *ritardando*; the singer keeps to his attack right up to the word 'Hand' in 17, but compensates, by making his *fermata* long (but still strong) and by taking a definite break before his *piano* at 18.

This new paragraph (contrived by the singer) of fourteen bars allows a respite from the warlike cries and clashes, it is feminine and tender, and for the first time the voice has a lyrical and *legato* line. In shape it terminates, save for the *fermata* which is now on the bar line, in reverse of 17, 18.

Uncertainty of 'Kein Ergrübeln' is underlined by the continuing *ritardando* and *diminuendo*, and the last note of 31 is clearly not to be sustained. But 'Schwert heraus' is a sudden, frightening *forte* and, in case there has been an understandable easing of pace, the hectic tempo of the opening is resumed. 'Each brother is felled by the other' (50–53) is the appalling climax, made more grim by the *chromatic* descent of the bass octaves in the accompaniment, symptomatic of the fighters sinking lifeless to the ground.

The interlude (54–55) appears as *sempre forte* with lively tempo maintained, but the singer is awe-stricken, his words 'centuries later' etc. should be foreshadowed by a *diminuendo* and a slackened pace. This last section is sung with bated breath to convey the horror of the haunted vale at midnight. Even the high phrase (64, 65) which was made mighty in the previous verses should now be *piano*.

Finally, the singer's 'the brothers are still fighting' should be allowed to die away with a long held note, a note not to be disturbed by the postlude. The pianist waits. Once the singer's tone has ceased, the player startles us by the fury of his last four bars. They crash like steel and hasten furiously to the bitter end without let-up.

DIE NONNE

(Fröhlich)

Op. 49 No. 3

In the garden a nun stands framed
in roses. Beyond the convent walls she
hears sounds of a wedding party with
dancing and singing. The bride appears
on a balcony with cheeks flushed by dancing.
With tearful gaze the nun reflects, 'Under
her crown of white roses she is so happy;
under my red roses, I am pale and
sick at heart.

An eight bar motif, previously heard as an introduction, is sung smoothly and colourlessly; it is as if an organ voluntary from the near-by chapel were accompanying the rueful thoughts of the nun. It has been her custom to wander in the garden so many times that she sings quietly and without nuance, in one eventful line.

Sounds of the bridal party come to her ears. *Mezzo forte* and a jocose movement suddenly displace the pallid tune, the placid D flat key is supplanted by a springy E major. In these fourteen bars one is tempted to quicken the tempo; it should be resisted; much of it is *staccato* and if articulation from voice and pianoforte are energetic, without exceeding the prescribed *mf*, it will be enough. The high point is 27 and 28 'das Tanzen und das Singen' and is the only passage in this section which is *legato*.

With the return to the tonic key, we return to the nun who again sings her refrain as she beholds the radiant bride. 'I exist' she says in effect, 'but this blushing girl lives'.

This sad conclusion is sung much slower and ends appropriately on the unresolved dominant seventh, to the word 'Freudenlose' (joyless).

LIEBESLIED

(Goethe)

Op. 51 No. 5

Would that I could reveal the secret of my heart! But I cannot, and that is the cause of my sadness. My life will henceforth be devoted to him, my thoughts centred only on him. My heart bleeds; for I can but love him in silence, all the time yearning to embrace him but I cannot, I cannot.

To sing and play this song is a joy, and I feel certain that Schumann loved it. With no disrespect to the poet it would be equally acceptable as a *morceau* for violin and pianoforte for the melodic line and accompaniment weave around one another with a fluency and expressiveness that we find in *Flutenreicher Ebro*. Though not on the same level as the latter, *Liebeslied* is full of yearning and flows with as much spontaneity and ease. It is a fervent duet between voice and the soprano melody in the accompaniment, with the singer's melodic line, after each short phrase, lovingly affirmed by the pianist.

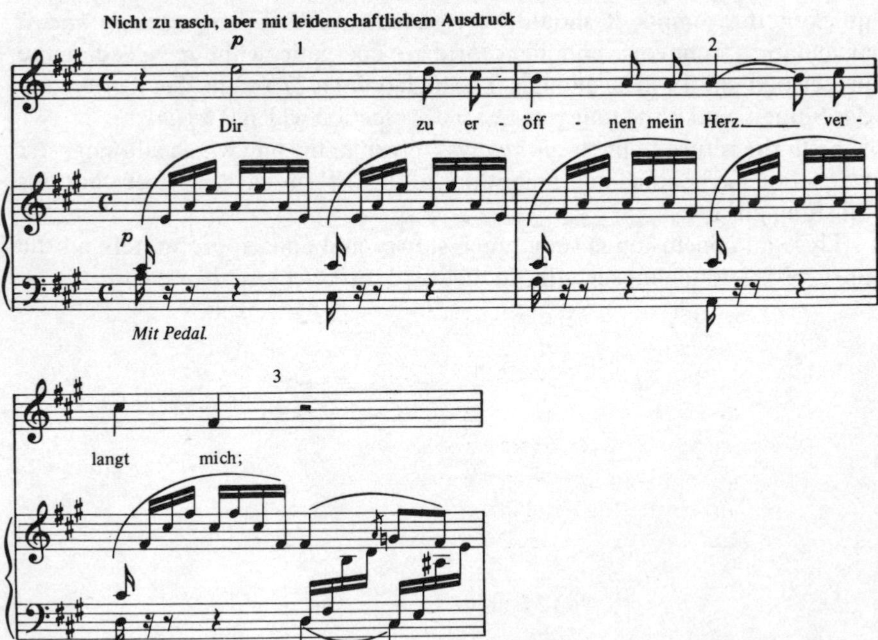

Discussion between them ceases half way through the song. The singer does not lose her urgency and the passionate *arpeggiando* figure under the voice continues, but as the vocal line soars higher, the pianoforte bass becomes more profound, with less emphasis in the treble.

I am not a stickler for uniformity, as the reader may begin to suspect by now, but the sudden cessation for one bar, only (36) of those flowing semiquavers in the accompaniment, changing to rather lumpy triplets, seems pointless and should be glossed over.

Lied der Suleika (which was certainly prompted by Goethe) has a similar cutting edge and a poignance to be heard in *Liebeslied*. Schumann set both in the same key; probably not unintentionally.

BELSHAZZAR

(Heine)

Op. 57

Midnight, and Babylon lay silent, sleeping.
But above at Belshazzar's palace, the king
and his followers made merry in noisy carousal,
draining goblet after goblet of sparkling wine.
Maddened to boldness, the drunken king
blasphemes and boasts of his might to the
applause of his vassals. At his command,
golden vessels, plundered from the sacred
temple of Jehovah, are placed before him.
With impious hand he seizes a jewelled chalice,
fills it to the brim, drains it and
shouts with foaming mouth, 'Jehovah, I
scorn you. I am the king of Babylon!'
No sooner had these dreadful words ceased echoing
round the hall than merriment faded and
the king's heart was gripped by fear. In the
deadly silence, on the white wall, appeared
the likeness of a human hand and it wrote
letters of fire. It wrote and was gone.
Pale as death, with trembling knees,
the king sat staring, his guests were dumb
with horror. None of the wise men could interpret
those fiery words.
That very night Belshazzar perished,
slain by his vassals.

Schumann informs us that evil is brewing by the two bar pianoforte introduction with its under-current of agitation, its diminished sevenths and sense of threat in the sweeping passages of the bass. The chromatic friction of the first two semiquavers in the treble (a characteristic) is made apparent.

Yet for the first ten bars the singer, in contradiction to the febrile accompaniment, describes the peaceful city in the valley: the voice can easily be submerged by an inconsiderate accompanist, and since he is telling the story he must dominate. Surges of tone in the pianoforte are made but they are short, quick to retreat.

In bar 11 an unrestrained *crescendo* erupts into

Tempo (𝅗𝅥 = 63) must be exact and the boisterousness of the dotted quavers and semiquavers is not to be tempered.

The scene Heine has depicted heretofore is no more than a vulgar brawl, it is Schumann who has been portentous; but now in the seventh couplet we are shocked by the blasphemy, while the music changes arrogantly to recitative.

'Ich' is accented and held, proclaiming that 'I, not you Jehovah, am king of Babylon' and it makes less sense if the word 'König' is given the same emphasis; it must have less strength and value.

Following this, is an interlude of four bars similar in pattern to the introduction but infinitely more demoniacal. It is a figure heard for the last time, for texture changes completely as terror begins to freeze the heart of the king. Awe inspires the singer as he gives expression to it.

The remainder of the song is all *piano*, (in the score) thirty eight bars of hushed and increasing terror up to the end. But it will not do for the singer to be too *sotto voce* for the pianoforte has apprehensive *staccato* bass octaves under its repeated chords, and the voice must carry over this. It is a fearful picture and the listener can be gripped by it, even though the singing is *piano* or *mezzo piano*, if enunciation is vigorous. The appearance of the white hand beginning 'Und sieh' (76) is depicted with mastery by Schumann.

The relentless repetitive rhythm of the vocal line is made the more grim by the chromatic creeping of the bass in threatening syncopation. While the latter crawls up, the treble moves down: a pincer movement of pitiless inevitability. These, to me, are the most remarkable moments in the song; an effect of 'closing in' (used by Schubert in *Winter's Journey*, 'Einen Weiser seh ich stehen' etc. from bar 69 in *Der Wegweisser* the Signpost).

After a long silence the singer unveils the final scene. He adopts a much slower tempo than before with no turbulent undercurrent, for the accompaniment is now dry and lifeless as a withered branch. The vocal line, notwithstanding, is *legato* yet utterance is punctuated by frequent breaks in tone, acute silences which in 96, 97, 98 are given *more* than their face value. The whole page of music is the declaration of an avenging angel and delivered with majesty, sustained and inevitable as doom.

DAS VERLASSNE MÄGDELEIN

(Mörike)

Op. 64 No. 2

Early, at cock-crow and before the stars
have paled, I must be down to light the fire.
I stare at the flames and flying sparks.
Suddenly I recall my dream of you, faithless
lover, and, lost in grief, my eyes fill with
tears.
The day has just dawned. Would it were ended!

It is inevitable that the unrivalled setting of these verses by Hugo Wolf should come to mind, incomparable for its searing sadness and desolation. Schumann has set it with feeling and understanding, which, if not so penetrating as the more famous song, is very moving.

By coincidence, each composer starts with the bare major third which turns out to be the relative of the tonic minor, and both of them are inspired to write in a style aptly pale and shrivelled. One feels with Wolf, that the girl is of peasant stock and the room sparsely furnished: this is not suggested in the song here, but it is sad and tender.

The vocal line falls despondently but rises slightly to 'springen die Funken' (sparks) and the treble in the pianoforte accordingly leaps to a height it will not reach again.

But it is the bass in the accompaniment that carries the design on which the whole conception is based. It has three cycles of protracted falling passages, bars 1 to 12, 13 to 26, and 27 to the end, each speaking with growing certainty of abandoned hope.

Though her melodic line moves with some independence of this, the singer should be aware what the pianoforte is saying and will find that it influences the colour of her voice and the mood she wishes to express.

There are two points where the singer can strive to give more emphasis than the composer has provided. Bar 19, 'Plötzlich' (suddenly) should be startling to some extent, and since the music's pattern precludes a quickening, more time can be given, as if her dream comes back to her with unexpected force, as indeed it has. Wolf writes 'etwas lebhafter' here (More lively) but the pattern of his music makes this feasible.

Then at bar 73 'O ging er wieder' Wolf gives this despairing outburst a sigh from the depths of the heart, and the singer is helped by a phrase which has a compass of a fifth, not gigantic, but enough for the desperation Wolf envisaged. Schumann does not give her such opportunity.

She should make all she can of it by an upsurge of anguished tone. If tone melts away, crushed and withered, it will be pitiful indeed, but the listener's heart will not be wrung.

It is not my intention to disparage this Schumann setting for it is an extremely good song. But in this instance his genius did not respond to Mörike as did Wolf's.

TRAGÖDIE

(Heine)

Op. 64 No. 3

1.

Flee with me and be my wife. Let my heart
be your home and your fatherland, even
though we journey far from here. If you
will not come I shall die and then you
will be alone as if you were in a foreign land.

A brave melodic line reflects convincingly the ardour and audacity of the lover; a splendid sweep, spurred on by the off-beats in the pianoforte treble.

The panting treble has to yield to solidity at 'Vaterland' (bar 7). The appearance of this word is an excuse for Schumann to give a hint, at least, that it is the start of a national anthem; earnest chords are given accents which tend to slow the forward drive which up to this point is inherent in the music's texture. The singer should not allow the impetus to be checked.

When the theme, as in the example above, is heard in G major it provides some ringing notes at the top of the stave and they should be enjoyed to the full. A little flexibility here is surely permissible (the qualification is important) where it is not to be considered on 'Vaterland'.

With every reason a *ritardando* is demanded on the singer's final phrase.

The postlude is spirited up to the very last chord. A *diminuendo* is marked but it is only a slight drop after the storming ascent of bars 31 and 32.

II

A night frost fell in spring, the tender
forget-me-nots perished.
A young man loved a maiden; in secret
they fled from her parents.
They roamed here, they roamed there
without fortune smiling on them,
They perished and are forgotten.

After the *brio* of the preceding song, the introductory chords are as chilling as a cold wind on a warm night. Schumann's laconic realization of the poem is eloquent, a mournful little tune heard three times, practically unsupported by the pianoforte.

The slow tempo permits the semiquavers to be sung smoothly and unhurriedly, and gives the singer time to unfold them with tenderness. (bars 5, 6)

The rests are rhetorical and their poetic significance goes for nothing if they are abridged. This ukase applies to the accompaniment as well, the chords on bar 9 (18 and 27 likewise) should on no account come prematurely.

Both *Tragödie* and *Der arme Peter* are trilogies. There is this difference; in the latter Heine needed three poems to tell his tragic story whereas in *Tragödie* the third song can be regarded as an epilogue. I have heard these two songs performed but never the third, for Schumann, regrettably, made it a duet for soprano and tenor and for this reason alone the little cycle is never heard in its entirety at Lieder recitals. But 'Entflieh mit mir' and 'Es fiel ein Reif' are superb songs and should be heard more often, sung as a pair.

MELANCHOLIE

(Geibel)

Op. 74 No. 6

When, when will come the day for my
life to be released from these shackles?
My eyes, tear-laden, have only beheld
sorrows, never a happy hour. When
they no longer see, it will be a blessed relief.

There is more drama in this sparing translation from the Italian than Schumann poured into many a nobler lyric. Even the terse introduction is arresting.

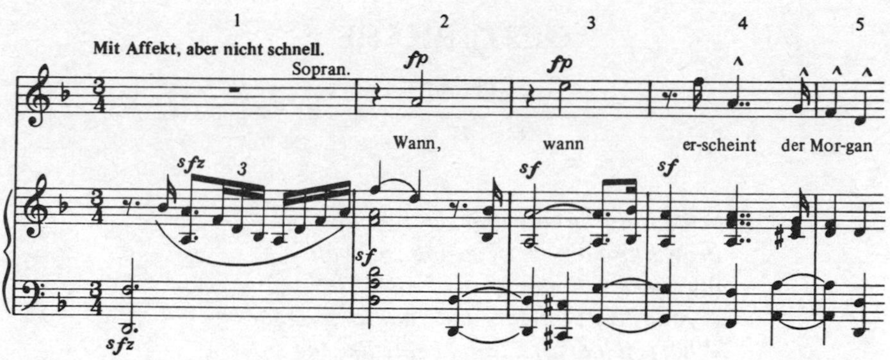

Its outburst is a challenge to which the voice responds with superb strength, in a style that reminds one of Gluck or Purcell. Declamation is operatic, an aria without a recitative, for though vehement and dramatic, it is statuesque. A constant, not to say majestic tempo is maintained so that the frequent intervals reaching their apogee in 26 to 29 will have accommodation to impress their stark impact. The tempo is marked *nicht schnell* which is equivocal; *Maestoso* would have been more helpful. I suggest ♩ = 48.

At this speed the reiterated 'wann denn' is expressive and the grace notes are not trivialized. Again, with its heavy *melisma*, the world-weariness on 'Leben' is explicitly and frustratingly suggested by the laboured motion. A breath can be taken after 'löst'. (9) Admittedly, the onus is on the singer for her attack should be unremitting even to the very end of her last phrase.

This passage (39, 40) is low in the voice and under it there are suggestions in the accompaniment of the prolonged 'Leben' (8), they need to be played with moderation so as not to cover the voice. With the postlude, on the other hand, intensity is renewed and it gathers force to the final chord.

GESTERNÄHE

(Halm)

Op. 77 No. 3

What is this breeze that gently cools my
brow like a breath of spring and wafts
my cheek with the scent of roses? It
is your dear thoughts and your longing for me.
What is it that affects my being like the
soft sweeping of harp strings? It is your
lips murmuring my name.
Though we are far apart, I sense your presence
and your longing to be with me.

There is indeed a sense of yearning in the singer's first phrase, its keenest impact is made on those F naturals; one feels grateful they are not humdrum F sharps! But it is spring time and the April airs in the accompaniment tell us that desire will be allayed.

Triplets appear frequently in the vocal line, they are assigned, intentionally of course, to words of sensibility, – 'Rosenduft' – 'holder Gedanke' – 'Schläfe kühlt' and are to be treated with consideration, *legato* and unhurried.

'Und was wie Harfenklänge' (19) becomes more excited, the accompaniment triplets change to 32nds (demisemiquavers) and thereby give the impression of increased speed, especially if each note is articulated clearly, but the tempo remains the same.

But it is from 27 ('I sense your presence') to the close that we arrive at a spirited *forte*. Alternative notes in 35, 36 are open to the singer; I prefer the high G sharp and A against the pianoforte's treble of F natural and E.

The postlude repeats the charming introductory figure and contentedly subsides.

AUFTRÄGE

(L'Egru)

Op. 77 No. 25

Not so fast, not so fast, little stream,
wait while I give you this message.
As you glide past my darling, greet
her, say I would have floated down
with you to crave a kiss if you had
waited for me.
Stay a moment, light-winged dove, take
this message to my sweetheart: a thousand
embraces for her and a hundred more;
say that I would have flown with you
if you had waited for me.
Wait not for me, laggard moon, you
know you will peep at my love. Tell
her I would have sailed with you
and begged a kiss but you move too slowly.

In the whole field of song there are few with more exuberance than this. It cannot be taken too quickly, always with the proviso that the player does not sacrifice clarity for speed. Every note sparkles and bubbles but its joyousness depends on lightness of touch, for though the burden of the song is largely born by the accompaniment, the singer must be able to deliver her message blithely and without effort.

With so much to say, it would be a mistake to attempt to sing the above *legato*; even when the silvery semiquavers are succeeded by quavers, playful *staccato* is wanted in bar 3.

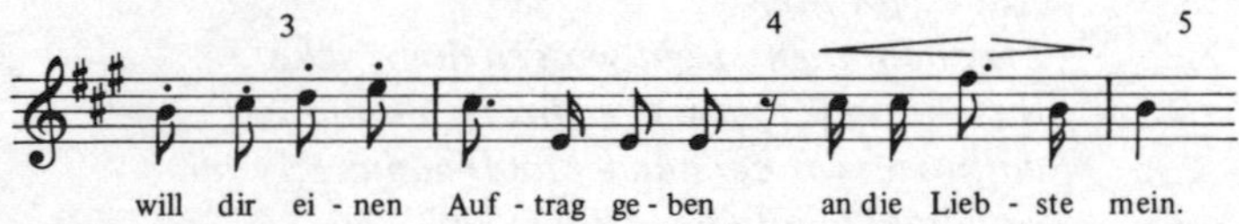

But at 'Liebste mein' *legato* is very desirable, also, let us say, with a tiny indulgence on the top note.

Each verse is identical – save for a charming little variation (bar 29) in the last, and has a *fermata* on the dominant seventh, to be tantalizingly enjoyed before we scamper off again.

A provisional top A (32) is accepted with avidity and made the more enjoyable if the *ritardando*, marked in the following bar, is anticipated.

Always the player uses the sustaining pedal sparingly.

Since the love messages are addressed to 'Die Liebste mein' one must assume that a man is singing. I have played it hundreds of times but invariably it was sung by a soprano. For this reason I am prejudiced and do not wish to hear it performed by the most counter of counter-tenors. The tessitura is not high, but the texture, airy lightness, shimmering delight are feminine.

It provides the only specimen in my experience, where the singer, finding the pianist endeavouring to cope with so many notes, does not urge him to play faster. On the contrary, here the player is continually charged not to sweep along so quickly. With refreshing independence the pianist ignores the singer's bidding. It is a novel situation which is so enjoyable for him that he is irresistably spurred on to feats of unheard-of velocity.

SONNTAG

(von Fallersleben)

Op. 79 No. 6

Sunday has come round again smiling peacefully. It can be felt everywhere, in valley and hill, in town and country, and calls us to pray together. Young and old are clad in their Sunday-best, all of them so friendly and they call 'Grüss Gott' to one another.

With a treble voice the hearer can imagine a little boy or girl piping away happily, therefore it asks for a woman singer. The deeper pitch of a man destroys the illusion. But it has no vehicle for your *prima donna* (the term is used pejoratively) for the design could not take the formal 'expressive' nuance or curve. The *melisma* on 'Aug' (9), 'mild' (10) and the lengthy (heiter') connote the wide-eyed wonder of a child.

The final bar of the first verse, the first bar of the second verse are musically identical and what is more, there is no break between them.

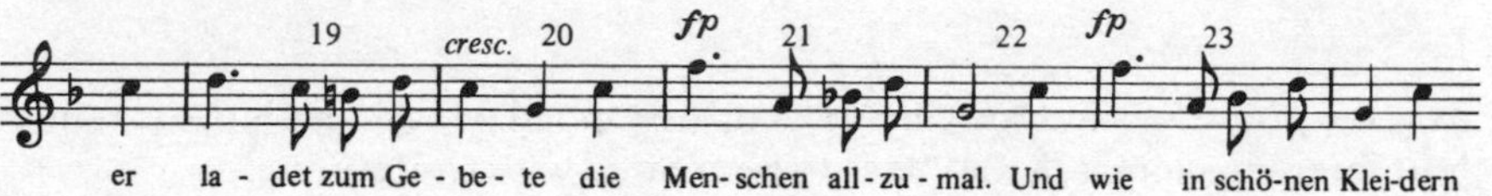

It is as if the juvenile warbler had no time or need for a pianoforte interlude! A charming Schumann touch.

All is innocent and sedate, and none the worse for that.

DER SANDMANN

(Klethe)

Op. 79 No. 13

With soft little shoes on my feet I slip quickly upstairs while the children are saying their evening prayers. From my sack, I drop two grains of sand on their eyes and they sleep the night through, watched over by God and his angels. Then quickly down the stairs again for there are many children for me to visit. Already some of them are smiling in their sleep: there was no need for me to bring my sack.

Schumann was unexcelled in such moods where playfulness and tenderness are combined.

Animation and intimacy are wanted. Within the frame of a *piano* energetic enunciation is essential. There is an inclination to assume an air of nanny-like condescension or archness, and the singer must be on the alert not to fall into this trap; it ruins the song. She takes the Sandman seriously, believes in the fairy tale and it is the listener who smiles.

A delightful touch in the second verse is the long interval (bars 14 and 16),

as if the grains of sand were being gently dropped on the child's eyes. While 'auf ihre Augelein' (28, 29) begs to be treated with tenderness.

The pit-a-pat of the sandman's slippered feet is heard in the pianoforte and, not unnaturally, is *staccato* : the treble however is smooth, as marked, and must be played with finger *legato*.

In the second half of each verse, where for a few seconds the Sandman is still, hovering over the cot of the sleeping child, the sustaining pedal is used more generously.

DES SENNEN ABSCHIED

(Schiller)

Op. 79 No. 23

Farewell, sunny meadows and pastures,
the summer is over and we cowherds must
be away. We shall be back when the
cuckoo calls, when the earth is clothed
with flowers and the springs gush
again in Maytime.

Sehr mässig (very moderate) gives the clue to the tempo and character here. It is very much in the nature of a country dance with the dancers more on their heels than on their toes. The singer should bear in mind that a rustic, simple and untutored, is giving voice to a bagpipe accompaniment.

The pianoforte introduction and interludes 'want' to be in two-bar phrases, but the composer wishes each bar to be an entity on its own; his wish is unmistakable and is so marked. While the drone in the bass is continuous, the pianist manipulates the treble separation on the bar line by making the last quaver *staccato*; by snatching the hand off the note he inevitably drops on the first of the following bar with an accent, but no matter. It should be played strictly in time, the cowherd is not well versed in the subtle art of *rubato*.

Ornaments in the vocal line are treated with the small note played quickly but *on* the beat, it gives an impression of yodelling. Mordents (half-shakes) in the pianoforte treble (bars 1, 2, 4 etc.) start, as the singer's, on the beat and are played as semiquaver triplets.

The disjunction in the pianoforte solos is brought into play most flagrantly and amusingly at bars 39, 40. Here, the singer, as if carried away by the prospect of spring's return, begins modulating to the luxuriant key of E major. He does not establish himself firmly here, for having arrived at the dominant of that key (an inquiring toe in the water) he unexpectedly leaps like a chamois back to the safe home key of C major.

ER IST'S

(Mörike)

Op. 79 No. 24

Spring lets its blue ribbon flutter in the breeze. Again that sweet familiar fragrance is wafted through the land, full of promise. Violets, as yet unseen, are dreaming and will soon be here. Hark, from afar the sound of a harp.
Spring, it is you, I hear you.

In Mörike's *Das verlassne Mägdlein* I evinced, while still finding much to appreciate in Schumann, a preference for the Hugo Wolf penetrating conception.

Wolf's setting of *Er ist's* is without doubt the most celebrated of all other essays and its impact is immediate: his spring comes with a flood, a conquering goddess sweeping all before her in one glorious assault. For the listener it is rousing, for the singer a prize and musically rewarding, for the accompanist it is dazzling and a joy to play. Compared to the modest primrose we now examine, it is an opulent chrysanthemum in full bloom.

This flowering of Schumann's is virginal and unpretentious, has a naïvete seeming to assert that the wonder of spring has never before been recognized, let alone tested and enjoyed.

A patter of repeated chords in the treble with light steps tripping down in the bass lead to the voice's entry.

To apprise us immediately that spring is in the air, the voice bursts joyously on the ear; not easy within the limitation of a *piano* and I suggest that the singer responds to the pianoforte's *crescendo* with a *mezzo piano*. A *forte* would be too much. The savour of the words can be enjoyed without pressure by clear and forward tone.

My interpretation of the song's meaning can be incapsulated in one phrase.

This is the core from which my love for the song springs. First of all it is beautiful, with voice and piano moving independently but intimately involved. Much more than that, however, is the hesitation, the maiden meditation asking, 'Can violets really be waiting there? Is it possible?' The uncertainty, so eloquently expressed by the questioning line of the voice, and the unresolved harmony are the personification of innocence. It cries out for restraint and space, and for this reason is marked *etwas zurückhaltend.* (Somewhat held back.) The singer allows time for its significance to be absorbed.

Harp chords are heard in a sudden C major and just as abruptly return to A major where the singer, no longer uncertain, sweeps up in uninhibited joy.

The passage speaks for itself, but after the exultation on her high note, I beg the singer to give 'Dich hab ich vernommen' a warm embrace, especially the word 'vernommen'.

In this lyric set by two master song writers, Schumann uses the expression *etwas zurückhaltend*, a sign seldom found in his *Lieder*: it was idiomatic with Wolf. An intriguing coincidence.

Why, it might be asked, do I suggest the maiden's awareness of spring is newly awakened when Mörike refers to the sweet fragrance as 'familiar'? By way of reply, I could ask why does Wolf promote the 'süsse Düfte' to a whirlwind in his postlude?

It is a case where both Master and humble scribe indulge in poetic licence.

SCHNEEGLÖCKEN

(Rückert)

Op. 79 No. 27

The snowflakes that fell yesterday have
frozen and to-day hang like little bells
from the frail stems. What is your message
to the silent woods, snowdrop bell?
Oh, cease your dreaming and swiftly
ring in the spring!

Nine bars, heard three times, of tinkling delight; it is the perfect miniature: a fourth verse would have been one too many, a verse less, one too few.

With all its simplicity it cannot be sung unmindfully, some thought is needed.

For example, the hiatus (3, 4) need not be an obtrusive gap: through the rests the breath can easily be held without slightest loss of relaxation. 'Flöckchen' and 'vom Himmel' are not separated in thought.

Only the smallest *crescendo* is made in bar 4 out of consideration for 'hängt nun geronnen' etc.

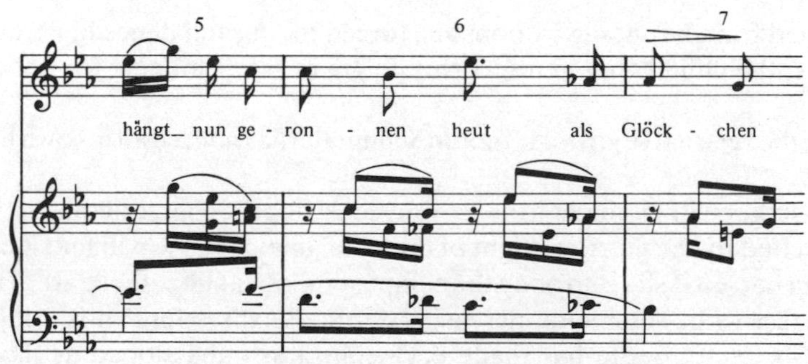

This phrase is so beautifully shaped that it brings the curved stem and hanging snowdrop before our eyes if softly sung. Imagination is aided by the chromatic fall of the bass in the pianoforte.

Perhaps more urgency (if this is not too forcible a term in so fragile a connection) might be accorded to the concluding 'kommt ungesäumt'. In any case the nuances, the delicate tracery, are left to the singer.

Throughout the accompaniment – marked *sehr gebunden* (very *legato*) – should be *pianissimo*, its texture is fine-spun and only at the verse's end do we hear a low bass note. The tinkling bells in the treble will be evident without emphasis.

KENNST DU DAS LAND?

(Goethe)

Op. 79 No. 29

Do you know the land where lemons bloom and golden oranges glow amidst dark leaves, where a wind gently blows from a blue sky through the myrtles and laurels?
Do you know the house with pillared roof, gleaming hall and salons where marble statues gaze at me asking 'What have they done to you, poor child?' Do you know it? There, my protector, would I go with you.
Do you know the mountain where mules pick their way up the cloudy trail? An ancient brood of dragons hides there and the rock falls sheer with the river flooding over. Do you know it? There, oh father, is our path. Let us go.

Snatched from her home by nomads, forced to sing and dance in a troupe of players, the child Mignon utters this poignant cry of longing for her native Italy.

Into the restrictive strophic mould Schumann has poured all his own hunger of soul.

The singer will, or ought to be, so moved during the course of the first verse, and excited by the glorious flight of the vocal line, that she will find it hard to restrain herself if she is to obey the composer's instruction, these are 'The last two verses to be sung with increasing depth of expression.' It is asking too much. In fact Goethe has made each stanza as impassioned as the next, neither more nor less. Without disrespect to Schumann, the singer should, in my opinion, follow the fine frenzy of the poet.

In the pianoforte introduction, the trenchant interval of an augmented sixth is premonitory.

Yet the singer's 'Kennst du das Land?' is posed softly and wistfully and her demisemiquavers (32nds) in bar 8 are meaningless if hurried. Warmth is kindled when the wind stirs,

and over rustling pianoforte triplets and with rising excitement the high A is taken glowingly, remembering that the climax is still to come.

The *crescendo* begun at 11 continues. It is now born along impatiently; this is only to be expected if we understand a little of Mignon's longing. This cannot be expressed by keeping meticulously to strict time.

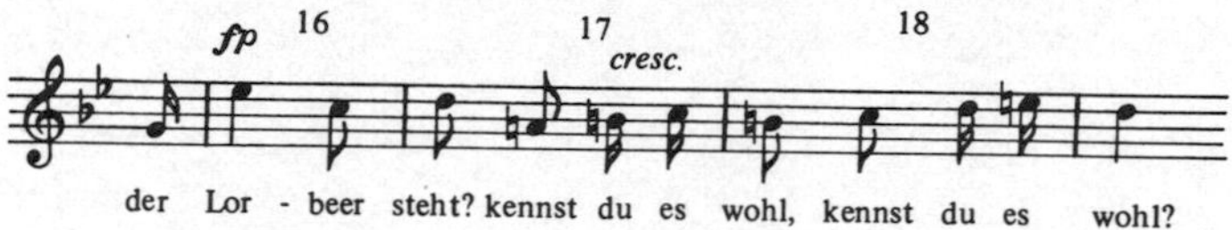

Here is quick interrogation, impetuosity. It would be unnatural for Mignon (bar 17) to sing the two words 'steht-kennst' with complacent attention to strict note values; she leaps quickly from 'steht' to 'kennst' arriving on the latter ahead of the beat as if she instinctively clutched the arm of her protector. A snatched half breath before 'kennst' adds to the urgency.

We are in the midst of an exciting *crescendo* and the zenith is now reached.

Expansion on the high G is only to be expected; it is largely under the accompanist's control. The ardour of those crushing discords is heightened by a small *tenuto* on the second syllable of 'dahin' in bars 20 and 21. This gives the climax the space it needs for its full impact to be felt: the following chords are hastened by way of compensation.

After its gradual climb from bar 10 to 24 the vocal line descends and the verse ends quietly as if the poor girl were exhausted by her own fervour.

A MISCELLANY OF SONGS

VOLUME III EDITION, PETERS.

DIE BLUME DER ERGEBUNG

(Rückert)

Op. 83 No. 2

I am a flower waiting silently in the garden
wondering in what fashion you will come to me.
If you come as a ray of sunshine I shall
relish your warmth, if as drops of rain,
I will nurse them in my chalice. If you pass
over me as a cooling breeze, I shall bow
my head to you.

Our composer shared Mendelssohn's prediliction for A major at the suggestion of spring, – *Er ist's*, *Geisternahe*, *Frühlingslied*. No mention is made of this dream-season in these gentle Rückert verses but, as in the riotous *Aufträge*, it is in the air. Again it begs for a soprano voice for the pleasing melody soars softly and sweetly over a harp-like accompaniment.

The phrases are short, frequently interrupted by rests, but the singer gives the impression that her line moves in a steady stream by not making it obvious that she is taking breaths. She can be helped materially by the pianoforte which, with a counter melody sings eagerly during her broken thread. This soprano voice in the accompaniment is played with definition and needs a different touch from the muted semiquaver *arpeggiandi*.

There is some resemblance in the vocal line to the better known *Lied des Suleika* (Op. 25 No. 9) which, incidentally, is in the same key.

DER EINSIEDLER

(Eichendorff)

Op. 83 No. 3

Calming night, climbing the hills, you bring
comfort to me. The breezes are sleeping, but
the evening hymn of one tired mariner is heard
from the harbour.
The years pass over like clouds and leave me
here, forgotten, but you comfort me, calming night,
as I sit here lost in thought.
The day has tired me, let me rest now from joy and
pain until eternal dawn lights the silent forest.

Eichendorff's beautiful lyric speaks of world-weariness and is reflected by the cadence of the music,

the singer's 'stille Nacht' is the embodiment of tiredness. Even the sailor, whose evening hymn permeates the song is worn out by wandering and is thankful to rest in harbour.

There is one precious moment of comfort;

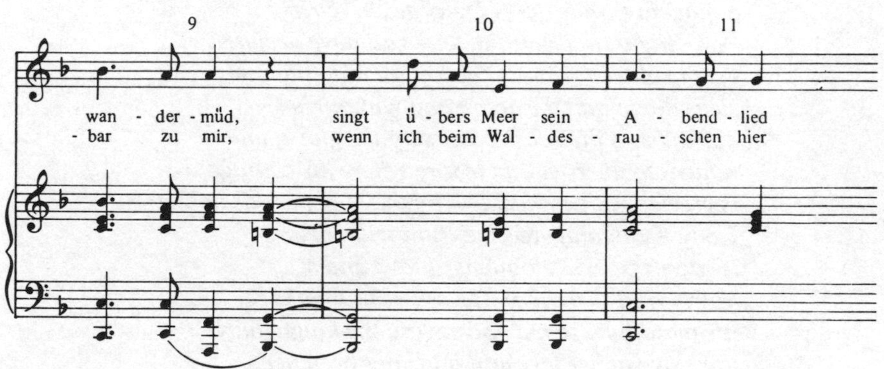

it is that strangely restful and unexpected discord heard alone in bar 9, and the singer gives it time that we may absorb it.

The dropping interval of a seventh, E to F, in the vocal line (5–6) is taken with care for the high E not only comes on the unimportant definite article in all three verses, but is the highest note in the song and the listener should not be made aware of the fact.

A sad mood, no doubt, but there is an unforced and haunting restfulness about it.

DER HANDSCHUH

(Schiller)

Op. 87

At the arena sat the king with the lords and ladies of his court. He signals, a gate is opened and in comes a lion with quiet tread, looks round proudly, yawns, stretches himself on the ground. On another imperious gesture, a second gate opens, a tiger leaps in. He sees the lion, gives an angry roar and slowly circles the lion, then at last lies down near him. Once again the gates open and two leopards leap into the arena and straightway attack the tiger whose slashing claws keep them at a distance. The lion rises and gives an intimidating roar: then silence, and the bloodthirsty beasts lie down in a ring. From the balcony a lady's glove is dropped between lion and tiger; fair Kunigunde with a mocking smile dares Delorges to retrieve it. 'Sir Knight, to prove the love you have declared get my glove for me.' The knight unhesitatingly steps down into the arena and without haste approaches the beasts, picks up the glove, and returns to the royal enclosure where his courage is greeted with enthusiasm by the king and his nobles. Lady Kunigunde receives him with melting tenderness, eyes eloquent of love and a murmured surrender. 'Lady, your thanks mean nothing to me'. So saying the knight hurls the glove in her face and quits her presence.

So that there is no misunderstanding the composer gives the direction *Mit durchaus freiem Vortrag* (with freedom of delivery throughout) though one look at the first section of the ballad is all that is necessary to perceive that the vocal line is recitative, pure and simple, up to bar 48.

King Franz's role is functional, only the entry of the lion quickens interest.

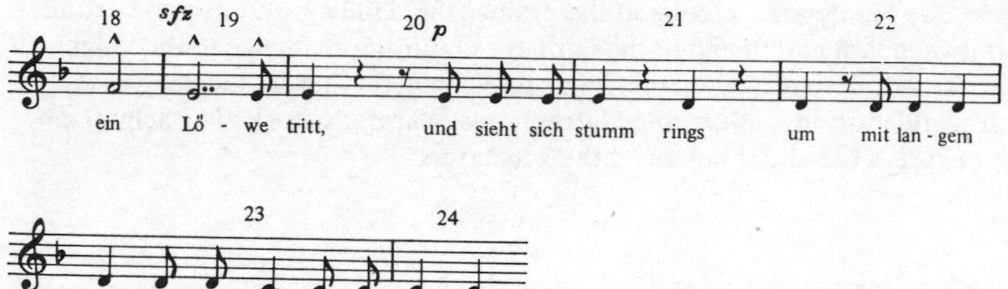

The majesty of the king of beasts, the apprehension he incites are depicted by the singer's awed tone. He ensures that his notes are markedly longer than the short chords of the accompaniment; remembers too that his rests between 'stumm' and 'rings' and elsewhere, are of dramatic importance. None of his notes are snatched as they are in the pianoforte. Very long pauses are wanted in 27 and 28 where the lion finally and with dignity reposes himself.

When the tiger is admitted, the wide springing intervals in the vocal line are enough in themselves to characterize its ferocious feline grace without the singer having to quicken his tempo. It settles, finally, near the lion and calmness reigns (the *fermata* on 48). This quiet is startingly shattered as a bounding movement in 6/8 announces the arrival of two leopards, who attack the tiger. The recitative is temporarily abandoned; slashing claws, vicious snarling are obvious in 55.

Only when the lion rises, roars, asserts his authority does the savagery of the leopards appear to subside and the music reverts (bar 60 and onwards) to recitative. The menace of the beasts, though held in check, is made apparent all through these moments of deceptive calm, and is felt even when our attention is drawn to the royal balcony. Snatched minatory chords in the accompaniment, preferable to a civilized *staccato*, aid the singer.

Lady Kunigunde's scene in the drama, the dainty glove dropped artfully between lion and tiger and the fair lady's taunting challenge to the knight is accorded, intentionally, the same feline 6/8 rhythm as the leopards. Its graceful motion is interrupted by recitative, carefully marked by Schumann, to express the silent horror of the spectators.

Frightening *sforzandi* on 'Tiger' and 'Leu'n' exploding from a whisper cannot be exaggerated. Though the pianist leaves these high-wrought effects to the singer, his bare octaves in unison with the voice add to the tension. On the other hand the pianoforte's discordant contribution, when the sweet lady taunts her champion, must be clearly heard (79 to 84) for these grating chords unmask the acid in her soul.

By comparison, the picture of the brave knight in 4/4 time is straightforward and uncomplicated, his retrieval of the glove is performed without haste or heroics. Disgust for the woman once desired is disclosed in recitative style (clashing snatched chords and diminished sevenths under the voice) and delivered by the singer with cold deliberation as the glove is returned in a manner its owner deserves.

HERBSTLIED

(von der Neun)

Op. 89 No. 3

Through the firs and pines, the dark
red beams of the sinking sun are glinting;
I am reminded that I have reached my
autumn days. Yet those trees whisper to me
and comfort me, the splendour of their
colour gives me hope even though the
sun's light has lost its power.

The first punctuation mark in the lyric does not appear until the seventh bar after the singer has sung three phrases.

An imperceptible breath after 'Tannen' is permissible but not after 'spinnt' nor after 'Wehmut'; these are instances where one sings *mentally* through the rests. This song is made much more acceptable if the brevity of the phrases is not too apparent. There is a risk, if the singer does not seek to disguise these short utterances, that the music will sound nervous; the furtive *leitmotif* in the pianoforte bass conspires to exacerbate this effect which one assumes the composer did not intend.

Not until the major mode is reached (32) will the singer find a long rewarding line where faith and hope take possession. He lets us know unmistakably that whatever misgivings assailed him, they are banished here in a series of smooth easeful phrases that are a welcome change after the dispersed comments of the opening; his tone increases steadily and he finishes with a resonant confidence on 'greiser Wipfel Farbenpracht'.

The message of the trees is depicted in the murmuring semiquaver accompaniment and runs throughout the song. Also noticed, but too frequently, is a rhythmical figure mostly in the bass.

It comes eight times in the first eleven bars, a *Leitmotif* that seemed to take possession of Schumann; the pianist would be wise to play it parenthetically rather than bully us with it.

Wielfried von der Neun (of the Nine Muses) was the poet. To use the words of Eric Sams, this was 'a pretentious pseudonym' adopted by Wilhelm Schöpff.

RÖSELEIN, RÖSELEIN

(von der Neun)

Op. 89 No. 6

Little rose, why must you bear thorns?
By a little brook I fell asleep as I
pondered over this and I dreamt I saw,
glowing in sunlight, a rose without thorn.
But when I woke the roses all round me
had their thorns as ever.
The brook laughed at me and my foolish fancy.

Schumann could scarcely be described as inspired when he set this little lyric. The vocal line, apart from the four bar minor recitative which poses the question expressively, is without design and seems to be tacked on to the accompaniment as an afterthought. For a motif or an allusive passage or a shapely tune in the voice part, one looks in vain. And yet the song has a certain charm.

This charm is engendered entirely by the pianoforte. It is here in bars 5 and 6, now in A major, that the only theme in the song is announced, and this shapely little air is heard again and again in various guises with one bright change to C major.

Only an unselfish artist will want to select this song in a recital programme, and preferably the singer should be a soprano or a *mezzo* for her line abounds in delicately pitched F sharps, all of them to be sung *pianissimo*. The fact that she wishes to sing *Röselein* is evidence that her priorities are in just order; first musician and then singer. And she will give us pleasure and enjoy the song herself if she listens to, and allows us to hear, the slender and graceful figuration of the accompaniment.

LIED EINES SCHMIEDES

(Lenau)

Op. 90 No. 1

There, my beauty, is your new shoe and when
it is well fixed, off you can go, fresh and eager.
I'll gladly see you again. Be guided as you
bear your master by that star shining on his
road, and carry him with each step nearer heaven.

The singer's tune is but eight bars in length and is heard four times to an accompaniment in block harmony which is as uniform as the vocal line. These are bare facts. My own experience, when introduced to this song, was of growing wonderment at my own reaction, for it fascinated me the more I rehearsed it. Brahms's *Der Schmied* (much more famous) with its mighty hammer blows rings through one's mind when first looking at this single page of music, but the songs are poles apart. Here the smithy is warm, a warmth kindled by the friendly understanding between horse and man rather than the furnace. Undeniably it is four square, the hammer blows in the pianoforte make this inevitable, but the singer makes the player wait for him wth the benedictory 'sei frisch und fromm'.

Schumann's explicit instruction 'The last verse *piano*' carries the implication that the three previous verses should be *forte*, and indeed there is an accent on every beat in the accompaniment. These are undoubtedly meant to be hammer blows but they are always in the background so that the singer can comfortably disclose their meaning; they have weight without stridence and the thick bass chords are calculated not to cover the voice.

MEINE ROSE

(Lenau)

Op. 90 No. 2

This lovely jewel of spring, the rose,
sags, is made pale by the sun's torrid rays.
I quench its thirst with water from the deep well.
You, rose of my heart, drooping and wan
with pain, would I could pour out my soul to you
as I pour water on this flower, even though
you might not revive.

A continual duologue between singer and the pianoforte's soprano voice is a feature of this delectable song. Too heavy for its stem the flower droops and in intimate sympathy voice and accompaniment follow each other in gentle falling drops.

Sensitivity is demanded of the singer; the falling line has to be handled with care.

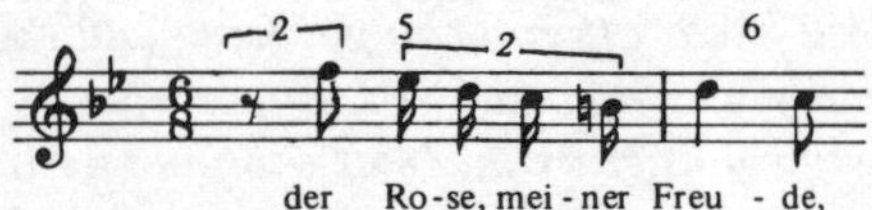

Conscious of the descent with its concomitant *diminuendo* the tendency is to give the highest note more tone, facilitating the ensuing decrease, but this is in poor taste for the crucial point of the phrase is 'Rose' not the definite article, therefore 'der' floats softly and easily and makes it possible to give the slight pressure 'Rose' needs.

The 32nd notes on 9

are sung with languor, typifying the hot rays of the sun; it is as if there were seven quavers to be counted in that bar instead of six. To give the words their true implication these notes, delivered slowly, render the phrase enervating;

on the other hand, sung as they are written with scrupulous exactitude they become undesirably brisk and invigorating. The singer must be courageous, as elastic as a pianist in a Chopin Nocturne.

The song is in A B A form. An enharmonic modulation to G flat (You, rose of my heart) can move forward slightly more urgently with a suggestion of passion. But I repeat, a suggestion only, for never need the singer's tone rise above a *mezzo piano*.

Being a repetition of the first verse, the third section resumes the *Langsam* of the opening, with even more languor.

To me the song is not so much Chopinesque in spirit as Wolfian. It is in the same family as *Bedeckt mich mit Blumen* though as compositions they do not bear the faintest resemblance. The tuberose fragrance, the heavy suffocating sweetness, the masochistic 'ich sterbe vor Liebe' (I die for love) in the Wolf song are only distantly related to this Lenau lyric. The music of each song is very beautiful. Schumann's is justifiably to scale, infinitely lighter in texture.

DIE SENNIN

(Lenau)

Op. 90 No. 4

Pretty cowgirl, sing your song once again
and awaken the hills, for your sweet
sounds go to their heart and they echo
your voice. One day love or death
will take you away and those hills will
stand sad and silent, but they will remem-
ber you and your songs.

Fresh air, rosy cheeks and innocence are conjured up by this free-ranging tune. Each constituent stage in its passage seems to be a votary to F sharp, for it is this resounding note that acts as a magnet and is the focal point towards which the others lead us back. In fact for twenty bars the vocal line echoes with F sharps; truly the reverberation that the girl's voice creates in the answering hills can well be imagined and the pleasing repetitiveness of the phrases adds to this illusion.

These refreshing tones, alas, cease when we are told of the destined departure of this fascinating creature, her resounding notes at the top of the stave are indeed missed.

The rolling *arpeggio* accompaniment is perfect for the gladsome tune though always kept at a lower dynamic level than the voice. But the bass, marked with stresses here and there, should be evident.

AN DEN MOND

(Byron)

Op. 95 No. 2

Son of the sleepless! Melancholy star!
Whose tearful beams glow tremulously far,
That show'st the darkness thou canst not dispel,
How like thou art to joy remember'd well!
So gleams the past, the light of other days,
Which shines, but warms not with its powerless rays;
A night-beam Sorrow watcheth to behold,
Distinct, but distant-clear-but, oh how cold!

Melancholy is apparent at once in the drooping vocal line,

with its slender nuances responding to the rise and fall of the phrases.

While it presents no difficulty for the singer, the accompanist has to consider how his harp-like chords as seen above (and in the preceding introduction) should be treated. In the score there is no suggestion of sustaining pedal, yet it will be found that without this help, the spread chords will sound dry and blunt: I advise a separate pedal (*una corda*) for each chord, with the soprano note singing plaintively. Once arrived on bar 8 where flowing semiquavers appear, a new pedal can be taken on each change of harmony.

Schumann divides Byron's octet into two strophic sections but the core of the poem lies in the last foot 'aber fern, so klar, doch ach! wie kalt!' and it is a pity that the composer found it necessary to repeat it, so many *wie Kalts* rob it of substance and sincerity. The singer should reserve his bitterness for the last time of asking so that 'wie kalt' in 42–43 has far more feeling than the rising phrase 40–41. The agony of desolation can be given more expression here. Of course it depends on the delivery of the word 'kalt'; the consonant 'k' should be heard with aggressive intensity.

Dichterliebe was the predominating influence in the creative life of Hugo Wolf, though none of his Heine songs compare with Schumann's. In this instance (under the title of *Sonne der Schlummerlosen* – translated by Gildemeister) Wolf's imagination and penetration were far more searching than that of his revered precursor. Schumann was not stirred so deeply by Byron (or by Körner's translation) nor does his music tear our heart-strings but it is grateful to sing and will be enjoyed by those unacquainted with the Wolf version.

NACHTLIED

(Goethe)

Op. 96 No. 1

Peace reigns on every summit.
Scarcely a breath stirs the treetops,
the birds are hushed in the woods.
Only wait, soon you too will be at peace.

The metronomic mark of ♩ = 96 as seen in Edition Peters is too fast for the *Sehr Langsam* which is asked. For study purposes the beat should be ♩ = 52 but, having decided on an acceptable tempo, 'common time' is eschewed.

To preserve the calm, the singer thinks and feels a very slow two beats to a bar. How slow he dares make his pace is for him to judge, for every phrase simply must be contained in one breath, without any evidence of struggle. He is treated indulgently in the second phrase, for where Franz Schubert in his renowned setting wants 'in allen Wipfeln spürest du kaum einen Hauch' disclosed in one broken line, Schumann allows a half bar rest after 'spürest du'.

At this point the modulation from the home key of C major melts into E minor with ineffable smoothness.

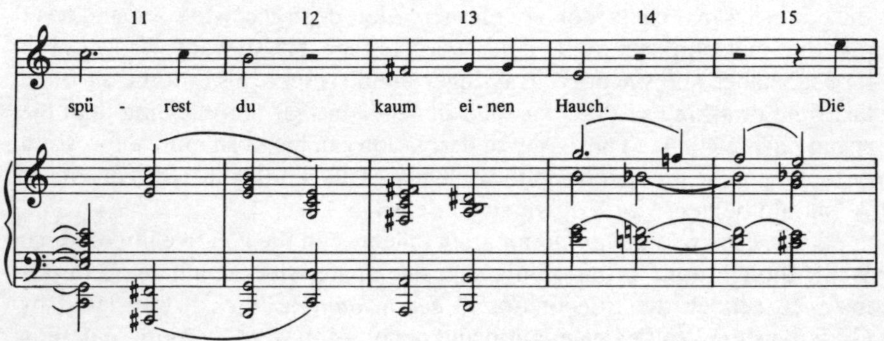

The sudden emergence of the pianoforte in the high treble in answering the allusion to the treetops, the whispered triplets that float on the air leading us so smoothly to 'Warte nur' cannot be played too gently or too relaxedly. And it is here in five bars of music, that the singer has three bars of silence (19, 21, 23); he does not permit us to be aware that he breathes in these intervals.

A moment of radiance awaits us, when from C major we are wafted into A major

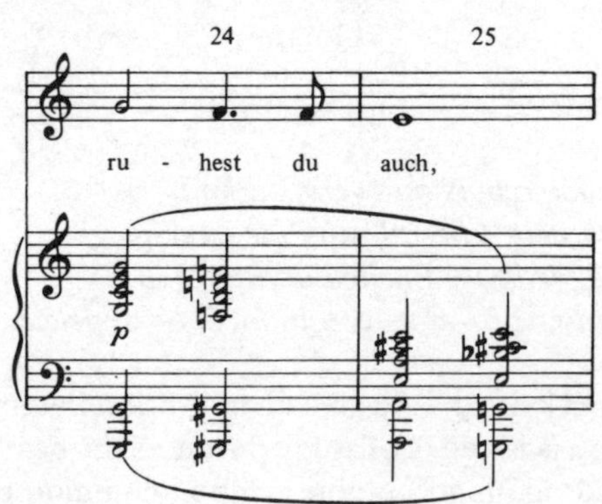

Its unexpectedness explains, perhaps, why it is so deeply moving.

Schubert's immortal *Wanderers Nachtlied* is so loved and so indelibly imprinted on our hearts, that other settings are overshadowed by it and in consequence unheard. To my sorrow, and so far as I am aware, this song is never performed, yet it is very beautiful.

IHRE STIMME

(Platen)

Op. 96 No. 3

The sound of your voice is a true reflection of your soul, its tone means more to me than words. My heart vibrates to your voice in complete sympathy.

Ihre Stimme (Her voice) carries a typically free-moving melody which dips, soars and wings away to a Mendelssohnian arpeggio accompaniment.

For a ringing tenor, it has a fine tune which lodges in the memory. This was my reaction after first listening to the song. Only on closer study does one realize that the commendable impulsion is make-believe passion. Admittedly the lyric cannot be called a fount of inspiration; fortunately, however, the hearer has little opportunity to become aware of the limitations that Schumann, with one qualification, glides over rather skilfully.

The exception is the coda, where the phrase which ought to have brought us to a close, is repeated. After all its previous flights and undulations the melody sinks down in chromatic steps, deflated. Paradoxically this is the very moment where the alert singer makes his winning stroke. Instead of obeying the natural tendency to reduce his tone on this falling passage, he gives us a shining *forte* as if he were singing *The Prize Song* and quickens his pace precipitously down that slope, to finish triumphantly. The postlude continues in this hot-blooded vein.

It may not be according to Platen, Schumann might not approve, but it saves the song.

NUR WER DIE SEHNSUCHT KENNT

(Goethe)

Op. 98A No. 3

Only he who has endured loneliness knows what I suffer. Cut off from everyone, I look southwards where, far away, he who loves me dwells. I am frenzied, flames consume my vitals. Only he who has suffered can know how I feel.

We have remarked that Schumann did not place much store in lengthy introductions and here the soprano makes immediate impact with a trenchant phrase. She delivers it without reticence for it is laden with emotion.

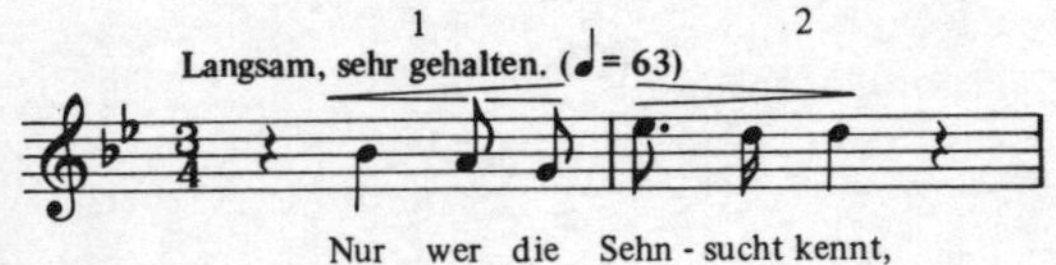

The cutting edge of this vocal line is thrown into greater prominence by the low *tessitura* of the accompaniment and made more poignant by the diminished seventh on 'Sehnsucht' (longing). *Langsam, sehr gehalten*, is instructed and the metronomic beat of ♩ = 63 gives quite enough impulse.

At 'seh ich ans Firmament' (bar 7) the tempo appears to quicken but this is an illusion caused by the pianoforte quavers in duple rhythm becoming triplets. This activity generates passion but not haste and the artists keep a tight rein on the tempo until asked to throw off restraint at 12. Here Schumann writes *Schneller*; 'he who loves me is far away' which begins the build-up for a truly piercing climax.

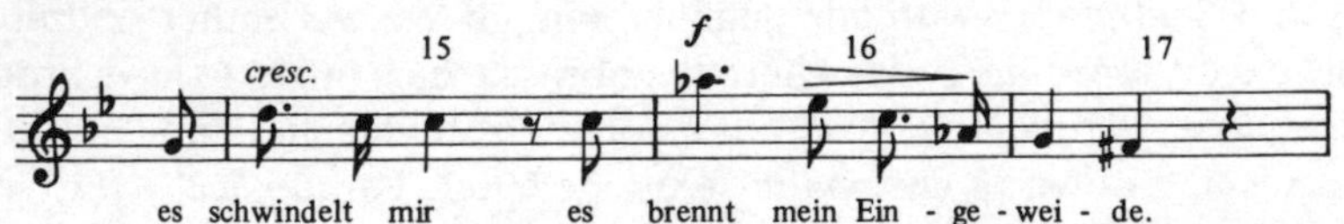

It is a scorching passage and is, one might say, the raison d'être for singing the song. Bars 12 to 17 must make a telling impression on the hearer and this can only be achieved by not obeying the instruction 'Quicker' too literally. With the *crescendo* growing bitingly 'brennt' is made momentous, provided the singer sees to it that the agony is protracted.

From the outset the singer's sights are set on the vital bars 16 and 17, her tone should have an incisive edge; the *piano* sign at the beginning is too complacent.

These seventeen bars carry all the more significance in relation to what ensues, for we now have a repetition of what has been already stated though less convincingly. It makes for an inevitable tailing away dynamically and emotionally to the end.

Goethe in his novel *Wilhelm Meister* makes Mignon's secret anguish a duet to be shared with the Harper. Schubert composed several settings, one of them for two voices, but his Op. 62 No. 4 is best known for its simplicity and bleak despair. Wolf is even more poignant; here indeed is a duet but it is shared by Mignon, with the tortured octaves in the pianoforte treble: Frank Walker (*Hugo Wolf*, J.M. Dent Ltd) describes it as 'rather repellent at first and then increasingly fascinating'. The most popular setting of all is Tchaikowsky's. Should it be condemned on this account? The writer confesses he loves it, though he is almost afraid to admit it.

These settings are each superb, Schumann's comes into the reckoning, for the first page of his song and the sweeping 'Es brennt mein Eingeweide' are reason enough for allowing us to hear it.

SINGET NICHT IN TRAUERTÖNEN

(Goethe)

Op. 98A No. 7

Sing not in such sad tones of the loneliness of night, for it was made for companionship. The day must be endured but it is at night by the flickering lamp light, to the song of the nightingale, to the clock's twelve mysterious strokes that lovers meet, lip to lip. Therefore, dear heart, remember every day has its vexations and the night its pleasures.

Philine is the counterpart of Puccini's (or rather Henry Murger's) Musetta, the grisette in *La Bohème*, and like her is a young woman of great attraction, infinite vivacity and excessive amiability. Her song is shallow but most amusing; the humour and sparkle of it are admirably caught by Schumann.

Words could not give a better account of the girl's character than this pianoforte introduction with its laughing *staccato*, playful *sforzandi*, occasional saucy grace note and, above all, its coquettish slurs. The latter marked meticulously and the player's observance of them add piquant contrast to the *staccato*. No sustaining pedal is wanted save at the words 'und die Nacht hat ihre Lust' which, no doubt to rub it in, comes three times in case we miss the point.

Thrown away with playful abandon, as it should be, the song still needs concentration from the singer, for the 32nd note must be clear and, like the *melismata*, is continually appearing and all these conspire to become tiresome if not delivered with consummate smoothness and clarity. Plenty of *forte* signs appear, but, like Philine herself, are relatively light.

AN DIE TÜREN WILL ICH SCHLEICHEN

(Goethe)

Op. 98A No. 8

I shall creep from door to door,
wait there quietly and humbly
till a kindly hand gives me food,
and then I'll move on.
After seeing me, any man will
think himself fortunate and
will shed a tear for me.
I ask myself 'Why'?

In the introduction, short though it is, the contrast between the measured tread of the bare bass octaves and the shambling gait of the treble semiquavers gives a positive picture of physical fatigue.

The semiquavers are weighty, not with increased tone, but weighty in the sense that they are dragging as if it were only force of will that propelled them.

Similarly though *pianissimo* prevails in the vocal line the tone must be solemn, not slender. Both Schumann's and Wolf's Harper songs are set in the bass clef for the voice. While a bass is able to sing as softly as a tenor, the profundity of the darker and deeper voice suggests that neither composer wanted the *pianissimo* to be too attenuated.

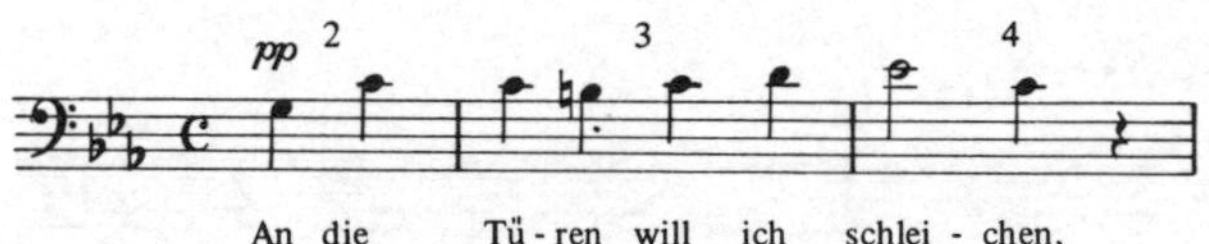

The singer is always *legato* (the accompaniment is designed to suggest the lagging and uneven gait) and he should make no *crescendo* up to 4.

After fourteen bars in the minor, a change to the major comes as a beatific ray of light. 'Scheinen' (16) with its pianoforte echo – 'wenn mein Bild vor ihm erscheint' – the eventual climb up to 'weint' (22) where the weary footfalls are resumed – all conspire to clutch the heart. These nine bars are quite magical; the singer makes it evident that they are the song's apex, but when he repeats 'I know not why he weeps', all that is asked of him is to sing in a uniform *pianissimo* for the Harper is bemused, too numbed to realize how pitiful an image is his.

The conception is superb. Wolf made use of syncopation throughout his setting as a constant reminder of the hesitating footsteps and uncertain progress of the Harper. Schumann's picture is just as felicitous. Strangely he achieves it without resorting to any syncopation (one of his favourite practices) whatsoever.

MEIN SCHÖNER STERN

(Rückert)

Op. 101 No. 4

Beloved star, I beg you let not your brightness
be dimmed by the darkness in me, rather remedy
this darkness by your splendour.
Beloved star, I beg you not to sink down to
this earthly level for my sake, rather raise me
nearer to the heavenly height where you shine.

The secret of this divine melody – is it in C minor, F major, B flat, or D minor? – owes something, I feel, to its ambiguity; subconsciously the ear is teased bar after bar by a continuous succession of discords, sweet discords that lead from one key to another but never to the home key of E flat (except by a passing allusion in bar 5) until we have heard seventeen bars or more. Frequent dissonances are heard whose effect, thought but a tone or semitone apart, far from being abrasive seem to act as balsam.

A taste of this comes in 5

where the accompaniment's affectionately accented F, rings through the voice's E flat; again in 10 the singer's 'mir' (a C natural) floats with the pianoforte B flat; and most of all at 12 when the E flat in the vocal line and the pianoforte's D natural a semitone lower, move hand in hand insistently and meltingly.

Self-abasement, or at least a prayer of humble access is suggested by these discords and they are delivered by the partners with compassion.

Smoothness and deliberation are demanded of the singer and he makes us unaware that consummate technique is involved as well as deep feeling. For instance 'Mein' (1) and 'Stern' (3) though an octave apart should carry a like tonal quality and weight. There is, one feels, a suggestion of world-weariness in the text and it is reflected in the music, hence an active response to the prescriptive rising and falling nuance is unwanted. If there is one note, one word, in that opening phrase which asks for more stress it is 'bitte' (4) but certainly not the high note on 'Stern'.

The even flow of the music can easily be impaired by the composer's insatiable desire for syncopation, it occurs – for no earthly reason one can see – on bar 15 in the pianoforte bass.

It must be played as softly and unobtrusively as possible. Apart from this one bar the accompaniment has bass octaves moving smoothily and coolly with repeated chords in the treble.

The player should not be too shy when his soprano appears to clash with the vocal line, these moments give the music its character.

There is no need whatever for the singer to attempt to vary the second verse, we are grateful to hear this heavenly tune twice.

In the postlude the sighs on the fourth beats of 36 and 39 can be allowed a little expressive space.

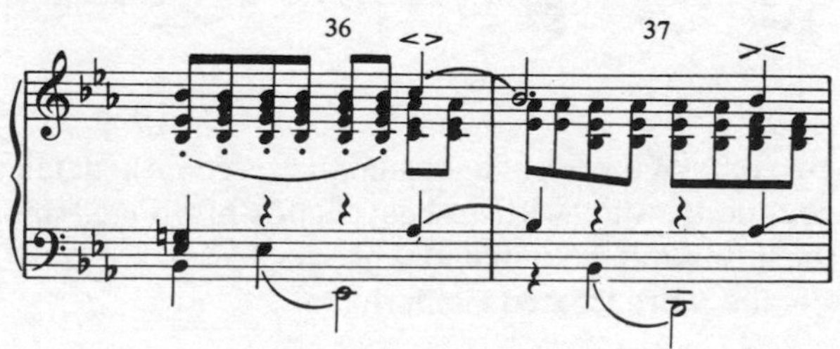

VIEL GLÜCK ZUR REISE, SCHWALBEN!

(Kulman)

Op. 104 No. 2

Good luck, dear swallows, for your long flight to the warm south. Gladly would I go with you to see the thousand wonders of each land you visit, yet, no matter how fair these may be, I should always want to return to our own dear Fatherland.

Of the seven songs set to Elisabeth Kulmann's words under this opus, easily the most acceptable is this miniature for a light soprano. One can imagine listening to the same child who sang *Schmetterling* and *Marienwürmchen* from Op. 79. Much of its charm lies in the accompaniment. The demisemiquaver fluttering of wings, constantly heard, is flicked away weightlessly and every note, almost, is made feathery *staccato*. Accents such as that seen in bar 4 (below) do not need fussy observance for the high treble chord of itself is sufficient without extra pressure. *Una corda* prevails except for 'Vaterland' (27) which is *forte* and only here at the third time of asking. Sustaining pedal is used with the utmost economy otherwise it becomes earthbound and stodgy.

In the first two bars of the vocal line, guidance is given in detail and should be obeyed throughout. 'Viel' with up-beat slightly prolonged smoothly joins 'Glück', but the latter and the remainder of bars 3 and 4 are given a sprightly *staccato*: bars 5 and 6 are treated similarly.

Lebhaft (lively) is the instruction but this does not necessarily mean fast, and if the singer takes too rapid a tempo, the piquancy of this amusing *legato-staccato* conjunction will be lost. The suggested tempo is ♩ = 66.

The only exceptions to this jaunty style of delivery are the crotchets which are naturally given full value. Schumann clearly indicates that he wants 'kührem' and 'Wunder' (9 and 16 respectively) sung with smoothness.

HERZELEID

(Ullrich)

Op. 107 No. 1

The tired branches of the willow droop in
the waters. A girl, pale of cheek
stares miserably down at the
slow moving stream and gently
drops a garland of flowers
in it. From the waters comes a
whisper – 'Ophelia, Ophelia!'

Weeping willow and drowsy stream take pattern from the unhappy girl, with a dejection eloquent of tiredness of life. One can picture, in the accompaniment, the branches hanging despondently. Sadly, in a succession of curved passages the vocal line falls and should be delivered colourlessly and resignedly. In each verse there should be only one rising inflexion; first to draw our compassionate attention to the ashen-cheeked maid; and again to sound the warning of the waters. Their haunting, melancholy plaint 'Ophelia, Ophelia' is breathed in a disembodied tone, the last whisper so soft and distant that one cannot recognize when the singing voice ceases. Perhaps it is silenced for ever by the deeper waters of the postlude, but its mournful threnody lingers in the mind.

IM WALD

(Wolfgang Müller)

Op. 107 No. 5

In the wood I see two butterflies fluttering
until they nestle together on the lip of
a flower, while I stand here alone, troubled.
Now two birds, startled from their warm
nest, chase one another while I stand
here alone, troubled.
Two deer come down the hillside but
seeing me, they turn tail and disappear
over the hill, while I stand here alone, troubled.

Schumann's precept that the poem was an orange from which the juice must be crushed is born out in this androgynous song. Müller's insistence on the loneliness and care, reiterated by the composer in each strophic verse, make so little impression on the music's mood that the only logical conclusion I can come to, is that the protagionist is a child. How else can the lively, frisky motion, skipping along with such innocent enjoyment and tireless energy be explained? There are other hints which lead to this deduction: the instruction *somewhat lively* with a metronome mark in Peters Edition of 𝅗𝅥 = 58; the vocal line at once vigorous and 'off-hand'; the fascination (open-mouthed?) at the sight of the butterflies, birds and deer; lastly the fairly consistent *staccato* in the accompaniment with that jolly triplet flight and *sforzando* in bars 4 and 5.

Well, the loneliness does not make its effect in the above phrase. 'But' the percipient reader will ask, 'each verse reinforced by the instruction

Zurückhaltend (hold back) refers to loneliness and worry, how do you explain this?' This question troubles me no more than it does the child who forgets his or her cares at the sight of the butterflies and birds.

By answer I will quote T.E. Brown, an English poet who wrote a jingle over a century ago, the first two lines of which run:–

Now the beauty of the thing when childer plays is
The terrible wonderful length the day is.

and the last two lines are:–

And when you look back it's all a puff
Happy and over and short enough.

which is another way of saying that the loneliness and worry, so much insisted on in the song, are the outcome of a childish tiff.

The late H. Walford Davies composed a most delightful song to the words 'When childher plays' and I warmly recommend it.

ABENDLIED

(Kinkel)

Op. 107 No. 6

So still is the evening, so hushed, that
angels' footfalls could be heard.
The darkness deepens. Put an end to
your sorrow, my heart. As the stars
pursue their courses, your path too will
be secure.

The triplets in the pianoforte are apparently conspiring to disrupt the calmness that the lyric advances.

An argument between singer and pianist, each grimly determined not to be deflected by his partner, was far from Schumann's intention. If we regard the accompaniment as earthbound, with the voice sailing serenely above it as the stars, we may come a little nearer to the composer's idea.

Much depends on the playing, for the accompaniment must always be dematerialized: this is difficult, for it is placed inconsiderately, in a resonant register of the instrument most of the time. One can say it is in block harmony, but the player would be wise to forget this designation with its innate suggestion of squareness.

Cross rhythm or no, the singer's line is supple, thus 'so still' (4, 5) is allowed space, to give meaning to the words. Bar 6 again is unhurried, so that the unanimity between voice and pianoforte is underlined ('verauscht'). This advice applies especially to 'wirf ab, Herz, was dich kränket' (16, 17) where the upper notes float reassuringly.

DER HUSAR, TRARA!

(Lenau)

Op. 117 No. 1

Hurrah for the hussar! What matter danger?
Ready at a glance to leap to his sweetheart's
side, ready both for wine and for his sabre to
drink deep of blood.
Hurrah! What is danger to him?
This refrain is his lullaby.

One is grateful to Nikolaus Lenau for having inspired our composer with his *Lied eines Schmiedes* and *Meine Rose* but there are times when his verse becomes boorish and flatulent. That this mustachioed animated sword-blade sings himself to sleep with this hullabaloo, is beyond my understanding.

Dislike the fire-eater though I may, I concede that his song is a useful one for a baritone at the end of a group. It clatters and trumpets away effectively, lasts but one minute and is over before the hearer has time to be irritated by its repetitiveness.

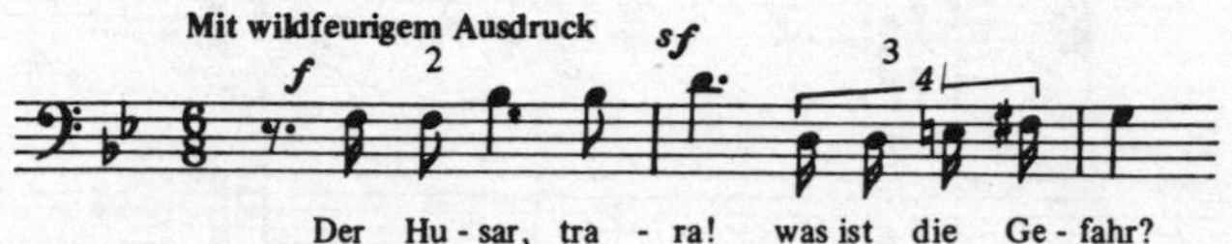

With 'violent expression' it is marked. Sung with audacious abandon and as if he believes every word of it the singer must allow 'was ist die Gefahr' to be enunciated with fierce clarity; it is the 'motto' of the hero.

In bars 9, 10 the higher notes are taken.

FRÜHLINGSLUST

(Heyse)

Op. 125 No. 5

Now roses are in bloom. The time has
come for Eros to set his nets and,
poor trembling butterfly, he has caught you.
Had I been caught by Love in the roses
as you, I would have died, but not being
fashioned for sorrow I can go on freely
singing to the tree tops.

The singer has a care-free lightsome line and she lets us know at once that her sympathy for the enmeshed butterfly does not discompose her joy of spring or the lilt of her song.

Whenever the jaunty dotted quaver occurs, as in 5 and 7, it has a rhythmic gusto which must be communicated. At the beginning the composer has inscribed the word 'happily' but it is not easy to give this impression if the singer's flight is earthbound by the pianist: since the melody has undistinguished patches (7 and 8), much depends on the player.

There is a solidity about the accompaniment which should be disguised; a feathery touch is wanted, and for this reason what appears to be an easy piano part becomes difficult. In addition a fast tempo is required, ♩. = 72 no less. We have observed that the more difficult the accompaniment, the quicker the singer will want the song to speed. You can depend on it, it was ever thus. Those of us, not sitting at the keyboard, are on the side of the angels – the singers.

ES LEUCHTET MEINE LIEBE

(Heine)

Op. 127 No. 3

My love gleams like a gloomy tale
told on a summer night.
'In the magic garden two lovers wander
beneath the fickle light of the moon.
The maiden stands, a perfect picture, and
her knight kneels before her. Suddenly a
giant, the scourge of the countryside appears
and the frightened maid flees. Down
sinks the bleeding knight and the giant
stalks away.'
When I am in my grave the story will be over.

This accompaniment is unusual for Schumann, with thick chords moving with lightness. *Forte* is wanted in the introduction with its two bars of sinister intent, but at bar 3 the treble chords should be eerie reminders of the shadowy inconstant moonlight, yielding to the voice, and allowing pride of place in the accompaniment to the accented bass with its portentous message.

A speed is advised which makes it possible to cover the cohesive chords in the treble; it should be no slower than ♩. = 66.

The singer is the narrator for four bars and sings straightforwardly but with a dark quality of tone over the restless accompaniment. The magic garden wants a different approach; it is sung mellifluously and smoothly, imbued with compassion.

When the nightingale is described, the pianoforte has a clearly indicated cross-rhythm; it is unnecessary at this point, and should not be emphasized, for later it plays a significant part when the ogre comes on the scene. Let us put off this evil moment at bars 7 to 14 and make what amenity we can of the little time that remains for the lovers to enjoy. The texture of the writing invites this tender treatment where the maiden is pictured.

This, and the following phrases are rudely interrupted by the stumping stride of the giant, and now the cross-rhythm (seen in 9–10) makes its destructive effect, clawing and rending at the vocal line.

In this pianoforte interlude the club wielded by the killer whistles through the air (those shrieking notes in the high treble) and lands on the victim with a sickening thud (the bass octave *sforzando* in 19 and above all in 21).

So far as the ballad is concerned that ends a distasteful story of the triumph of evil. It remains, however, for the pianist to draw the curtain which he does in a succession of wailing chromatic octave passages – noxious winds blowing over the prostrate knight.

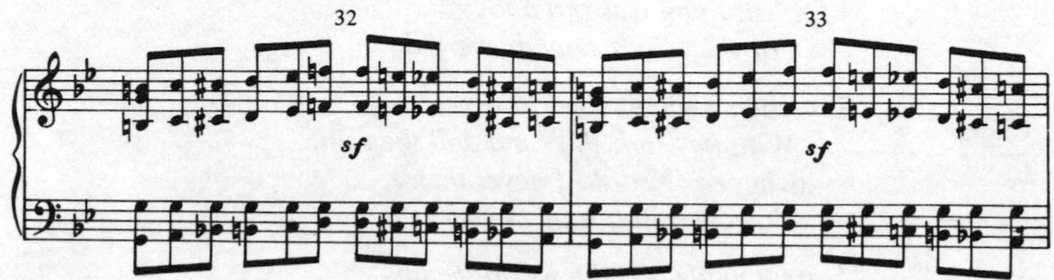

Horror is made apparent in the surging rise and whimpering fall; the *crescendo* and *diminuendo* cannot be overdone, nor can the terror of it be held in check. From 30 an *accelerando* begins and its momentum maintained until the penultimate bar of the postlude.

It is an unique lyric for Schumann to have adopted and he handled it in a way which was, for him, unusual. He does not wear the cloak and dagger with comfort, horror is simulated. All the same it is a capital song for a fine singer and accompanist and justifies an occasional appearance in a recital programme.

SCHLUSSLIED DES NARREN

(Shakespeare)

Op. 127 No. 5

When that I was and a little tiny boy,
With hey, ho, the wind and the rain,
A foolish thing was but a toy,
For the rain it raineth every day.

But when I came, alas! to wive,
With hey, ho, the wind and the rain,
By swaggering could I never thrive,
For the rain it raineth every day.

A great while ago the world begun,
With hey, ho, the wind and the rain,
But that's all one, our play is done,
And we'll strive to please you every day.

This is a most engaging idea of Feste's closing song from *Twelfth Night*. It is angular, clownish, and the German translation (Schlegel und Tieck) with their 'hop heise' makes a very fair make-shift for 'with hey, ho' etc.

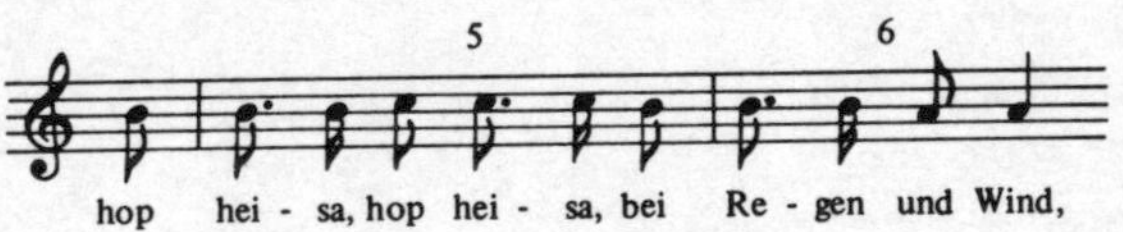

It is sung with zest until, and quite suddenly, it changes to a mock lugubriousness 'for the rain it raineth every day'. This quick transformation from merriment to dolour can be made very facetious, subject to the singer's imagination, and Schumann has catered for it by a decided retardation, and by allowing the refrain 'it raineth every day' to sink very low in the voice. Compensation is made in the last verse, (verses two and four of the original are omitted) 'our play is done' is marked 'Quickly' and should be sung with great good humour and as fast as clear enunciation allows.

The pianist uses no sustaining pedal where *staccato* is wanted. He hardly waits for his partner to finish the last syllable of 'gefalle' (28) before he is off on his postlude like a shot, making an *accelerando* so that the last three bars are dashed off in double quick time.

TIEF IM HERZEN TRAG ICH PEIN

(Geibel)

Op. 138 No. 2

Torment racks my heart but I conceal it from the world, it is a sweet agony felt only by the soul. It is hidden deep inside me like the spark hides within the flint.

Sung with smoothness and control, this passage puts the singer on course for the whole song. Its distinctive feature is the interval in bar 4 (here a sixth) and it should be considered as the expressive high point. It is accomplished without *crescendo*, indeed 'trag ich pein' should be less in tone than 'Tief'. This emotive stretch is heard in the next phrase (9) 'stille sein' and is wider and even more restrained than before. We hear it repeatedly in the vocal line and the accompaniment becomes affected by the 'sweet agony' in 15, 22 and above all in 48–49.

This is not, simple though it appears, an easy song to sing for each phrase is long and must be performed in one breath. The singer will instinctively obey the nuances enjoined by the composer, but it may be noticed that the 'featured stretch' I have harped upon has no expression marks whatsoever.

O WIE LIEBLICH IST DAS MÄDCHEN

(Geibel)

Op. 138 No. 3

What an adorable girl she is! Tell me,
sailor, whether your ship and its sails can compare with her?
What an adorable girl she is! Tell me,
knight at arms, whether your charger and your battles
can compare with her?
What an adorable girl she is! Tell me, young
shepherd, whether your lambs, fields and hills can
can compare with her?

A strophic song of three verses without the slightest variation and with the refrain tacked on at the end for good measure seems a recipe for tedium. Actually it is delightful and bounces along with freshness and joy of life with each verse leading up to a ringing and sustained top G (there have been several *en passant*) where the singer can really spread himself. An admirable vehicle for a tenor though his finest moment vocally is his resounding B flat on bar 40 which comes in the section which I disrespectfully alluded to as 'tacked on'.

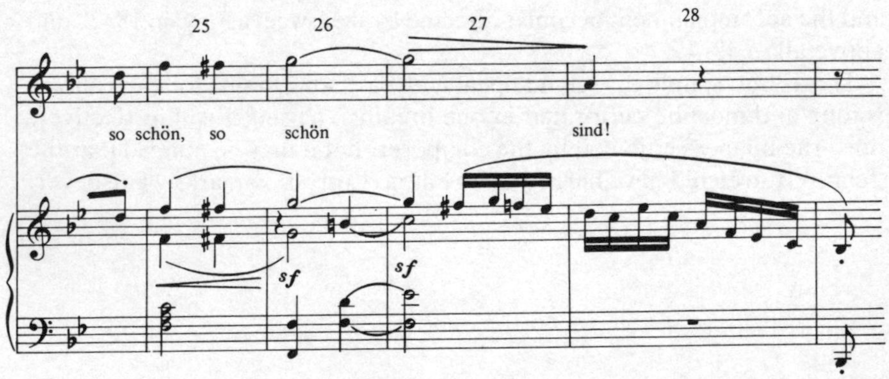

Enjoyable to play too, with its bouncing *staccato* and playful interludes, of which the above example is typical.

WEH, WIE ZORNIG IST DAS MÄDCHEN

(Geibel)

Op. 138 No. 7

Oh, the girl is so angry!
She leads her flocks into the fields and
is as beautiful as the flowers, but
as angry as the sea. Oh! Oh!

'Weh', repeated so often in the text, is not to be taken literally as 'Woe is me' nor does it imply a sigh in the accepted sense but rather a French 'O, la, la!' as if a parent or older guardian were regarding with astonishment and some pride the tantrums of a very pretty but rather spoiled girl. In fact the grace notes in the accompaniment, coupled with off-beat accents, suggest a chuckle.

The singer's utterances are disconnected all through the song and whether or not he breathes between them makes no matter for the instruction is 'sehr markiert' and the vocal line spiky. If the tempo is too quick (it is marked *Nicht schnell*) it can easily be mistaken for an angry outburst. On the other hand, if it is taken too slowly, the repeated 'Weh' which is heard nine times in the last nine bars, begins to sound dismal.

There should be no *rallentando* at the end, and the two *fermati* in the final bar must be curtailed.

Having made myself as obscure as possible with my 'Not too fast' and 'Not too slow', let me retire as gracefully as possible with a word to the wise regarding this song. It smiles.

PROVENZALISCHES LIED

(Uhland)

Op. 139 No. 4

Provençal valleys were first to hear the
song of the troubadours for there, child of
springtime and gallantry, it was born.
Blessed valleys of Provence, the glorious song
of your troubadours is even more vivid than
your flowers. That honoured circle of
minstrels sang of the days of chivalry, of
valiant knights and elegant ladies.
How nobly their praises were sung.

'Mit Anmut', (with grace) is the advice above the tenor's entry; to this should be added 'panache'. This is sung in one's imagination to the accompaniment of the harp, sung with freedom and abandon, as if the singer accompanied himself. An observance of four-square rhythmical pedantry stifles the song at birth.

A swagger is suggested by lingering on the *Auftakt* (the 'leading-in' quavers of bar 2) and then by sweeping on to 'ist' where once again we make a slight *tenuto*: (this prominence given to 'ist' makes no literal sense at all but it is an instance where musical demands take precedence over verbal metre); on again to 'entsprossen' where again we wait, simply because the pianoforte (as in bar 2) must be allowed its elastic *Auftakt* since it repeats the singer's opening air and treats it in exactly the same way.

This suspenseful 'wait' comes frequently, sometimes with voice and pianoforte together, sometimes separately and cries out for brave expression.

Life-enhancing breadth is afforded to the high notes; the F's and G's in 'Kind des Frühlings' (8, 9) – 'Herzensglut' (21) – 'Mutter' (25) should ring out impetuously.

The pianist spreads his chords with gusto, every note should be heard, but the quaver rest between these harped chords, though important, does not ask for an abrupt *staccato*, this would be too aggressive, therefore a sensitive touch on the convivial sustaining pedal is needed.

Schumann gives preference in the second verse to the ladies rather than their consorts. The gallant knights yield pride of place, musically at least, to the fair ones.

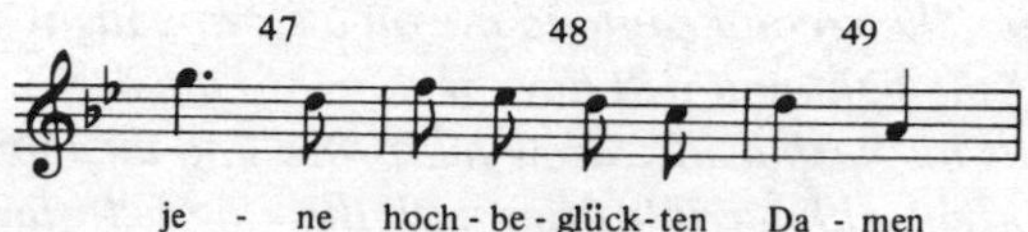

It is a phrase already heard in the first verse but now is invested with pride and pageantry, with a generous expansion for the high note and a picturesque swagger down to 'hoch beglückten Damen'.

From 55 to 70 the music loses some impetus, but this can be made less obvious if extra *verve* is poured into it.

The spirit of 'Sänger liebe, hoch und herrlich' is nullified by an unwarrantable and sudden drop of the vocal line in the middle of the phrase.

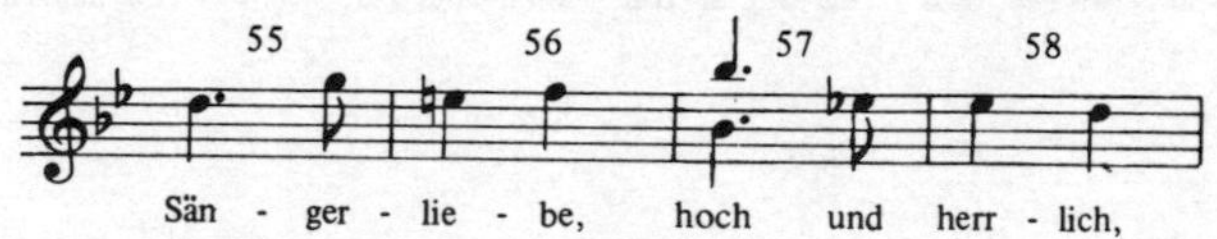

it should soar up to 'hoch' and any tenor who can heroically but comfortably take the B flat an octave higher should do so.

Once again the postlude revivifies the song. It is played with the same freedom and flourish that was heard from the singer. Bars 79, 80, 81 should be hastened a little prior to the *rallentando* on the last two bars.

BALLADE

(Uhland)

Op. 139 No. 7

In his great hall sat King Sifrid and called
'Which of you harpers can sing me the finest ballad?'
A once a young man stepped forward, harp in hand
and sword at side. 'Three songs I know. The first tells
of my brother who was treacherously stabbed to death
by you. The second came to me on a stormy night and
tells of the fight you will have with me to the death. Now!'
He puts his harp aside, drew his sword and they fought
and fought with terrible cries until the king fell, slain.
'Now for my third song, and the finest of all which I shall
never weary of singing: King Sifrid lies dead in a pool
of blood.'

With the pianoforte introduction so premonitory, a metronomic mark of ♩ = 58 is not slow enough or sufficiently majestic to accommodate the oratorical pauses or silences of the impressive address which follows.

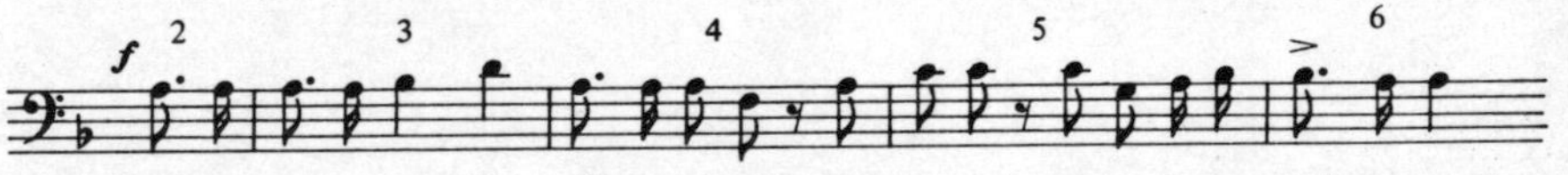

It is marked 'Mit grosser Kraft' (with great power) but this does not signify that a stentorian tone is wanted; a *forte* is enough, for the strength is made evident by the rhythmic control. This becomes clear by a sudden and fearful change from the home key of D minor to F sharp minor when the young harpist sings. Now a *fortissimo* is truly essential. This clarion outcry would have made less impact had the singer rashly given too much voice at the beginning.

Those vital rests give sinew to the music: space must be accorded the octave C sharps in the bass; space too, on the voice's 'Drei'. The singer listens to give the pianist time to make his triplet in the bass clear and menacing, for if it is played hurriedly it will be trivialised.

Space, or time allowance, is the very essence of the song;

imagine being impelled by jaundiced convention to arrive promptly 'to time' on the low *piano* 'hast' after the thunderous 'aber'! Schumann's magnificently dramatic effect would be brought to naught. This huge leap must be carefully considered by the pianist; after his *sforzando* there should be a moment's daylight before his *piano* chord on 'hast', so that no overtones cover the voice.

The design is constant throughout the second verse in which King and Harper duel to the death, although the composer asks for a quicker tempo. (♩ = 68 is suggested). We can hear Carl Loewe's pianoforte making a running commentary on the fight as the battle rages with steel clashing on steel, and the cries of the combatants, but Schumann had no taste for melodrama and his stately measure, though speedier, is not greatly disordered by this sanguinary affair. It is brought at short notice, to a conclusion: the King is quickly dispatched, a dead man before he finds time to say 'Mamma mia'.

Although not marked, the third verse should resume the ceremonial tempo of the opening, with the singer in noble voice and the harp chords richly spread.

The postlude is *sempre pianissimo* until the penultimate bar, which demands a *crescendo* as the passage mounts up and up to a triumphant final chord.

It is a pity this ballad is so seldom heard, the singer with a good bass will find it rewarding.

MÄDCHEN – SCHWERMUT

(Bernard)

Op. 142 No. 3

Dew on the flowers seems like tears
to the girl who weeps. The whispering
rustle of spring is as a wail for love
that is lost. Even the stars in heaven
shed no gleam in the joyless world
of the maid who knows no hope.

The shrivelled nature of the accompaniment and the inert colourless vocal line are expressive of forlorn sadness. Discords add to the distress on 'Blumen' (10) and 'zart' (30) and in neither instance should the singer be under pressure to hasten her tied note. The pianist also allows the discord on bar 12 to be heard before he completes the cadence.

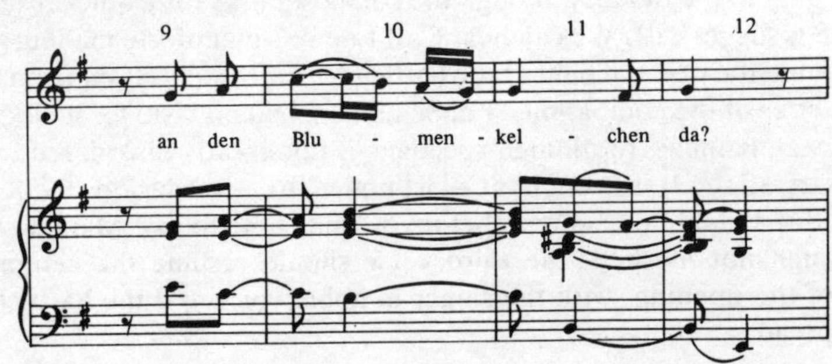

But it is on bar 47 'Himmelszelt' that the jarring dissonance is most painfully manifested and is noticeably prolonged as marked.

Intense feeling is apparent in the postlude

Bar 64 becomes slower and slower, dwindling away to nothing, leaving the bare chord in the bass to sigh forlornly.

The utter loss of hope that the poet endeavoured to express is akin to *Das verlassene Mägdlein* one of Hugo Wolf's masterpieces. We do not claim such glory for this song, the poet is no Mörike nor does it show Schumann at his best, but to some extent it reflects the misery the composer was enduring when he wrote it.

MEIN WAGEN ROLLET LANGSAM

(Heine)

Op. 142 No. 4

My carriage rolls along slowly through
green woods, through valleys where flowers
are gleaming in the sunshine. I sit and
muse and day-dream of my loved one.
Then three weird phantoms float through
my window, they mock me, grimace at me,
then sniggering, disappear like mist.

Relaxation and complacency are inherent in the leisurely movement of the accompaniment. It glides so smoothly on this warm summer day and with such regular and delightful monotony that the passenger is lulled.

The singer makes his entry at 8 after an introduction (with an accompaniment of similar pattern as that shown above) of unusual length. Much more unusual however, is the instruction 'Nach dem Sinn des Gedichts' (consistent with the poem's meaning) a direction which, shortly, will be beyond the performers' power to obey.

With a change, unprepared but by no means disturbing, there is a modulation to D flat.

The rolling movement is no longer heard, all is quiet, as if the man had become tranquillized by the gentle rhythmic sway, and sinking into a pleasing torpor, allows his thoughts to dwell luxuriously on his beloved. An eight bar interlude still in D flat returns us to the song's opening motif and the voice joins in smoothly and casually with

This announcement is extraordinary, not to say frightening. But the astonishing element is not the appearance of the three ghastly shadows, for Heinrich Heine is capable of anything; the surprise is that the music is not ruffled in the slightest degree nor is the passenger the least bit disconcerted.

How, the question arises, are singer and accompanist to follow the composer's precept that they interpret the music 'according to the poem'? The utmost the singer can do at 31 is to sing *mezzo forte* as marked, and at the very least *look* surprised, but if any attempt is made by the pianist to introduce some *bizarrerie* it will be out of character with the musical pattern.

In fact the postlude of 28 bars continues with the carriage moving on placidly. Not perhaps quite as placidly, for the flow is disturbed when the second motif is heard, for the *pianissimo* is interrupted by quite startling *sforzandi* (53 and 59)

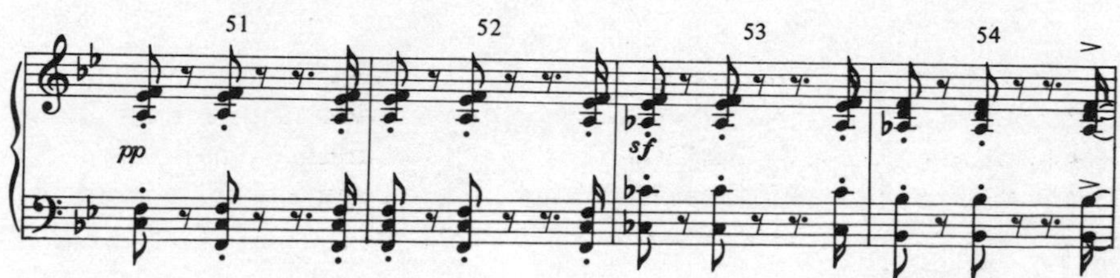

Schumann perhaps feels he did not give the bogies the recognition that they deserve, so in this impressive postlude he makes amends with these convulsive 'starts' as if his passenger recollects the intruders with a shudder. They are only administered, being in the postlude, as an afterthought.

The song, despite this criticism, is a pleasure to hear and to perform. It is far removed, as I said in my preface, from the Richard Strauss version (Waldesfahrt Op. 69 No. 4) where ample accommodation is provided for the horrors, much to the dismay of the pianist who has to cope with them on his own with very little help from the singer.

GENERAL INDEX

Excluding references to Robert Schumann himself. For titles of songs, see separate index.

INDEX OF SCHUMANN SONGS